9.95

ECONOMIC LITERACY

A Complete Guide

EDITOR

Stephanie Schwartz Driver

Marshall Cavendish
Reference

NEW YORK

Other Marshall Cavendish Offices:
Marshall Cavendish Ltd. 5th Floor, 32-38 Saffron Hill, London EC1N 8 FH, UK • Marshall Cavendish International (Asia) Private Limited, 1 New Industrial Road, Singapore 536196 • Marshall Cavendish International (Thailand) Co Ltd. 253 Asoke, 12th Flr, Sukhumvit 21 Road, Klongtoey Nua, Wattana, Bangkok 10110, Thailand • Marshall Cavendish (Malaysia) Sdn Bhd, Times Subang, Lot 46, Subang Hi-Tech Industrial Park, Batu Tiga, 40000 Shah Alam, Selangor Darul Ehsan, Malaysia

Marshall Cavendish is a trademark of Times Publishing Limited

All websites were available and accurate when this book was sent to press.

Library of Congress Cataloging-in-Publication Data

Economic literacy : a complete guide.
    p. cm.
Includes bibliographical references and index.
ISBN 978-0-7614-7910-9 (alk. paper)
1. Economics.
HB171.E2424 2009
330--dc22
                        2009009462
Printed in Malaysia

12 11 10 09 1 2 3 4 5

Marshall Cavendish
Publisher: Paul Bernabeo
Production Manager: Michael Esposito
Development: MTM Publishing
Cover Design: Patrice Sheridan
Indexer: AEIOU, Inc.

Photo credits: Alamy: Jupiter Images/Pixland 192; AP/Wide World: 8,13,23,41,48,51,58,65,73,80,85,146,158,176,183,186,202; Corbis: 29,71; Paul Almasy 171; Patrick Bennett 163; Bob Daemmrich/Sygma 121; FK Photo 148; Randi Faris 76; Owen Franken 155; Farrell Grehan 36; Hulton 126; R.W.Jones 131;Palmer Kane 137; Tim Kiusaalas 150; Thom Lang 33; Brian Lee 91; Russell Lee 14; Richard T. Nowitz 195; Jose Luis Pelaez 169; Steve Raymer 143; Roger Ressmeyer 17, 136; Tony Roberts 10; Richard Hamilton Smith 35; Ted Spiegel 148; William Taufic 110; Bill Varie 111, 112; Adam Woolfitt 185' Tim Wright 47; Corbis AFP 81,98,217; AFP Scott Olson 17; AFP Martial Trezzini 32; Corbis Bettman: 6, 19, 25, 38, 39, 55, 62, 107, 115, 161, 175, 179, 194,207,209; Corbis Reuters New Media: 30, 66, 87, 116, 117, 152, 154, 162, 173; Getty Images:AFP 81; Congressional Quarterly 201; Cover Don Emmart; Chris Hondros 64; Hulton 7,26,28; Photodisc 188; Taxi 187; Library of Congress: 27,199

Alphabetical Table of Contents

Contributors

Editors

William R. Childs
Ohio State University

Scott B. Martin
Columbia University

Wanda Stitt-Gohdes
University of Georgia

Editorial Consultants

Judith Olson-Sutton
Madison Area Technical College

Don Wentworth
Pacific Lutheran University

Contributors

Carol Alaimo, Arizona Daily Star; J. Isaac Brannon, Office of Management and Budget; Stephen Buckle, Vanderbilt University; Stephanie Buckwalter; Karen Ehrle, University of Wisconsin–Milwaukee; Peter C. Grosvenor, Pacific Lutheran University; Joseph Gustaitis; Carl Haacke, Skylight Consulting; Stephen Haessler, Marquette University High School; Bradley K. Hobbs, Florida Gulf Coast University; Tracy Hofer, University of Wisconsin–Stevens Point; John Keckhaver, University of Wisconsin–Madison; Mikhail Kouliavtsev, Temple University; Marilyn Lavin, University of Wisconsin–Whitewater; David Long, International Baccalaureate program, Rufus King High School, Wisconsin; Rich MacDonald, St. Cloud State University; Donna Miller; Andrew Morriss, Case Western Reserve University School of Law; Alan Murray, Wall Street Journal; Carl Pacini, Florida Gulf Coast University; John Riddle; Mark C. Schug, University of Wisconsin–Milwaukee; Mary Sisson, Crain's New York Business; Andrea Troyer, University of California–Irvine; John Troyer, Carlson School of Management, University of Minnesota; Connie Tuttle; Randall E. Waldron, University of South Dakota; John Washbush, University of Wisconsin–Whitewater; David Wessel, Wall Street Journal; Chris Woodford

Introduction

If the global economic downturn that began in 2008 has taught us anything, it is that world economies are intricately interrelated. Prior to 2008, economists debated the idea of decoupling, or the notion that some emerging economies, especially those in China, India, and Brazil, might be strong enough to develop independently of other nations. However, in the wake of the sharp global downturns of 2008 and 2009, "globally, the idea of decoupling is dead," said British economist Martin Wolf.

Economic Literacy takes steps to demystify complex global economic issues. It offers the background to events both current and historical, helping to clarify today's news headlines as well as chapters in history textbooks. It looks at topics such as tariffs, balance of trade, deregulation, inflation, microeconomics and macroeconomics, and income distribution to explain the ways economies around the world are constructed and interrelated. It investigates international organizations such as the European Union, OPEC, OECD, and the World Bank to explain their roles politically and economically.

Articles in this volume also explore the theoretical underpinnings of world economic systems, looking at socialist, communist, and capitalist approaches to economic organization and also at the tools of monetary policy that governments deploy to steer their national economies.

Around the world, concerns about environmental, social, and governance issues have become paramount. Developing economies confront the social and environmental costs of rapid economic growth. Corporations and governments in more developed countries try to integrate environmental sustainability into their business practices and political policies. In the twenty-first century, the costs of mismanagement and corruption continue to expose the importance of sound corporate governance and business ethics, and the value of an economically literate public.

Economic data change daily. In order to assure the long-term usefulness of this reference work, the citations for further reading and research with each of the 52 articles are reliable, Web-based resources that publish current information on an ongoing basis. The colorful and easy-to-interpret charts and graphs that illustrate most topics are designed to guide students in understanding and interpreting the statistical displays furnished online by governments, financial institutions, international organizations, and other interest groups.

—*Stephanie Schwartz Driver*

Arbitration

Arbitration is a method by which two parties involved in a dispute agree to have a neutral third party, the arbitrator, hear both sides of the argument, consider the facts, reach a decision and, when appropriate, make a monetary award. As part of the arbitration process, both parties customarily agree to abide by the decision of the arbitrator. While arbitration carries the weight of a legal proceeding, arbitrators are not necessarily lawyers or judges. Arbitrators may be persons with specialized knowledge in a field pertinent to the particular arbitration hearing.

Arbitration is often used as a way to avoid a long, costly court battle. Rather than have their case heard in a public court of law, the parties agree to have their differences privately arbitrated. Arbitration is usually quicker and less expensive than the trial process.

Sometimes arbitration may be the only available course. For example, credit card companies may ask their customers to sign an agreement that requires the customer to submit disputes to arbitration when differences are not routinely resolved. In some cases, employers ask prospective employees to sign arbitration agreements as a condition of their employment. Arbitration clauses may be included in any contract between two parties; the parties involved can be two individuals, an individual and a company, two companies, a labor union and management, or even two nations.

Although decisions reached through arbitration proceedings are usually binding on both parties, nonbinding arbitration does exist. In nonbinding arbitration, each party retains individual rights to have the case heard in a court of law.

History of Arbitration

Resolving international differences through arbitration dates to the first Hague Conference in 1899. The 26 nations participating agreed to consider questions of disarmament, methods of warfare, and the establishment of a permanent vehicle for the resolution of international disputes. Along with the other participating nations, the United States agreed to the creation of a Permanent Court of International Arbitration. However, arbitration was not made mandatory. In 1907, at the urging of President Theodore Roosevelt, a second Hague Conference was called. The apparatus for voluntary arbitration was enlarged at that time.

In 1925 the United States Congress passed the Federal Arbitration Act. As

In an 1886 cartoon by Joseph Keppler, two men set the hands (labor) of the clock (business). Arbitration, as the pendulum, swings in between them.

originally envisioned, the act addressed arbitration of commercial contract disputes. Over time, however, federal arbitration procedures have been used to resolve civil rights violations, securities fraud, antitrust claims, and employment disputes. The commercial aspect of the act remains important, however, and enforcement of arbitration agreements and awards, both in interstate commerce and in international contracts, is addressed in the federal act.

The Arbitration Society of America, the Arbitration Foundation, and the Arbitration Conference joined forces in 1926 to form the American Arbitration Association (AAA). That year, the Actors' Equity Association was one of the first organizations to include an arbitration clause in its contracts between actors and managers. Today, the AAA offers a wide range of services for alternative dispute resolution (ADR). A nonprofit organization, the AAA annually provides assistance to more than 100,000 persons seeking remedies outside the courtroom. AAA handles disputes in business, labor relations, employment, automobile accidents, and in other areas.

Mediation is another approach to conflict resolution. In mediation, a neutral third party hears both sides of the argument and may offer suggestions on better ways to communicate about the conflict, or ways to see the other's point of view, but does not offer a specific, binding resolution. Thus, a mediator helps the parties arrive at their own solution while an arbitrator provides the solution.

Why Arbitrate?

Arbitration or mediation offers many advantages in dispute resolution. For many people, avoiding the cost and complexity of a lawsuit is advantage enough; but there are others. In addition to the cost of a lawsuit, cases brought before the judicial system can take months or even years to be heard. Once a decision is reached, if a party to the lawsuit chooses to appeal the ruling, still more time may be added to the process.

Unlike a trial by jury, where the parties involved do not choose the members of the jury charged with weighing the evidence, arbitration allows the parties to choose their arbitrators from a pool of neutral individuals who have expertise in the field. Because courts must abide by complex rules of evidence and procedure, an arbitration hearing can seem quite informal. During arbitration, the parties involved in the dispute have the opportunity to present their story in a relaxed and private setting.

Because the hearings and awards in arbitration are kept private, less opportunity arises for the acrimony that sometimes accompanies the publicity surrounding a high-profile court case. This is especially important if the parties involved must continue to work together after the dispute is settled.

Both arbitration and mediation as methods of dispute resolution are gaining more adherents. Arbitration clauses are increasingly being written into contracts of every kind across virtually all industries. The methods of ADR have even made it to the classroom; the value of constructive conflict resolution is being recognized by a growing number of educators in both elementary and high schools. Workshops are being offered, journal articles written, and teachers are using ADR techniques to address conflicts among students.

In some schools, students are being trained in ADR methods to enable them to act as mediators when a conflict erupts among their peers. Before a dispute reaches that step, the students involved in the conflict are encouraged to negotiate their differences in an attempt to reach an understanding. If negotiation fails to produce results, student mediators become involved. Finally, if the situation cannot be resolved through mediation, a teacher is brought in to arbitrate the dispute.

A demonstration by United Farm Workers (UFW) in support of legislation that would give the union greater control during arbitration of contract negotiatons. A poster depicting Cesar Chavez is in the background.

Further Research
American Arbitration Association
www.adr.org

The home page of one of the largest arbitration organizations in the United States provides links to information on all aspects of arbitration and mediation. Its subsidiary, the International Centre for Dispute Resolution, has links with arbitration organizations in 43 countries to help U.S. institutions handle disputes abroad.

Association for Conflict Resolution
www.acrnet.org

The ACR is a professional organizing representing mediators, arbitrators, and other professionals in the field.

—*Connie Tuttle*

Balance of Payments

Individuals produce, trade, and borrow to satisfy their economic needs. These exchanges can become complicated; therefore, many people keep careful records of their transactions. These records tell them how much they have earned, the amount of their debts, what they own, and so on. Reviewing these documents will reveal their financial strengths and will show potential problems. National economies can be understood and evaluated in the same way, in a process economists call the balance of payments. This is the record of all transactions that take place between the residents of one nation (including individuals, businesses, and governmental units) and the residents of all other nations. (A related concept, the balance of trade, focuses more narrowly on goods exchanged between nations.)

The balance of payments has three components: goods, services, and money. All are exchanged with other countries in equal trades. Therefore, if all of one nation's exchanges are totaled, the inflows and outflows must be equal. If one nation buys more goods and services from another nation than it sells to that country, the difference is made up by the second nation gaining assets from the first. For example, if Americans buy computers from Taiwan and make no other exchanges with Taiwan, the Taiwanese retain the dollars that they realized from the sale. They may keep this money in a bank or buy something with it. The result: The United States gains computers and Taiwan gains dollars or property in the United States.

The table shows the different parts of the United States' balance of payments in 2007. The top half of the table is called the Current Account; it records trades in goods and services. It shows that the United States sold $1,148 billion worth of merchandise and $497 billion of services to people in other countries. However, after totaling U.S. imports and other transactions, the table reveals that the United States has a $713 billion trade deficit; the United States buys far more from other countries than it sells to them.

The bottom half of the table records the Capital Account. It shows the flow of money for the purchase or sale of financial and real assets that occurred in 2007; financial assets include stocks and bonds, while real assets include factories, office buildings, and so on. Many foreigners invest in the United States, buying financial and real assets, and Americans also frequently invest abroad. The Capital Account shows how the United States paid for its trade deficit. Capital inflows—foreign borrowing and purchases—exceeded

The 2007 balance of payments for the United States. Foreign investment makes up for the deficit in U.S. exports.

U.S. Balance of Payments 2007
(in billions of dollars)

THE UNITED STATES OF AMERICA

Current Account

U.S. merchandise exports	1,148
U.S. merchandise imports	−1,968
Balance of trade	−819
U.S. exports of services	497
U.S. imports of services	378
Balance of services	119
Balance of goods and services	−700
Net investment income	82
Net transfers	−113
Balance of current account	−713

Capital Account

Capital inflows into the United States	2,058
Capital outflows from the United States	−1,290
Balance of capital account account transactions, net	−1,843
Current and capital account balance	−731
Total balance	0

Note: Numbers are rounded to the nearest billion.   *Source:* U.S. Bureau of Economic Analysis

capital outflows by $1,843 billion, more than making up for the Current Account deficit.

This demonstrates one reason why the balance of payments calculations can result in controversy: Overspending on imports by a country results in foreigners owning assets in that country. This became a great concern in the United States from the late 1980s when other countries' nationals bought such properties as Rockefeller Center in New York City and Pebble Beach golf course in California. Many people were also concerned that jobs were leaving the United States as fewer people bought goods produced in the United States.

Another reason why balance of payments calculations can be controversial is related to the concept of national wealth. Eighteenth-century economists, called mercantilists, argued that a nation's wealth should be measured by how much gold and silver it had. Having more specie made a nation more powerful, they reasoned, therefore governments should actively interfere with trade and the economy to create a trade surplus. The result was that European kings frequently attempted to manage their economies by granting monopolies, imposing heavy taxes on trade, and other policies.

Adam Smith was the most famous opponent of this view. He convincingly argued that the mercantilists were wrong because increasing the supply of specie resulted in inflation, or an increase in prices. Instead, Smith asserted that a nation's wealth was best measured by what it could produce and proposed a policy called laissez-faire, or hands off. Smith's policy called for minimizing government involvement in the economy and allowing individuals the right to trade freely.

Economists generally agree that a nation's balance of payments is a matter of perspective. A trade deficit suggests that a nation's industries are not competitive and may suffer job losses as a result. On the other hand, consumers gain because they are able to buy foreign goods that are more appealing because of price or quality. Whether deficits are helpful or harmful depends on how long they last and the events causing them.

Further Research
Bureau of Economic Analysis
www.bea.gov/international
The International Investment Division of the BEA compiles data on U.S. direct investment abroad and foreign direct investment in the United States for the U.S. government.

—David Long

The famed Pebble Beach golf course in California was bought by Minoru Isutani in 1990; two years later he sold it to a Japanese golf resort company, the Lone Cypress Co., for approximately $500 million. A consortium of U.S. investors, including Arnold Palmer and Clint Eastwood, bought the course in 1999.

Balance of Trade

The balance of trade is the difference between the amount of goods that a country sells to other countries and the amount it imports from other countries. If a country sells more than it buys, it has a trade surplus. If it buys more goods from abroad than it sells, it has a trade deficit. A nation's balance of trade depends on several factors, including the spending habits of its citizens and how competitive its leading industries are.

The consequences of a persistent trade deficit can be serious. One concern is that such a deficit indicates an economy that is not very competitive. If a country cannot produce appealing goods at reasonable prices or fails to produce new and innovative goods, it will tend to export less and import more. The result: Employment will fall as domestic industries fail, thereby reducing incomes. Another concern is that nations seem to lose wealth when they run consistent trade deficits. Trade deficits result in foreigners gaining assets—money or property—in the deficit nation. This sale of a nation's assets can cause discontent and resentment among voters, because foreigners seem to be buying the country.

U.S. Balance of Trade 1955 to 2008
(in million dollars)

	Exports	Imports	Balance on goods		Exports	Imports	Balance on goods
1955	14,424	-11,527	2,897	1982	211,157	-247,642	-36,485
1956	17,556	-12,803	4,753	1983	201,799	-268,901	-67,102
1957	19,562	-13,291	6,271	1984	219,926	-332,418	-112,492
1958	16,414	-12,952	3,462	1985	215,915	-338,088	-122,173
1959	16,458	-15,310	1,148	1986	223,344	-368,425	-145,081
1960	19,650	-14,758	4,892	1987	250,208	-409,765	-159,557
1961	20,108	-14,537	5,571	1988	320,230	-447,189	-126,959
1962	20,781	-16,260	4,521	1989	359,916	-477,665	-117,749
1963	22,272	-17,048	5,224	1990	387,401	-498,435	-111,034
1964	25,501	-18,700	6,801	1991	414,083	-491,020	-76,937
1965	26,461	-21,510	4,951	1992	439,631	-536,528	-96,897
1966	29,310	-25,493	3,817	1993	456,943	-589,394	-132,451
1967	30,666	-26,866	3,800	1994	502,859	-668,690	-165,831
1968	33,626	-32,991	635	1995	575,204	-749,374	-174,170
1969	36,414	-35,807	607	1996	612,113	-803,113	-191,000
1970	42,469	-39,866	2,603	1997	678,366	-876,485	-198,119
1971	43,319	-45,579	-2,260	1998	670,416	-917,112	-246,696
1972	49,381	-55,797	-6,416	1999	684,553	-1,029,987	-345,434
1973	71,410	-70,499	911	2000	772,210	-1,224,417	-452,207
1974	98,306	-103,811	-5,505	2001	718,712	-1,148,231	-429,519
1975	107,088	-98,185	8,903	2002	682,422	-1,167,377	-423,725
1976	114,745	-124,228	-9,483	2003	713,415	-1,264,307	-550,892
1977	120,816	-151,907	-31,091	2004	807,516	-1,477,094	-669,578
1978	142,075	-176,002	-33,927	2005	894,631	-1,681,780	-787,149
1979	184,439	-212,007	-27,568	2006	1,023,109	-1,861,380	-838,270
1980	224,250	-249,750	-25,500	2007	1,148,481	-1,967,853	-819,373
1981	237,044	-265,067	-28,023	2008	1,291,337	-2,112,490	-821,153

Source: U.S. Census Bureau

Economists and politicians therefore try to create trade surpluses to increase the wealth and power of their nation. In the second half of the twentieth century, the world steadily moved toward more open trade. Treaties like the North American Free Trade Agreement (NAFTA) and organizations like the European Union are predicated on the gains expected from free trade. These include access to goods and services that otherwise would not be available, lower prices for consumers, and the chance to create jobs by exporting goods and services to other countries.

However, free trade is not universally recognized as a positive force because capitalism is based on competition. Businesses that can satisfy consumers on price, quality, and innovation will profit and prosper. Those that cannot will be forced into bankruptcy and their workers into unemployment. Foreign trade increases the amount of competition and therefore presents a threat to both business profits and workers' jobs. Accordingly, both workers and employers have an incentive to appeal for government action against foreign trade. Consumers, a far larger but less united group, have less incentive to act and are thus less involved.

Almost all nations have trade barriers in place to protect domestic industries against foreign competitors, frequently citing a balance of trade deficit as the reason for government action. Common strategies include tariffs (taxes on imported goods that raise their prices) and quotas (set limits on the amount of goods foreign competitors may import).

These strategies benefit domestic employers and, to a lesser extent, their workers. Their costs can be quite large, however. In various studies of different industries, economists have found that protecting jobs through tariffs costs more than retraining the workers in other fields. This gap between intentions and results leads many economists to conclude that

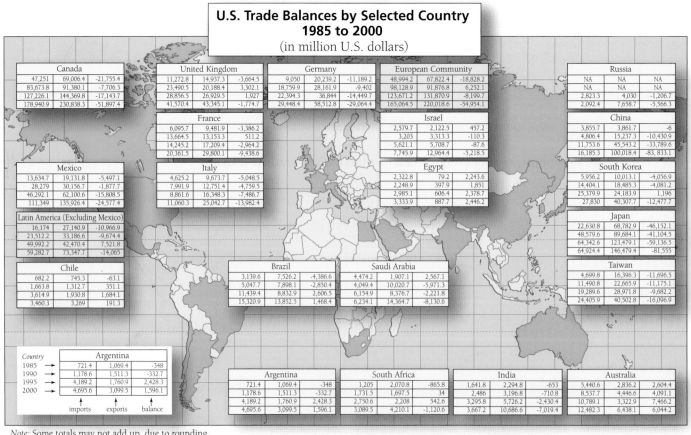

U.S. Trade Balances by Selected Country
1985 to 2000
(in million U.S. dollars)

Canada

47,251	69,006.4	-21,755.4
83,673.8	91,380.1	-7,706.3
127,226.1	144,369.8	-17,143.7
178,940.9	230,838.3	-51,897.4

United Kingdom

11,272.8	14,937.3	-3,664.5
23,490.5	20,188.4	3,302.1
28,856.5	26,929.5	1,927
41,570.4	43,345.1	-1,774.7

Germany

9,050	20,239.2	-11,189.2
18,759.9	28,161.9	-9,402
22,394.3	36,844	-14,449.7
29,448.4	58,512.8	-29,064.4

European Community

48,994.2	67,822.4	-18,828.2
98,128.9	91,876.8	6,252.1
123,671.2	131,870.9	-8,199.7
165,064.5	220,018.6	-54,954.1

Russia

NA	NA	NA
NA	NA	NA
2,823.3	4,030	-1,206.7
2,092.4	7,658.7	-5,566.3

France

6,095.7	9,481.9	-3,386.2
13,664.5	13,153.3	511.2
14,245.2	17,209.4	-2,964.2
20,361.5	29,800.1	-9,438.6

Israel

2,579.7	2,122.5	457.2
3,203	3,313.3	-110.3
5,621.1	5,708.7	-87.6
7,745.9	12,964.4	-5,218.5

China

3,855.7	3,861.7	-6
4,806.4	15,237.3	-10,430.9
11,753.6	45,543.2	-33,789.6
16,185.3	100,018.4	-83,833.1

Mexico

13,634.7	19,131.6	-5,497.1
28,279	30,156.7	-1,877.7
46,292.1	62,100.6	-15,808.5
111,349	135,926.4	-24,577.4

Italy

4,625.2	9,673.7	-5,048.5
7,991.9	12,751.4	-4,759.5
8,861.6	16,348.3	-7,486.7
11,060.3	25,042.7	-13,982.4

Egypt

2,322.8	79.2	2,243.6
2,248.9	397.9	1,851
2,985.1	606.4	2,378.7
3,333.9	887.7	2,446.2

South Korea

5,956.2	10,013.1	-4,056.9
14,404.1	18,485.3	-4,081.2
25,379.9	24,183.9	1,196
27,830	40,307.7	-12,477.7

Latin America (Excluding Mexico)

16,174	27,140.9	-10,966.9
23,512.2	33,186.6	-9,674.4
49,992.2	42,470.4	7,521.8
59,282.7	73,347.7	-14,065

Japan

22,630.8	68,782.9	-46,152.1
48,579.6	89,684.1	-41,104.5
64,342.6	123,479.1	-59,136.5
64,924.4	146,479.4	-81,555

Chile

682.2	745.3	-63.1
1,663.8	1,312.7	351.1
3,614.9	1,930.8	1,684.1
3,460.3	3,269	191.3

Brazil

3,139.6	7,526.2	-4,386.6
5,047.7	7,898.1	-2,850.4
11,439.4	8,832.9	2,606.5
15,320.9	13,852.5	1,468.4

Saudi Arabia

4,474.2	1,907.1	2,567.1
4,049.4	10,020.7	-5,971.3
6,154.9	8,376.7	-2,221.8
6,234.1	14,364.7	-8,130.6

Taiwan

4,699.8	16,396.3	-11,696.5
11,490.8	22,665.9	-11,175.1
19,289.6	28,971.8	-9,682.2
24,405.9	40,502.8	-16,096.9

Argentina

Country				
1985 →		721.4	1,069.4	-348
1990 →		1,178.6	1,511.3	-332.7
1995 →		4,189.2	1,760.9	2,428.3
2000 →		4,695.6	3,099.5	1,596.1
		imports	exports	balance

Argentina

721.4	1,069.4	-348
1,178.6	1,511.3	-332.7
4,189.2	1,760.9	2,428.3
4,695.6	3,099.5	1,596.1

South Africa

1,205	2,070.8	-865.8
1,731.5	1,697.5	34
2,750.6	2,208	542.6
3,089.5	4,210.1	-1,120.6

India

1,641.8	2,294.8	-653
2,486	3,196.8	-710.8
3,295.8	5,726.2	-2,430.4
3,667.2	10,686.6	-7,019.4

Australia

5,440.6	2,836.2	2,604.4
8,537.7	4,446.6	4,091.1
10,789.1	3,322.9	7,466.2
12,482.3	6,438.1	6,044.2

Note: Some totals may not add up, due to rounding.
Source: U.S. Census Bureau, Foreign Trade Division, Data Dissemination Branch, Washington, D.C.

the costs of protectionism far outweigh the benefits.

A second drawback of trade barriers is that they often result in international friction. Nations commonly accuse each other, often with reason, of cheating and threaten retaliation. Nations commonly subsidize, or give loans or other funds, to producers of certain goods. This allows those companies to offer cheaper prices and reap greater profits, often driving their foreign competition into bankruptcy. Cheating makes sense to politicians because they have more incentive to please their potential campaign donors and voters than the citizens of other countries.

A series of international trade agreements called the General Agreement on Tariffs and Trade (GATT) strives to address these issues. The 1994 GATT agreement called for international reductions in tariffs, quotas, and other trade barriers between 1995 and 2005. The World Trade Organization (WTO) was created in 1995 to quickly and fairly resolve trade disputes. Formerly, nations had very little recourse to solve trade issues and often resorted to retaliating against tariffs or quotas with similar measures, leading to trade wars and economic losses. Ideally, the WTO acts as a neutral third party to mediate disputes.

Further Research

U.S. Trade Deficit Review Commission

govinfo.library.unt.edu/tdrc/reports/finalrept-contents.html

"The U.S. Trade Deficit: Causes, Consequences and Recommendations for Action." is a report that examines U.S. trade policy and its ramifications.

World Trade Organization

www.wto.org

The home page of the World Trade Organization offers resources for students, including trade statistics, country reports, news, and other essential information.

—*David Long*

Steelworkers in Chile protest U.S. tariffs on steel imports, which were imposed to protect the U.S. steel industry from foreign competition.

Business Cycles

Business cycles involve patterns of expansion and contraction in employment, production, and price levels that occur in an economy over time. Consider the biggest dip in U.S. economic history, the Great Depression. Between 1929 and 1932, stock prices as measured by the Dow Jones Industrial Average fell about 89 percent and did not recover their value for many years. Unemployment soared from 7.7 million in 1937 to 10.4 million in 1938, an increase in the unemployment rate from 14 to 19 percent in one year, and this was eight years after the stock market crash. Bank failures climbed from 167 in 1920 to more than 4,000 in 1933. Indeed, the country lost about one-half of all commercial banks to bankruptcy during the Depression. Industrial production also declined sharply. Factories produced at about one-half of their capacity, and investment in new equipment collapsed from $16 billion to less than $1 billion.

Business cycles affect the economies of all nations. Since World War II, the United States has experienced nine business cycle contractions and expansions. Fluctuations in business activity are repetitive, and cycles in the United States affect other economies as well—from Japan, Great Britain, Germany, and Brazil to Canada, Indonesia, South Korea, and Italy.

Debates on Business Cycles

Business cycles have many names and competing explanations for their occurrence: observed patterns include Kitchin's 40-month cycle, Juglar's 8-year cycle, or Kondratieff's 50-year waves. Some experts explain cycles by looking at the fluctuations of inventories; others identify changes in the level of investment in capital technology as the cause. In general, economists rely on two broad schools of thought when trying to understand fluctuations in the business cycle: the classical school and the Keynesian school.

Classical thinkers assume the economy obeys the laws of supply and demand. Markets work to bring themselves into balance. Price fluctuations reflect real changes in the economy and, if allowed to operate freely, provide enough information to savers and investors so that saving and investment decisions promote stability. According to this school of thought, business cycles are

In March 1939, during the Great Depression, people wait in line to receive food from a relief program in San Antonio, Texas.

self-correcting unless misguided government economic policies make matters worse.

The classical formulation holds that economies tend toward long-run stability in employment, prices, and output, because what is manufactured generates sufficient income to be taken off the market. Supply creates its own demand. Gluts and shortages are temporary and actually perform useful signaling functions in a decentralized, self-regulating system that continuously adjusts itself. Ineffective tax hikes and disruptive tinkering with monetary policy exacerbate the fluctuations in business cycles. The Depression,

U.S. Business Cycles 1854 to 2001

Business cycle dates		Duration in months			
Trough	Peak	Recession	Expansion	Cycle	
		Trough from previous peak	Trough to peak	Trough from previous trough	Peak from previous peak
December 1854	June 1857	–	30	–	–
December 1858	October 1860	18	22	48	40
June 1861	April 1865	8	*46*	30	*54*
December 1867	June 1869	*32*	18	*78*	50
December 1870	October 1873	18	34	36	52
March 1879	March 1882	65	36	99	101
May 1885	March 1887	38	22	74	60
April 1888	July 1890	13	27	35	40
May 1891	January 1893	10	20	37	30
June 1894	December 1895	17	18	37	35
June 1897	June 1899	18	24	36	42
December 1900	September 1902	18	21	42	39
August 1904	May 1907	23	33	44	56
June 1908	January 1910	13	19	46	32
January 1912	January 1913	24	12	43	36
December 1914	August 1918	23	*44*	35	*67*
March 1919	January 1920	*7*	10	*51*	17
July 1921	May 1923	18	22	28	40
July 1924	October 1926	14	27	36	41
November 1927	August 1929	13	21	40	34
March 1933	May 1937	43	50	64	93
June 1938	February 1945	13	*80*	63	*93*
October 1945	November 1948	*8*	37	*88*	45
October 1949	July 1953	11	*45*	48	*56*
May 1954	August 1957	*10*	39	*55*	49
April 1958	April 1960	8	24	47	32
February 1961	December 1969	10	*106*	34	*116*
November 1970	November 1973	*11*	36	*117*	47
March 1975	January 1980	16	58	52	74
July 1980	July 1981	6	12	64	18
November 1982	July 1990	16	92	28	108
March 1991	March 2001	8	120	100	128

Note: Figures printed in red are wartime expansions (Civil War, World War I and II, Korean War, and Vietnam War), the postwar contractions, and the full cycles that include the wartime expansions.
Sources: National Bureau of Economic Research and the U.S. Department of Commerce, *Survey of Current Business*, Washington, D.C., Government Printing Office, 2002.

The duration of the peaks and valleys of business cycles.

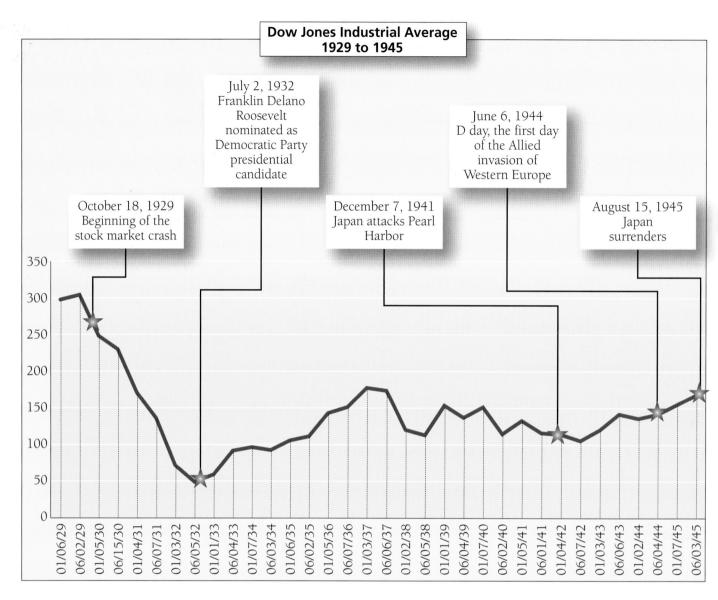

**Dow Jones Industrial Average
1929 to 1945**

October 18, 1929
Beginning of the
stock market crash

July 2, 1932
Franklin Delano
Roosevelt
nominated as
Democratic Party
presidential
candidate

December 7, 1941
Japan attacks Pearl
Harbor

June 6, 1944
D day, the first day
of the Allied
invasion of
Western Europe

August 15, 1945
Japan
surrenders

Experts often look to the stock market when analyzing business cycles. This chart shows the activity of the Dow Jones Industrial Average during the Great Depression and World War II.

according to the classical school, was made much worse by the bad timing of tax increases, cuts in the money supply, and enormous increases in tariffs.

By contrast, British economist John Maynard Keynes claimed that capitalism was chronically ill. The illness predisposed the economy toward instability in prices, output, and employment. The sickness of capitalism was attributable in part to the disconnected nature of the plans of savers and investors. Mismatches in savings and investment decisions could become a source of long-term disruption for the real economy of goods and services and for production, distribution, and consumption. Acknowledging some of the self-correcting market tendencies described by the classical school, followers of Keynes believed that some sort of governmental

demand-management policies were required to keep capitalism healthy. According to this line of thinking, an optimal combination of monetary and fiscal policy would promote stability in the labor and financial markets during periodic imbalances. To make good savings and investment decisions, individuals and businesses needed help and assistance from the public sector.

Stocks and Cycles

An important question emerges in the course of this argument between the classical and Keynesian schools. What is the relationship between stock market fluctuations and the real economy of jobholders who make consumption decisions and savers who make investment decisions? Studies indicate stock prices do affect consumption and investment decisions, but only slightly. A 10 percent sustained increase in stock market values in one year is associated with a 4 percent increase in consumption spending during the next three years. The connection between investment spending and stock values is even weaker.

Apparently, however, stock market bubbles matter much more. When the prices of shares outstrip the underlying value of the issuer, as happened in the 1990s and in 2007, it can cause serious problems in the real economy. Stock market bubbles are the product of unbridled optimism (reflected in the popular misconception that recessions are a thing of the past in the new economy), frenzied speculation (the dot-com craze or the explosive growth in financial engineering and derivative investment vehicles from 2005 to 2007), or just plain "irrational exuberance," as Federal Reserve chairman Alan Greenspan asserted. Falling stock prices can wreak havoc as workers are laid off, consumption plans postponed, and investment projects cancelled. The intoxicating euphoria of the run-up is replaced by the hangover of gloom and doom.

Can stock market prices predict changes in the business cycle? The answer is uncertain. Insofar as stock price indexes like the New York Stock Exchange Index or the Standard and Poor's 500 Index accurately measure the mood of the investment community, they may be said to show some kind of connection between stock market and business cycle fluctuations. However, the precise connection is unclear. Most of the American recessions since 1945 were preceded by general decreases in stock price measures. Yet stock market prices alone do not always predict recessions. Stock market indexes sometimes fall sharply without being followed by a business cycle downturn, as was the case in 1987 when a 508-point drop in the Dow Jones Industrial Average was not followed immediately by a downturn in the economy. Although the exact connection is unclear, the general level of stock prices is deemed important enough to be included in the government's top 10 leading economic indicators that, taken together, may predict future directions of business activity.

Volatility in the stock market is one indication of economic dislocation.

The economists' quarrel over the causes of business cycles has become increasingly important. Substantial differences result when the government does little or nothing, on the one hand, or adjusts taxes and spending levels to mitigate the effects of a recession, on the other. These policy choices matter a great deal. Business cycles in the United States, Japan, Venezuela, and the European Union are increasingly interconnected as globalization brings markets closer together. The United States committed itself to achieving full employment and stable prices in the Full Employment Act of 1946 and in its subsequent amendments; dealing with the business cycle is the law of the land. So, in addition to being the subject of debate between economists, the roller coaster ride of the business cycle is important to people concerned with their jobs or with how far their paychecks will take them during the ride.

Further Research
Irrational Exuberance
www.irrationalexuberance.com
Robert Shiller, professor of economics at Yale University, has studied speculative bubbles in the stock market and in real estate. This Web site explains some of his theories and offers links to information about his research.
National Bureau of Economic Research
www.nber.org/cycles.html
The Business Cycle Dating Committee of the NBER tracks business expansions and contractions (recessions).

—*Stephen Haessler*

Business Ethics

A product designer considers making public the fact that the company he works for has decided to manufacture a product that could have dangerous defects. A government purchasing manager considers awarding an important contract to a high bidder because she has made investments in that bidder's company. A chief executive officer (CEO), concerned about his corporation's decreased competitiveness, contemplates moving operations to a foreign county with cheaper labor, which would result in the layoff of thousands of his company's U.S. employees.

These situations all involve businesspeople making decisions about actions that have an ethical dimension. These individuals have moral choices to make, choices that involve business ethics. Ethics is a branch of philosophy that examines moral judgments and the principles underlying those judgments. Business ethics is a form of applied ethics: it considers how ethical principles influence business judgments and vice versa. On a more practical level, a code of business ethics helps businesspeople to distinguish right behavior from wrong and to practice doing right at the same time that they fulfill their functions in the world of business.

Present-day business decisions cannot be made without some consideration of their ethical dimensions. CEOs, mid-level managers, professional staff, and factory and plant workers are all confronted with choices every day; their decisions may affect an entire corporation, industry, or community. Despite media reports that tend to revel in the scandalous behavior inside the largest corporations, the image of business as completely unconcerned about and unconstrained by moral considerations is not true. The smooth functioning of business requires that shareholders and managers, employers and employees, sellers and buyers, and corporations and the communities in which they are based engage in relationships of trust with one another. Businesses suffer when those relationships of trust are damaged by questionable or unethical practices, as evidenced by the decline of the U.S. stock market in 2002, when investors were made wary—and poorer—by the shady business dealings and accounting practices of large corporations, including Enron, Tyco International Ltd., and WorldCom.

Key Issues in Business Ethics

Business ethics is a vast field that examines business practices from a variety of perspectives. Often, it involves the application of philosophical theories like utilitarianism, which says that ethical actions are those that result in the greatest good for the greatest number of people. Another important principle used in business ethics is Kant's categorical imperative, which identifies ethical acts as those whose rules the

Areas of Business Affected by Ethics	
Area affected	*Examples*
Employee–employer relations	Fair and just wages
	Hiring and promotion
	Workplace safety
	Monitoring of employees
Corporate relations with suppliers and customers	Fair contracts
	Honestly performed contracts
	Fair and reasonable pricing of goods
Corporate relations with society at large	Truthful advertising
	Impact on environment
	Impact on welfare of community
	Influence on political and international affairs

actor would want willed into universal law. It asks: What would happen if everyone did that? For instance, a manager who bribes foreign officials to secure tax breaks for his company might justify the act by arguing that bribery is the only way to do business in that country, and that bribery has allowed him to increase profits for the company's shareholders—a duty with which he has been entrusted as agent for those shareholders. However, a universal law that allowed everyone to use bribery to serve the special interests of his or her employer would significantly impede business; thus in this application of Kant's theory, bribery cannot be considered ethical behavior.

While these and other philosophical principles form the basis of many arguments about and discussions of business ethics, business ethicists investigate such a wide array of issues that it is impossible to formulate one theory that can be successfully applied to all situations. In one area, business ethics considers the rights and responsibilities of employers in relation to employees. Key questions include: What constitutes fair and just wages, hiring and promotion practices, and monitoring of employees? To what extent is an employer obliged to protect employees' health, safety, and right to privacy, and what responsibility do employers have to prevent sexual harassment or discrimination in the workplace? To what extent is an employee obliged to avoid conflicts of interest, remain loyal, and protect confidentiality? At what point are such duties superseded by an employee's obligations to consumers and society in general, as in the case of whistleblowers alerting the public to a company's wrongdoing?

Business ethics also investigates the relationship between corporations and their suppliers and customers. Here, concerns about fair contracts, waste or fraud in the performance of contracts, and the fair and reasonable pricing of goods come into play, as well as the morality of initiating and maintaining business relationships through gifts, entertainment, and bribery. Another key

The philosopher Immanuel Kant's theory of the categorical imperative is the basis for many aspects of business ethics.

question in this area involves advertising: What constitutes deceptive advertising practices? To what extent are corporations and the advertising agencies they hire responsible for presenting a thorough and accurate portrayal of their products? What are the ethics of creating desire for goods that are unlikely to provide the popularity, beauty, wealth, and status that advertisements often imply?

Business ethicists also debate corporate practices that have sweeping consequences for society. To what extent should corporations be responsible for their effect on the environment and for the health and safety of individuals living near their plants and factories? Corporations have become powerful enough to determine the fates of entire communities in many cases, so should they be responsible for bettering those communities through charitable donations and business practices that help to reduce poverty, urban blight, and racial and gender discrimination? What are the ethical implications of corporate downsizing, involvement in political action committees, and investment in countries whose governments abuse civil and human rights?

Many of these questions are integral to the discussion of and debate about corporate social responsibility, a concept that emerged after World War II in response to the growing influence of corporations on American life. Proponents of corporate

Eight Guidelines for Managing Ethics in the Workplace

1. *Recognize that managing ethics is a process.* Ethics is a matter of values and associated behaviors. Values are discerned through the process of ongoing reflection. Therefore, ethics programs may seem more process-oriented than most management practices. Managers tend to be skeptical of process-oriented activities, and instead prefer processes focused on deliverables with measurements.... Ethics programs do produce deliverables, e.g., codes, policies and procedures, budget items, meeting minutes, authorization forms, newsletters, etc. However, the most important aspect of an ethics management program is the process of reflection and dialogue that produces these deliverables.

2. *The bottom line of an ethics program is accomplishing preferred behaviors in the workplace.* The best of ethical values and intentions are relatively meaningless unless they generate fair and just behaviors in the workplace. That's why practices that generate lists of ethical values, or codes of ethics, must also generate policies, procedures, and training that translate those values to appropriate behaviors.

3. *The best way to handle ethical dilemmas is to avoid their occurrence in the first place.* That's why practices such as developing codes of ethics and codes of conduct are so important. Their development sensitizes employees to ethical considerations and minimizes the chances of unethical behavior occurring in the first place.

4. *Make ethics decisions in groups, and make decisions public, as appropriate.* This usually produces better quality decisions by including diverse interests and perspectives, and increases the credibility of the decision process and outcome by reducing suspicion of unfair bias.

5. *Integrate ethics management with other management practices.* When developing the values statement during strategic planning, include ethical values preferred in the workplace. When developing personnel policies, reflect on what ethical values you'd like to be most prominent in the organization's culture and then design policies to produce these behaviors.

6. *Use cross-functional teams when developing and implementing the ethics management program.* It's vital that the organization's employees feel a sense of participation and ownership in the program if they are to adhere to its ethical values. Therefore, include employees in developing and operating the program.

7. *Value forgiveness.* An ethics management program may at first actually increase the number of ethical issues to be dealt with because people are more sensitive to their occurrence. Consequently, there may be more occasions to address people's unethical behavior. The most important ingredient for remaining ethical is trying to be ethical. Therefore, help people recognize and address their mistakes and then support them to continue to try to operate ethically.

8. *Note that trying to operate ethically and making a few mistakes is better than not trying at all.* All organizations are comprised of people and people are not perfect. However, when a mistake is made by any of these organizations, the organization has a long way to fall. In our increasingly critical society, these organizations are accused of being hypocritical and they are soon pilloried by social critics. Consequently, some leaders may fear sticking their necks out publicly to announce an ethics management program. This is extremely unfortunate. It's the trying that counts and brings peace of mind—not achieving an heroic status in society.

Source: Reprinted by permission from Carter McNamara, *The Complete Guide to Ethics Management,* The Free Management Library, http://www.mapnp.org/library/ (January 2, 2003).

social responsibility contend that corporations have a responsibility not just to their shareholders, but also to all who have a stake in the corporation's activities, including

It shall be unlawful for any domestic concern, or for any officer, director, employee, or agent of such domestic concern or any stockholder thereof acting on behalf of such domestic concern, to make use of the mails or any means or instrumentality of interstate commerce corruptly in furtherance of an offer, payment, promise to pay, or authorization of the payment of any money, or offer, gift, promise to give, or authorization of the giving of anything of value to—

(1) any foreign official for purposes of—

(A) (i) influencing any act or decision of such foreign official in his official capacity, (ii) inducing such foreign official to do or omit to do any act in violation of the lawful duty of such official, or (iii) securing any improper advantage; or

(B) inducing such foreign official to use his influence with a foreign government or instrumentality thereof to affect or influence any act or decision of such government or instrumentality,

in order to assist such domestic concern in obtaining or retaining business for or with, or directing business to, any person;

(2) any foreign political party or official thereof or any candidate for foreign political office for purposes of—

(A) (i) influencing any act or decision of such party, official, or candidate in its or his official capacity, (ii) inducing such party, official, or candidate to do or omit to do an act in violation of the lawful duty of such party, official, or candidate, or (iii) securing any improper advantage; or

(B) inducing such party, official, or candidate to use its or his influence with a foreign government or instrumentality thereof to affect or influence any act or decision of such government or instrumentality,

in order to assist such domestic concern in obtaining or retaining business for or with, or directing business to, any person.

employees, suppliers, consumers, and the communities they affect. Hence, business managers must shape their policies according to how they will affect not just profits but also their broad group of stakeholders, with each group given equal weight in the decision-making process. Where earlier theories of the corporation reflect Adam Smith's concept that businesses act as an "invisible hand" in society, providing social benefits via economic growth, the concept of corporate social responsibility charges businesses with providing social good in more tangible and purposeful ways.

The free-market or shareholder theory of the corporation holds that corporate managers have neither the obligation nor the necessary knowledge to provide social good. As agents entrusted by shareholders to maximize profits for the corporation, managers' ethical duties go no further than to shareholders and to acting within the constraints of governmental regulations imposed upon them. Indeed, the government is responsible for the social good, not corporations, and the two should be kept separate in their functions, with the government regulating corporations in keeping with the ethical standards of society. Other arguments against the theory of corporate social responsibility contend that the theory raises more questions than it answers: Who gets to determine what kinds of social good corporations should provide? How much of a corporation's resources should be allocated to socially responsible projects? Is corporate social responsibility truly feasible in the real world, where companies spending resources to improve social well-being might lose their competitive edge and even go out of business?

Despite these arguments, the general trend has been for corporations to embrace

The Foreign Corrupt Practices Act was passed in 1977 to regulate the behavior of U.S. companies doing business abroad.

the idea of corporate social responsibility, perhaps because the two sides of the debate are not so at odds with each other as they first appear. Many theorists argue that "doing good" is, in fact, the best way to ensure the long-term success of a company—and hence fulfill duties to shareholders. After all, with the media, government, and investment community more carefully scrutinizing corporate behavior, businesses engaging in unethical or questionable practices often face litigation, stricter and more expensive forms of governmental regulation, anxious, less productive employees, and skittish shareholders. For example, in 1996, Texaco Corporation was involved in high-profile discrimination litigation that triggered a boycott of the company, leading to a marked decrease in share value. Research has shown that companies that are considered socially responsible often enjoy healthy profits and long-term growth. Good ethics—or at least the appearance of good ethics—is increasingly understood to be good for business.

The Law and Ethical Gray Areas

Bad behavior in the business world is, unfortunately, inevitable. As some individuals will always be ready to cross ethical lines, the

task of the legal system, as an embodiment of society's moral standards, is to make engaging in such damaging behavior unprofitable for businesses. In the United States, a vast network of state and federal regulations sets standards for corporate behavior in finance, contracts, employee and employer rights and obligations, workplace safety, product safety, and the environment. Ethics laws are constantly evolving: for example, the corporate accounting scandals of 2001 led directly to enactment of the Sarbanes–Oxley Act, which went into effect in July 2002 and was aimed at reining in some of the worst accounting abuses. Despite increased regulation and emphasis on auditing standards, Bernard Madoff was able to perpetrate his giant financial fraud, revealed in 2009, demonstrating that determined fraudsters can evade even enhanced oversight.

One important function that the law serves is to create a level playing field on which companies can compete. By requiring that all companies in a particular industry play by the same rules, less socially responsible companies do not achieve a competitive advantage over those that, for example, implement pollution controls or workplace safety programs and rules.

Yet the law must also protect and facilitate commerce. Often, state and federal regulations have as much practical as moral justification: for instance, most would agree that bribery and fraud are unethical, but such practices are also not in the best interests of the U.S. economy, so the law strictly prohibits them. In other contexts, it is less clear to what extent U.S. law should intervene to set ethical standards. Strict U.S. regulations and standards, plus increased litigation that often favors individuals over corporations, are criticized for requiring so much of companies that they have difficulty competing.

For instance, corporations are expected to adhere to high standards in relation to their effect on the environment, a heated issue that is often treated as its own area of business ethics. Critics argue that environmental regulations imposed on business and industry are unnecessarily costly to implement, thus encouraging companies to move operations to countries with lower standards. Others claim that more incentives could be provided to corporations to encourage them to go beyond the minimum required by law. Another ethical question arises when corporations devote resources to lobbying against environmental and other forms of regulation: How much influence should corporations be allowed to have on our legislative bodies?

Although these concerns are important, more often the law sets the minimum moral standard for corporations to meet, which, critics contend, often leaves too much room for companies to act in ethically questionable ways. For example, the Federal Trade Commission's prohibition of deceptive advertising goes a long way to prevent advertisements that contain lies; ethicists, however, question the more subtle forms of deception that businesses and advertisers sometimes practice. Laws can be difficult to enforce, or may even conflict with existing laws and ethical considerations. For instance, though law and public policy generally protect consumers against unsafe products, no universal standard exists for determining the line between safe and unsafe. When is an inherently dangerous product safe enough to be considered marketable? Should different standards be applied in the case of goods that are needed desperately and quickly, for example, new medications that treat deadly illnesses?

Along the same lines, workplace safety laws require that employers report workplace hazards to employees, but sometimes what constitutes a reportable hazard is unclear. This has become a particular concern because workplace safety laws often conflict with laws protecting employees' privacy rights: In the case of employees who have tested positive for drug use or AIDS, which employee right takes precedence, the right to a safe workplace or the right to privacy? How does the long-standing "employment at will"

doctrine, which protects employers' rights to hire, fire, and promote at their discretion, conflict with antidiscrimination and sexual harassment policies? Often, these murky waters can be navigated only on a case-by-case basis through litigation, as the U.S. legal and judicial systems struggle to delineate clearer ethical frameworks that respond to social concerns while still protecting commerce.

The Case of Multinationals

The rise of multinational corporations has introduced a host of new and complicated ethical issues that are separate from the ones raised by corporations with operations confined to a single country. Multinational companies typically have a base in a home country at the same time that they establish factories or plants in a host country—often an impoverished nation that offers cheaper labor, tax breaks, inexpensive land, and ready access to natural resources. While multinationals are credited with helping to improve and expand impoverished nations' economies, critics argue that they often do more harm than good by engaging in bribery, exploiting poor countries' land and mineral

Bernard Madoff (center) is escorted to court in 2009 to face charges in his $65 billion investor fraud case.

Major Provisions of the Sarbanes–Oxley Act of 2002

- Chief executive and financial officers are required to certify periodic financial reports and are subject to criminal penalties based on the certifications.
- In most cases, companies are prohibited from extending personal loans to executives.
- Protections for whistle-blowers are enhanced.
- The statute of limitations for securities fraud is extended.
- New criminal securities fraud statute enacted.
- Maximum penalties for willful violations of the securities laws are increased to fines of up to $5 million and imprisonment of up to 20 years.
- Maximum term of imprisonment for mail and wire fraud, and for destroying documents in a federal investigation or bankruptcy, is set at 20 years.
- Maximum term of imprisonment for any accountant who fails to maintain audit work papers for five years is set at 10 years.
- Criminal penalties for intentional interference with an official proceeding are enhanced.

The Sarbanes–Oxley Act was passed in 2002 to address some of the worst excesses of late-twentieth-century corporate behavior.

resources, taking advantage of lax or nonexistent pollution controls, violating worker and human rights, and generally aggravating the poverty and instability of host countries. They have even been charged with worsening labor conditions in their home countries. For instance, labor conditions in the U.S. garment industry changed dramatically after many of its companies became multinationals: the relatively few factories that remained on U.S. soil were forced to revert to sweatshop conditions to remain competitive with overseas factories.

The stakes get higher when the host country's government is considered corrupt or is a notorious violator of human rights. For instance, before apartheid was abolished in South Africa in 1993, U.S. corporations with South African operations were criticized for helping to support that country's oppressive regime. Although many of these corporations claimed that they served as a powerful instrument of social change in that country, the public outcry against them resulted in large-scale U.S. disinvestment.

A key question in the case of multinationals is the ethics of doing in host countries what is considered unethical or illegal in the home country. Adhering strictly to the moral and legal standards of home countries is not possible or even desirable in many instances. For example, imagine if a U.S. law required U.S. corporations to pay foreign factory workers the same wage as U.S. workers. In addition to the obvious economic disadvantages this law would present for U.S. corporations, such a law would also encourage skilled labor to seek employment at the U.S. companies, thus decreasing the pool of skilled labor for host countries' businesses. At the same time, many ethicists agree that simply "doing what the Romans do" in host countries is, more often than not, morally wrong. Many impoverished nations may desire to enact or even have existing laws that address bribery, pollution, and labor exploitation, but such nations may simply lack the means to create or enforce such regulations. Certainly, multinationals should not have the burden of correcting all the social problems of a host country, but the general consensus is that these powerful corporations should not take advantage of or further perpetuate any country's problems in the pursuit of profit.

Many governments of host countries—assisted by U.S. legislation like the Foreign Corrupt Practices Act, which prohibits U.S. companies from engaging in bribery or other acts of coercion in foreign business dealings—have made some headway in establishing ethical and legal standards for multinationals. The real need is for the international community to agree on laws that would regulate multinational companies—a task complicated by the challenge of enforcing those laws effectively.

Further Research
Business for Social Responsibility
www.bsr.org
Web site of a nonprofit organization that provides resources and news on business ethics and ethical companies.
Global Corporate Governance Forum
www.gcgf.org
The World Bank's multinational trust to foster research and initiatives.
—*Andrea Troyer*

Capitalism

Capitalism is an economic and social system based on private ownership of the means of production and on the distribution of goods and services through the coming together of supply and demand in the competitive free market.

The abstract concept of capitalism is made concrete in specific historical and cultural situations. Accordingly, a number of models of capitalism have evolved, all of which are characterized by a mixture of private, state, and communal modes of ownership, and by various kinds of modifications of the market. Therefore, no one definitive model of capitalism exists; capitalism is frequently best defined against noncapitalist models, like agrarianism or communism.

Historical Origins

Merchants, trade, and markets have always existed, but capitalism as a coherent system has its roots in early modern Europe, where it gradually emerged as the successor to the feudalism of the Middle Ages.

Historians and sociologists have commonly associated the transition from feudalism to capitalism with a succession of important events and processes. First, Europeans conquered the New World in the late fifteenth and early sixteenth centuries, gaining access to abundant resources and expanded markets. The humanist ideas of the Renaissance created a new emphasis on individualism in European thought, while the sixteenth-century Protestant Reformation intensified the spirit of individualism. The Reformation also freed economic activity from the strictures of the Roman Catholic church and contributed to the breakup of European Christendom into modern nation-states.

The seventeenth- and eighteenth-century revolution in scientific thought, exemplified by the work of the English mathematician and physicist Isaac Newton, laid the foundations for the technological innovations that multiplied human productivity. Finally, the eighteenth-century Enlightenment undermined traditional sources of authority and created an intellectual climate sympathetic to the development of a coherent capitalist philosophy.

A Capitalist Philosophy

From the sixteenth to the eighteenth centuries, the mercantilist system made merchant corporations the agents of the state and made national wealth accumulation the central objective of economic policy. During the Enlightenment, mercantilism was subject to rigorous intellectual criticism, first by the French physiocrats, who argued for free markets in agriculture and opposed the French state's efforts to encourage industry, and then by the Scottish moral philosopher Adam Smith.

In *The Wealth of Nations* (1776), Smith argued for a system of political economy in which theoretically unlimited growth would be achieved by the invisible hand of the free market and the division of labor into increasingly specialized tasks. Individual consumers and entrepreneurs thereby replaced the state as the focus of economic activity. Smith's design rested on a number of core philosophical assumptions about human nature. First, it presupposed individualism and self-interest as predominant human traits. Second, it conceived of humans

An engraving of Adam Smith from 1790.

as social creatures who engage in exchange for mutual advantage. Third, it assumed that people are motivated by a spirit of competition. According to Smith, therefore, a free-market economy would be superior to other models of political economy because it worked with the grain of human nature.

The Capitalist Century

Capitalism, both as an idea and as an economic system, had its heyday during the Industrial Revolution in nineteenth-century Britain. The techniques of industrialism greatly facilitated the specialization of labor and generated unprecedented rates of economic growth. Meanwhile, European imperialism, combined with improvements in transport and communications, spread industrial capitalism around the globe.

The immense economic growth came at great social cost. The process of urbanization resulted in slums with massively inadequate sanitation that led to disease; the inequality of bargaining power between workers and employers led to exploitation and poverty. The capitalist economy was also prone to recurrent crises as periods of expansion were followed by recessions and bouts of high unemployment. Several responses were made to the profound social problems of industrialism. Reformers and philanthropists, usually motivated by Christian principles, or by an aristocratic sense of social responsibility, demanded legislation that addressed issues like child labor and excessive working hours.

Meanwhile, socialist philosophers and political activists began to develop anticapitalist ideas and organizations, and workers began to organize in trade unions to improve pay and workplace conditions. Public health problems led to direct government intervention in the areas of sanitation and housing, and as the demand for skilled workers grew, the state also became directly involved in the provision of public education. Consequently, by the end of the nineteenth century, the world's first industrial capitalist state had significantly modified the theoretical model developed by Smith, though Britain continued to champion international free trade.

However, from the perspective of the United States and Germany as emerging countries, the British advocacy of free trade merely reflected Britain's interests as the world's leading industrial capitalist power. Alexander Hamilton in the United States and Friedrich List in Germany both advocated systems of protective tariffs behind which their young countries could industrialize and challenge the economic predominance of Britain.

In the United States, toward the end of the nineteenth century, dominant corporations organized themselves into trusts and used their political influence to protect themselves from potential competitors. During

Peace through Trade: The Corn Laws Controversy

Throughout the nineteenth century, advances in capitalist theory and practice were mutually reinforcing. In 1817 the English economist David Ricardo made a compelling case for extending the principle of economic specialization to international trade. His arguments had an important effect on what came to be known as the Corn Laws controversy.

In 1815 landowners, working through the Tory Party in the British Parliament, secured the passage of tariffs on cheap agricultural imports of maize (corn) and grain. This protected the landowners' interests but also inflated food prices, resulting in worker demands for higher wages, which in turn reduced the profits of the emerging class of industrial capitalists. Consequently, the Anti-Corn Law League was formed in Manchester in 1839, under the leadership of manufacturers Richard Cobden and John Bright. The league, and the growing political influence of the industrialists, secured the repeal of the Corn Laws in 1846. Over the course of its campaigns, the leadership of the league also advanced a theory of peace through free trade, according to which international economic interdependence would make war undesirable or even impossible.

The arguments concerning the Corn Laws remain relevant. The free trade versus protectionism debate continues in the era of globalization.

An illustration of an Anti-Corn Law meeting in 1844.

In this cartoon from 1873 entitled "The American Juggernaut," financiers and politicians ride a large train— the nineteenth-century symbol of corporate power—that crushes American workers.

what became known as the Progressive Era, this corporate influence was challenged both by advocates of liberal capitalism and by radical populist movements. The result was government regulation and the development of antitrust laws. For the most part, however, government attempts to regulate the economy did not seriously inhibit free market activity, and the U.S. economy continued to expand.

Capitalism in Crisis

In the first half of the twentieth century, capitalism faced a succession of deep crises: world war, communist revolution, and economic depression. World War I (1914–1918) had three major consequences for capitalism. First, it shattered the nineteenth-century confidence that the spread of free trade would ensure international peace. Second, the demands of modern technological warfare led to increased government intervention to harness the economy for the war effort. Third, the United States emerged from the war economically strengthened, and New York replaced London as the center of world finance.

In October 1917, the Bolsheviks seized power in Russia and put a halt to the country's incipient capitalist economy. Led by Vladimir

Lenin, they created the Soviet Union as the world's first communist state, in which the economy was taken over by the government. Under Joseph Stalin's leadership after 1928, the Soviets embarked upon a rapid program of centrally planned industrialization and agricultural collectivization.

The Great Depression (1929–1939) posed four major threats to the future of the capitalist system. First, it undermined public confidence in the system itself. Second, leading capitalist economies responded to the Depression with protective tariffs, doing further damage to the international trading system on which capitalism relied. Third, the Soviet Union, being insulated from the world economy, avoided the Depression, thus increasing the international prestige and credibility of communism. Fourth, the collapse of the German economy paved the way for the rise of the Nazi Party, which promoted nationalist and anticapitalist policies of economic management.

The economic crisis of the 1930s induced major changes in Western capitalist economies. In the United States, the New Deal of President Franklin Delano Roosevelt, elected in 1932, reformed the American financial system to prevent further speculative excesses of the

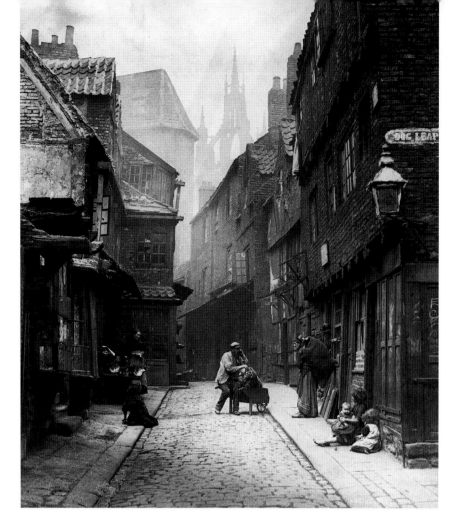

A slum in Newcastle, England, circa 1880; the abominable living conditions of urban workers inspired progressive reform movements both in England and the United States.

and theoreticians like Keynes emerged as the new orthodoxy in capitalist economics.

Welfare Capitalism

By surviving these crises, capitalism proved itself adaptable and durable. In North America, Western Europe, and Scandinavia, the first three decades after World War II were an era of Keynesian consensus during which mainstream parties of the Left and the Right adopted policies of macroeconomic demand management. The Keynesian model was internationalized at the Bretton Woods conference in 1944, which put in place a new architecture of global finance. The Bretton Woods agreement stabilized exchange rates by pegging them to the U.S. dollar and founded the World Bank to fund development projects and the International Monetary Fund to stabilize the international economy by avoiding or managing currency crises. The agreement also gave rise to a new regime of international free trade, the General Agreement on Tariffs and Trade (GATT), which was designed to prevent a return to the rivalrous protectionism of the 1930s.

In Western Europe and Scandinavia, governments established cradle-to-grave welfare states and mixed economies, in which some strategic industries were taken into public ownership. The government also established a range of models of corporatism, under which national economic policy was negotiated between representatives of governments, employers' organizations, and trade unions. These efforts seemed to overcome earlier instabilities of the capitalist system, and governments were freed to pursue social projects like educational reform, public housing, and initiatives to reduce economic inequality. In the United States, postwar welfare provision was less generous and comprehensive than in Europe but underwent significant expansion in the Great Society program of President Lyndon Johnson (1963–1968) with programs like Medicare and Medicaid.

The Noncapitalist Postwar World

The communist sphere expanded significantly after World War II with the Soviet occupation of Eastern Europe and the 1949 revolution in

kind that led to the stock market crash of 1929. Roosevelt also established a series of national job-creation agencies, including the Civilian Conservation Corps and the Public Works Administration. This period also saw the introduction of unemployment insurance and of Social Security, and it marks the origin of the American welfare system.

The theoretical basis for government economic intervention came from the British economist John Maynard Keynes, who argued that governments could take an even more active role in insuring against sharp booms and busts in the economy by manipulating the money supply and adjusting taxes to increase or decrease investment activity. This "Keynesian revolution" challenged the prevailing economic orthodoxy and advocated controversial policies like deficit spending.

The Depression was followed by World War II (1939–1945), which did more than any previous war to expand government direction of the economy. Consequently, after the war, the ideas of politicians like Roosevelt

Capitalism

1776
In *The Wealth of Nations,* Adam Smith argues for the free market and the division of labor.

1800s
Industrialization is in full swing in Europe and the United States.

1890
The Sherman Antitrust Act strives to limit corporate power.

1918
At the conclusion of World War I, New York replaces London as the center of world finance.

1929
Wall Street crash begins the Great Depression.

1932
Franklin Delano Roosevelt elected president; the New Deal programs of his administration create jobs and increase government involvement in the economy.

1944
Bretton Woods conference stabilizes exchange rates and founds the World Bank and the International Monetary Fund.

1963–1968
Great Society program of the Lyndon B. Johnson administration.

1971
President Richard Nixon devalues the dollar, effectively ending the Bretton Woods exchange rate management system.

1980s
British prime minister Margaret Thatcher and U.S. president Ronald Reagan lead a "neoliberal" revolution in Britain and the United States.

1985–1991
Soviet president Mikhail Gorbachev introduces perestroika (economic liberalization) to the Soviet Union.

1993
North American Free Trade Agreement is signed by the United States, Canada, and Mexico.

1991
Breakup of Soviet Union.

1995
World Trade Organization is created to liberalize world trade.

China. Both Moscow and Beijing began to aid communist liberation movements in the colonial world and to exert significant influence over the political and economic organization of postcolonial states. The Soviet model of economic planning even inspired noncommunist leaders of former colonies, for instance, Jawaharlal Nehru in India.

Elsewhere in the developing world, governments of various political complexions

Two icons of late-twentieth-century capitalism, U.S. president Ronald Reagan and British prime minister Margaret Thatcher, meet at the White House in 1987.

The Neoliberal Revolution

The Keynesian era came to an end over the course of the 1970s. In 1971, with the U.S. economy suffering the strains of the war in Vietnam, President Richard Nixon effectively ended the Bretton Woods exchange rate management system when he devalued the dollar. With the outbreak of war in the Middle East in 1973, Western economies were hit by an Arab oil embargo, levied as a protest against the West's support of Israel. By mid-decade, Western capitalist economies were experiencing "stagflation"—the simultaneous increase in both unemployment and inflation—which undermined the theoretical credibility of Keynesian economics. Governments responded with unpopular and unsuccessful public spending cuts and attempts to control wages and prices; many leaders were replaced in subsequent elections.

Monetarist economists, notably Milton Friedman at the University of Chicago, identified inflation as the central economic problem and prescribed deflationary economic policies based on the restriction of the money supply. They also advocated privatization, deregulation, welfare cuts, and measures to curb trade union powers. These ideas formed the basis of the so-called neoliberal revolution, led by British prime minister Margaret Thatcher (1979–1990) and U.S. president Ronald

sought to accelerate their countries' development with policies of economic nationalism. This strategy, exemplified by the Institutional Party of the Revolution in Mexico, aimed to develop indigenous industries with policies of protectionism and import substitution, not unlike those pursued by Germany and the United States in the nineteenth century. At the same time, many countries, principally on the continent of Africa, remained agricultural economies with premodern forms of economic organization.

In post-communist Russia, a vendor sells communist paraphernalia on a Moscow street in 1993.

Reagan (1981–1989). The more left-wing governments of Australia and New Zealand introduced monetarist economic policies, signaling that neoliberal economic ideas had spread across the political spectrum.

Toward the end of the decade, even communist countries were introducing economic reforms, for example, the perestroika of Soviet general secretary Mikhail Gorbachev (1985–1991) and the Chinese government's market socialism, the liberalization of a socialist economy. At the same time, many developing countries renounced economic nationalism and aimed at development through international trade. Mexico, for example, signed the North American Free Trade Agreement (NAFTA) with the United States and Canada in 1993. African political leaders also began to emphasize trade over aid in their economic development strategies.

Contemporary Capitalism

When Soviet communism collapsed between 1989 and 1991, no viable alternative to capitalism came forward. There remained, however, a variety of capitalist models. The Anglo-Saxon model of the United States, Britain, Australia, and New Zealand emphasizes market incentives, privatization, and economic deregulation. By contrast, the European social market model is characterized by greater state intervention in the form of regulated labor markets, high government expenditure on education, detailed structures of employer–union cooperation, and fiscal incentives for training and for research and development. The Asian model features a close structural relationship between finance and industry and a degree of economic planning, of which the Japanese Ministry of International Trade and Industry (MITI) is the prime example.

During the 1990s the term *globalization* emerged to describe the process of world economic integration driven by a combination of free trade and the revolution in information technology. In 1995 a series of GATT negotiations culminated in the creation of the World Trade Organization, an intergovernmental organization whose primary goal is the progressive liberalization of world trade relations.

Critics of globalization, who span the political spectrum, contend that the new capital mobility has increased the power of multinational corporations at the expense of national governments, resulting in the erosion of labor and environmental standards. The debate in the twenty-first century between advocates and opponents of free trade resembles the original arguments about the nature and purpose of capitalism in the nineteenth century.

Thousands converged on Seattle in 1999 to stage protests against the World Trade Organization, which held its meeting that year at the Washington State Convention Center. More than 40,000 anti-globalization protesters participated in coordinated actions.

Further Research
The Adam Smith Page
www.utdallas.edu/~harpham/adam.htm
This Web site, from the University of Texas–Dallas, includes biographic and bibliographic information relevant to Adam Smith.
Globalization 101
www.globalization101.org
A student's guide to globalization by the Levin Institute of the State University of New York.

—*Peter C. Grosvenor*

Cartel

A cartel is a group of producers in a particular industry that band together to coordinate their output and prices, sometimes with government support. For cartel members, success requires eliminating competition within the group and preventing new competitors from entering the market. To the extent that they succeed in their anticompetitive practices, cartels typically make prices higher. For this reason, they are generally regarded as undesirable within market economies.

The word *cartel* derives from the Italian word *cartello*, meaning "placard." The French borrowed the word as *cartel* in the sixteenth century and used it to mean "a written challenge or letter of defiance." Its modern meaning in English, suggesting defiance of market competition, has evolved from this French usage.

Cartels originated in Germany in the 1870s, when Germany's economy was growing rapidly. The German government encouraged the formation of cartels prior to and during World War I to foster the production of armaments and other war-related materials. Following the war, in the 1920s and 1930s, German firms formed cartels in many basic industries. The most prominent example was I. G. Farbenindustrie, a group of firms producing chemicals and dyes. At the onset of World War II, the German economy was dominated by cartels, which the government continued to encourage and supervise, again in support of the nation's mobilization for war.

Cartels also may be international, with firms from different countries combining efforts to dominate world markets for their products. Until the late 1930s international cartels existed primarily in the pharmaceuticals and steel industries. However, beginning in the 1960s, some cartels were formed by the governments of oil-rich countries. The most famous of these is the Organization of Petroleum Exporting Countries (OPEC); its 12 members include several Middle Eastern states, including Iraq and Saudi Arabia, as well as countries in Africa, Southeast Asia, and South America.

Increased profits are the goal of cartels. Participating firms enter into agreements to "fix" prices—that is, to raise them above the level that would prevail if the firms competed

Former secretary general of the Organization of Petroleum Exporting Countries Alvaro Silva Calderon of Venezuela at a press conference at the Geneva offices of the United Nations.

with one another in an open market. Such collusive arrangements may be explicit, with firms openly agreeing to form a cartel, or they may be tacit (understood), marked by a pattern of behavior rather than any binding, formal agreement.

To raise prices collectively, cartel members must reduce industry output. This sometimes involves dividing the market into segments and assigning responsibility for supplying each segment to a particular firm. In these cases, the cartel operates as if it were one firm, a monopolist.

Cartels are illegal in the United States because they are deemed anticompetitive. Formal contracts to restrict competition cannot be enforced in court. To succeed, then, cartels must rely on informal arrangements that provide incentives for the member firms to conform to the cartel's policies. In practice, such cooperation can be difficult to initiate and maintain because each firm has an incentive to cheat—to lower its price slightly by expanding its output at the expense of other firms, thus capturing a larger share of the market.

In the United Kingdom and other countries of Western Europe, some cartels exist legally, but they are monitored by governments to ensure that their monopolistic practices do not become outrageous. Although U.S. companies are prohibited by law from forming cartels domestically, they are permitted by U.S. law to "export" a cartel, that is, to coordinate their actions in other markets where they compete.

Cartels have played a major role in the development of several key industries, including textiles, pharmaceuticals, and petroleum products. Some argue, moreover, that cartels provide important benefits (contending, for example, that they stabilize markets, reduce costs of production, eliminate high tariffs, and distribute profits equitably). Against these arguments, market-oriented economists and policy makers maintain that, by restricting the competitive process, cartels increase costs for consumers, thus reducing individual well-being and the standard of living for

society in general. Accordingly, legal authorities in market-oriented economies will most likely continue to look with disfavor on cartels.

Cartels, historically common in the pharmaceutical industry, continue to be formed.

Further Research

American Bar Association

www.abanet.org/antitrust/

The ABA provides research and resources on U.S. and international competition law.

Canadian Bar Association

www.cba.org/CBA/sections_competition/main/

Research and resources on Canadian law.

Federal Trade Commission

www.ftc.gov/bc/antitrust/index.shtm

The FTC is charged with enforcing antitrust laws in the United States. Its Web site provides guidelines on enforcement of the laws.

International Competition Network

www.internationalcompetitionnetwork.org

The ICN is an international body dedicated to competition law enforcement.

—*Mikhail Kouliavtsev*

Commodities

In broad terms, commodities are any products that can be traded and that are used for commerce. More narrowly, commodities are products that are traded on an authorized commodity exchange. Major commodities of this kind include wheat, rice, corn, pork bellies, oilseeds, sugar, coffee, cocoa, tea, oil, natural gas, cotton, wool, jute, sisal, rubber, copper, zinc, lead, and tin.

The practice of buying and selling commodities in an open marketplace began in ancient times. The Agora in Athens and the Forum in Rome were originally commercial marketplaces; medieval fairs were their successors. These regional fairs were gradually replaced by the establishment in cities of specialized trading centers. In Japan, commodity exchanges arose in the eighteenth century. In these markets the purchase of commodities was generally made on the basis of immediate delivery ("spot" trading). Gradually, however, the merchants developed the practice of forward contracting, or futures, which is today one of the most crucial functions of a commodity exchange.

Commodity futures, which are contracts for delivery of specific commodities at a stated price at a specified future date, perform several important functions. The buying and selling of futures tends to even out price fluctuations (caused, for example, by seasonal availability) by allowing the market to mirror expectations about future harvests (or other variables in supply) and changes in demand. Futures are not usually employed for the buying or selling of the actual commodity, but for hedging price fluctuations. Hedging is a method by which individuals or businesses gain protection against future price changes.

For example, say that a coffee dealer knows that six months down the line he will buy 10,000 pounds of coffee to send to a processor, and he has promised to sell that coffee to the processor at a certain price. To protect himself, the coffee dealer buys coffee futures contracts representing 10,000 pounds of coffee. If the price of coffee is higher six months later, the value of the futures contracts rises too. By selling the futures at a higher price than he paid for them, the coffee merchant offsets the extra money he has to pay for the coffee. Hedging thus not only helps to even out gains and losses incurred by fluctuating prices, it also helps contribute to an even flow of business.

The number of commodity markets is not fixed. There are major commodities exchanges in more than 20 countries. In addition to the Chicago Board of Trade, major commodity markets include the Chicago Mercantile Exchange, the New York Cotton Exchange, the New York Commodity Exchange, the New York Mercantile Exchange, the New York Metal Exchange, the New York Sugar Exchange, and the London Metal Exchange. Important commodity markets are located in Winnipeg, Canada (rye, barley, and oats);

Kinds of Commodity Futures	
Livestock / meat products	• Propane
Examples:	• Unleaded gas
• Cattle	**Financial and index futures**
• Hogs	Examples:
• Pork bellies	• Dow Jones industrial average futures
Grains, cereal / oilseed	• NASDAQ 100 index futures
Examples:	• NYSE composite index
• Canola	• S&P 500
• Corn	**Currencies**
• Cotton	Examples:
• Flaxseed	• Australian dollar
• Oats	• British pound
• Rice	• Canadian dollar
• Soybeans	• Japanese yen
• Wheat	**Miscellaneous commodities**
Metals	Examples:
Examples:	• Butter
• Copper	• Cocoa
• Palladium	• Coffee
• Silver	• Lumber
Soft commodities / energy	• Milk
Examples:	• Orange juice
• Heating oil	• Sugar
• Natural gas	

The interior of the Chicago Board of Trade.

Brazil, India, and Egypt (cotton); and Australia, New Zealand, and South Africa (wool).

Most commodities do not pass through commodity exchanges but are sold by direct contact between exporter and importer, who agree on a contract. Commodity exchanges are of great global importance, nevertheless. Commodity markets are the hubs where buyers and sellers trade information and opinions, and their mutually reinforcing expertise tends to determine world prices of a particular commodity. The basic function of a commodity exchange is to ensure the regular and reliable flow of commodities by establishing accepted markets and determining current prices. Properly organized commodity markets strive to establish prices that are in line with demand and that do not fluctuate widely; in addition, as commodities often must be transported great distances from their point of origin to their point of use, commodity markets make certain that products are delivered reliably. Commodities markets are probably best known as the places where futures contracts are traded.

The futures market relies on individuals who are willing to accept risk. Futures attract speculators, persons who usually have no direct contact with the specific commodity but who get into the market in the hopes of making a profit by buying low and selling high. Because of the high risk and great potential profits of their activities, speculators have often been considered as buccaneers who add little value to business. Yet speculators play an important role in the commodities world. They are willing to bear the risk that hedgers seek to avoid and thus act as a kind of insurance underwriter.

Further Research
Chicago Board of Trade
www.cbot.com
Home page of the Chicago Board of Trade offers stock performance information, news, and market data.
New York Mercantile Exchange
www.nymex.com
The home page of the largest commodities futures exchange.
TFC Commodity Charts
futures.tradingcharts.com
This site provides performance measures as well as educational resources.

—*Joseph Gustaitis*

Communism

Communism is a political ideology that maintains that all property, and the wealth derived from its use, should be owned collectively and equally by the whole community. It is a recurrent idea in the history of political thought; in practice, communisim has taken two principal forms: primitive and modern.

Primitive communism has existed in certain highly egalitarian preindustrial societies. Some of these are known to us only through the archaeological record, while others continue to exist in parts of the developing world. Primitive communism can also refer to small-scale experimental communities, for example, those created at New Lanark, Scotland, and New Harmony, Indiana, by the nineteenth-century utopian socialist Robert Owen.

Modern communism has its origins in the writings of the German revolutionaries Karl Marx and Friedrich Engels. They analyzed history as a series of class struggles that would culminate in the revolutionary overthrow of the bourgeoisie (ruling class) by the proletariat (working class). Marx wrote that the new society created by this revolution would come to be organized on the principle of "from each according to his capacity, to each according to his needs."

In *The Communist Manifesto* (1848), Marx and Engels rejected the small utopian experiments of the past and called for a large-scale revolution. They also listed a number of immediate demands, including a progressive income tax, free education, and the abolition of inheritances. "The proletarians have nothing to lose but their chains," they declared. However, the actual experience of modern communist societies in the twentieth century differed markedly from Marx's vision.

The Russian Revolution

The first state to be created on the principles of modern communism was the Soviet Union. The regime of Tsar Nicholas II began to lose its legitimacy after Russia's defeat in the Russo–Japanese War (1904–1905) and failure to meet the political demands of the Revolution of 1905. The regime was weakened further by defeats in World War I, and the tsar abdicated in February 1917. Radical workers, inspired by Marxist revolutionaries, formed workers' councils (or *soviets*) across the country. The revolutionary communist Bolshevik Party, led by Vladimir Lenin, took control in October 1917.

Lenin withdrew Russia from the war, shut down all political opposition, and set about creating a communist state. He transferred ownership of industry, commerce, and

In 1975, a banner of three icons of communism hung in Moscow's Red Square: from left, Vladimir Lenin, Friedrich Engels, and Karl Marx.

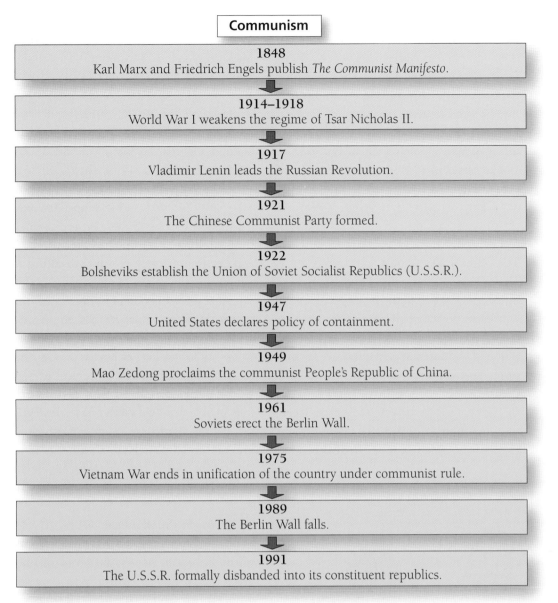

Communism

1848
Karl Marx and Friedrich Engels publish *The Communist Manifesto.*

1914–1918
World War I weakens the regime of Tsar Nicholas II.

1917
Vladimir Lenin leads the Russian Revolution.

1921
The Chinese Communist Party formed.

1922
Bolsheviks establish the Union of Soviet Socialist Republics (U.S.S.R.).

1947
United States declares policy of containment.

1949
Mao Zedong proclaims the communist People's Republic of China.

1961
Soviets erect the Berlin Wall.

1975
Vietnam War ends in unification of the country under communist rule.

1989
The Berlin Wall falls.

1991
The U.S.S.R. formally disbanded into its constituent republics.

banking to the state. When these actions, coupled with a civil war, threatened economic collapse, Lenin was forced to introduce the more market-based New Economic Policy (NEP) to stimulate production.

The Bolsheviks established a new political entity—the Union of Soviet Socialist Republics (U.S.S.R.)—in December 1922. Lenin's death in 1924 triggered a power struggle between Joseph Stalin, who wanted to pursue a policy of "socialism in one country," and Leon Trotsky, whose priority was an international communist revolution. By 1929, Stalin had emerged as leader; Trotsky went into exile and was later assassinated.

Stalin instituted a series of Five Year Plans to accelerate industrialization and to collectivize agriculture. In the process, millions of *kulaks*—independent peasant proprietors—were killed. In the mid-1930s, Stalin completed his control over the Communist Party, and he established the party's totalitarian dominance over society through the creation of an extensive secret police network. He also used the Comintern (or Third International) to establish Soviet control over Communist Parties in other countries.

As World War II was beginning, Stalin, wanting to expand Russia's territory, entered into the Nazi–Soviet Pact (1939), under which the Soviet Union and Germany agreed to partition Poland. By the end of 1940 Stalin had also annexed the Baltic states and parts of Finland. The Nazi–Soviet pact did not hold, however, and German forces invaded Russia in June 1941; Stalin then joined the Western Allies. By 1945 Soviet forces had pushed westward against the Germans, occupying and installing communist governments in most of Eastern Europe and the Balkans. Alarmed by a new threat of Soviet domination in Europe, the United States in 1947 declared its policy of containment, under which it would resist any further expansion of Soviet power, and the cold war began.

The Chinese Revolution

The Chinese Communist Party (CCP) was formed in 1921. Initially it cooperated with Sun Yat-Sen's nationalist republican movement, the Kuomintang, against imperial rule and the foreign penetration of China. After Sun died in 1925, his successor, Chiang Kai-Shek, sought to annihilate the CCP. Encircled by Chiang's forces in 1934, the communists began the famous Long March, led by Mao Zedong. Thereafter, Mao

Fidel Castro (center) and fellow revolutionaries enter Havana, Cuba, on January 1, 1959.

concentrated on building a revolutionary organization among the rural peasantry. Mao proclaimed the communist People's Republic of China (PRC) on October 1, 1949.

The communists quickly established control over the whole country and occupied Tibet in 1950. The PRC relied on Soviet aid and adopted the Stalinist model of economic planning. In 1958, frustrated with the slow pace of economic development, Mao launched the "Great Leap Forward." This rush to boost industrial and agricultural productivity through state mandates was an unmitigated disaster, resulting in famine and the deaths of millions.

After a brief period of normalization following this disaster, Mao established personal domination through the "Cultural Revolution" (1966–1976)—a long campaign to purge the party of critics and establish control over all aspects of Chinese life. As many as half a million people are believed to have died as a result of hardships and punishments imposed by Mao's regime during this time. When Mao died in 1976, he left China at the brink of fundamental change.

Third World Communism

As the Asian and African colonial empires of the European powers began to disintegrate at the end of World War II, communism presented itself to leaders of important anticolonial movements as an ideology of national liberation. This view was strengthened whenever the United States, pursuing its policy of containment, intervened in anticolonial struggles to prop up collapsing imperial regimes or postcolonial dictatorships. Both the Soviets and the Americans couched their Third World interventions in ideological language; in reality, both acted on the basis of cold war strategic calculations.

In the Korean War (1950–1953), the United States led a United Nations campaign to repel an invasion of South Korea by the communist North. The United States then sided with the pro-Western government in South Vietnam against Ho Chi Minh's North Vietnam, which was supported by the

Soviet Union and China. The result was the Vietnam War (1964–1975), which ended with the unification of Vietnam under communist rule. Elsewhere in Southeast Asia, the Pathet Lao brought communism to power in Laos, and in Cambodia Pol Pot's Khmer Rouge instituted a murderous brand of agrarian communism.

Communism also made inroads into Latin America. In Cuba, Fidel Castro and Che Guevara overthrew the Batista dictatorship in January 1959 and embarked on a thoroughgoing communist revolution that served as a model for Third World revolutions elsewhere. To the Kennedy administration, Cuba exemplified the threat of communist expansionism and, in October 1962, an American naval blockade forced the Soviets to withdraw their missiles from the island.

In Africa, the United States and the U.S.S.R. competed to install compliant governments in unstable countries, often exacerbating local conflicts in the process. For example, the two superpowers supported opposing sides in the civil wars that broke out in the mid-1970s in the former Portuguese colonies of Mozambique and Angola. In the Middle East, the United States traditionally supported Israel and the religiously conservative oil-rich states of the Persian Gulf, while the Soviets backed the Palestinian cause and various radical Arab states.

Tensions within the Communist World

During the cold war years, the communist world itself was seriously weakened by internal tensions. Sino–Soviet relations were damaged by a border dispute and by rivalry for leadership of the communist world. By 1971, the rift was sufficient for U.S. president Richard Nixon to visit Beijing, driving a permanent wedge between China and the U.S.S.R.

The Soviet Union's recurring problems in Eastern Europe were highlighted in Yugoslavia, where President Josip Tito's communists owed their position not to Soviet imposition but to their leading role

in the resistance to the Nazi occupation. Titoism therefore emerged as an independent communist model, characterized by an economy relatively liberal by communist standards—that emphasized worker self-management over centralized planning. Expelled from the communist bloc in 1948, Yugoslavia went on to play a leading role in the creation of the Non-Aligned Movement.

Other Eastern European countries had less success resisting Soviet control. In East Berlin in 1953, demonstrations against increased work quotas were put down by the East German authorities. In 1961, to solidify control over East Berlin, the Soviets built the Berlin Wall, which became the ultimate symbol of the cold war. In 1956, when Hungary tried to assert a greater degree of national independence by withdrawing from the

President Josip Tito of Yugoslavia in 1962.

Soviet-dominated Warsaw Pact, the Soviets invaded. The "Prague Spring" of 1968, Czechoslovakia's experiment in liberal communism, was crushed by Soviet tanks. In Poland in 1980, shipyard workers formed Solidarity, an independent trade union movement, which challenged the communist government's economic policy. Solidarity was banned after the imposition of martial law in late 1981.

Within the Third World, conflict among communists was usually the result of communism's encounter with preexisting local antagonisms. A series of border skirmishes between China's ally Cambodia and Soviet-backed Vietnam began in 1975 and ended in 1979 with the Vietnamese invasion of Cambodia and the destruction of the Khmer Rouge government. Also in 1979,

the Soviet Union invaded Afghanistan to prevent ethnic and religious opposition groups from overthrowing that country's communist government.

The Decline and Fall of Communism

Communism failed for four main reasons. First was economic inefficiency. Industry and agriculture were state-owned, and economic activity was planned from the center by a bureaucratic hierarchy. Economic decisions were, therefore, made subordinate to political considerations. The Soviet economy was subject to what has been called "diseconomies of scale" and characterized by the production of shoddy goods, continuous economic shortages, and the inefficient distribution of goods and services. Officially, unemployment was abolished in the Soviet Union. However,

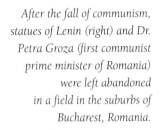

After the fall of communism, statues of Lenin (right) and Dr. Petra Groza (first communist prime minister of Romania) were left abandoned in a field in the suburbs of Bucharest, Romania.

underemployment was extremely common. Some workers did little more than punch time cards on their way in and out.

Experiments in economic liberalization like those made under Nikita Khrushchev (1953–1964) stimulated innovation and productivity, but they also jeopardized the political dominance of the Communist Party. Consequently, Khrushchev gave way to Leonid Brezhnev (1964–1982), who used state directives to focus the economy on heavy industry, regardless of consumer demand for other goods and services.

Second, the ideals of communist internationalism clashed with the realities of a world divided into nation-states. Marxist–Leninist ideology could not override nationalism and the desire for self-determination. Third, despite state censorship, communications technology made the citizens of communist countries aware of the higher living standards and greater political freedoms of the West. Fourth, after 1980, greater Western defense spending placed unbearable strains on the inefficient communist economies, as did the unwinnable war the Soviets had undertaken in Afghanistan.

All these problems confronted Mikhail Gorbachev (1985–1991), the last leader of the Soviet Union. Gorbachev aimed to democratize Soviet politics through a policy of *glasnost* (opening) and to liberalize the economy through a policy of *perestroika* (restructuring). The Gorbachev program also fueled demands for reforms in Eastern Europe, where communist governments began to fall in the face of a series of "people's revolutions." On November 9, 1989, the end of communism was marked by the fall of the Berlin Wall. The Soviet Union itself then began to break up into its constituent republics and formally came to an end on December 31, 1991.

Communist Parties exist today in several countries throughout the world, but communism is no longer a major force in world politics. China, Cuba, and North Korea are the only remaining countries dominated by communism. The brutal suppression of the pro-democracy demonstrations in Tiananmen

A McDonald's restaurant in downtown Beijing.

Square in 1989 demonstrated that the Chinese Communist Party remains intolerant of political dissent. However, China has increasingly turned toward a liberalized, market-oriented economy, encouraging free enterprise and joining the World Trade Organization. Cuba also remains under Communist Party rule, but it also has liberalized its economy and has taken steps toward normalizing its relations with the United States. North Korea remains a closed and isolated communist society, though it has improved its relations with capitalist South Korea. In eastern Europe, voters in some countries have supported Communist parties, but these parties appear to be influenced increasingly by democratic thought and market-oriented economic policy.

Further Research

Classic Works in Economics and Economic Thought

www.oswego.edu/~economic/oldbooks.htm

Links to transcribed and excerpted texts.

Marxists Internet Archive

www.marxists.org

A volunteer-run Web site, including a student's section with background information and a comprehensive archive of original source material.

—*Peter C. Grosvenor*

Consumer Confidence Index

Because economists cannot see into the future, they look to so-called leading indicators to predict upward and downward movements of the economy. Leading indicators reflect the economic indicators that fall before a recession and rise prior to a recovery. Consumer confidence is such an indicator. As consumer spending makes up about two-thirds of total spending in the United States, accurate predictions about consumer spending play an important role in predicting broader economic trends. Measures of consumer confidence are also used to gauge reactions to economic and political events, like wars and declines in the stock market.

Several regional, national, and international measures of consumer confidence are available. The Conference Board's Consumer Confidence Index (CCI) and the University of Michigan's Index of Consumer Sentiment (ICS) are the primary national measures. Both of these measures gather and assess consumers' opinions about current and future economic conditions—both of the general economy and their own financial situations.

The CCI is calculated by the Conference Board's Consumer Research Center. The Conference Board is a not-for-profit organization started in 1916 to conduct research and examine issues important to business and society. The Conference Board began tracking consumer opinions every other month in 1967. In 1977, the Conference board began monthly mailings of a five-question survey to 5,000 households. The Board conducts the survey during the first 18 days of each month, averaging 3,500 responses. Consumers are asked what they think about: (1) current business conditions, (2) business conditions six months in the future, (3) current employment conditions, (4) employment conditions six months in the future, and (5) their expectations of their total family income six months in the future.

The CCI is an average of the relative value of responses to all five questions. The relative value is the number of positive answers divided by the sum of positive and negative answers. Results are released on the last Tuesday of the month. In addition to the monthly national index, a confidence index is also calculated for each of the nine census regions.

The other consumer confidence index, the Index of Consumer Sentiment (ICS), is produced by the Survey Research Center at the University of Michigan. The center has been tracking consumer sentiment since 1946. At first the center produced an annual survey; in 1952 the survey became

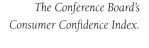

The Conference Board's Consumer Confidence Index.

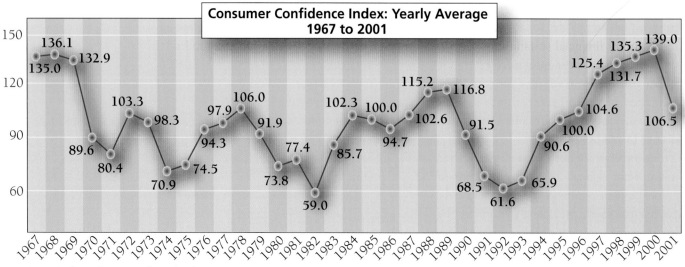

Source: © The Conference Board. Used with permission.

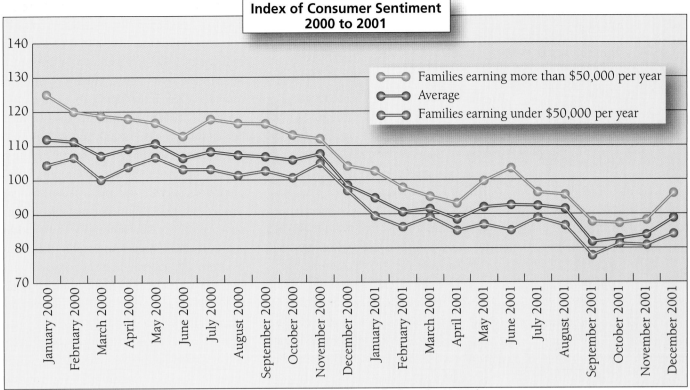

Index of Consumer Sentiment 2000 to 2001

Legend:
- Families earning more than $50,000 per year
- Average
- Families earning under $50,000 per year

Source: The University of Michigan. "Survey of Consumers," http://www.sca.isr.umich.edu/main.php (December 30, 2002).

a quarterly; and in 1978 the survey became a monthly. The Survey Research Center asks about a longer time horizon: one to five years instead of six months. Unlike the Conference Board, the center does not compile regional indexes.

At the beginning of every month, the University of Michigan's Institute for Social Research polls 500 families by telephone. The survey asks 50 questions about personal finances, general business conditions, and household buying plans. The index is based on responses to five questions. Consumers are asked to: (1) compare their current financial situation to their situation a year earlier; (2) predict what their financial situation will be a year in the future; (3) predict business conditions in the country as a whole a year later; (4) predict business conditions during the next five years; and (5) say whether it is a good or bad time to buy major household items.

Like the Conference Board, the Survey Research Center calculates a relative score for each question. The details of the calculation, however, are different. A relative score is the percent of favorable responses minus the percent of unfavorable responses, with the difference added to 100. The index is the total of all the relative scores divided by the base period value and added to a correction factor. This method "flattens out" the movement of the ICS compared to the CCI, as illustrated in the graph.

The ICS questions that involve making predictions are used to derive an Index of Consumer Expectations (ICE), which is part of the Leading Economic Indicators Index. Other components of the Leading Economic Indicators Index are manufacturing levels, interest rates, and employment. The Conference Board has compiled the Leading Economic Indicators Index since 1995; earlier it was done by the Commerce Department.

Movement of the indexes anticipates some changes in the business cycle and is therefore of great interest to businesspeople and policy makers. Movement that is not related to the business cycle, however, must be identified separately. Therefore, both indexes are adjusted seasonally for changes in consumer confidence that may be normal, annual occurrences. Without such

The Index of Consumer Sentiment is prepared by the Survey Research Center at the University of Michigan as a reflection of consumer confidence.

Holiday shopping in Little Italy in New York City. Consumer confidence indexes are adjusted for normal increases in spending, like those that occur during the holiday season.

adjustment, the indexes might seem to suggest that confidence takes a huge leap every year in November and December, whereas data related to those months may merely reflect planned holiday spending.

Unlike other measures, an index is unitless; it is measured in points, not dollars or tons or inches. It has meaning only when compared with itself. Each measure sets a base year when the index equals 100. The CCI has a base year of 1985. The University of Michigan's base year is 1966. Monthly reports of an index will indicate its movement up or down, by how much in both absolute and percentage terms, and how the current month's index number compares with historical values. For both measures, what has happened on average over the previous six months is a better

indicator of consumer opinion than one month's figure.

Which index is more useful depends on the question being asked. The Conference Board's focus on employment conditions provides good information about the labor market. If responses indicate positive feeling about the current and future job market, then consumers probably will be buying more than if they are unemployed or fear they will be laid off in the near future. Positive responses can also anticipate rising wages from a tighter labor market—that is, a market with more jobs than workers to fill them.

The University of Michigan's focus on the longer term and household goods provides slightly different information. Positive answers to the final question about purchase of household goods may result in more washing machines, refrigerators, and cars being bought in the near future. Positive answers to questions about future economic conditions may not result in higher spending today; they may indicate that consumers will wait until the economy is stronger before buying more.

Neither index by itself is a perfect predictor of recessions or recoveries. Both indexes provide a snapshot of consumers' opinions about the economy, based upon reactions to events, news, and commentary. One month's rise or fall in an index is not as significant as the direction the index has taken over the previous few months. Along with other leading indicators, however, consumer confidence indexes present a picture of general and household economic conditions.

Further Research
The Conference Board
www.conference-board.org
The home page of the research organization posts leading international economic indicators and offers links to further information.
Surveys of Consumers: The University of Michigan
www.sca.isr.umich.edu
This Web site contains archival and historical data from the Reuters/University of Michigan Surveys of Consumers. Current data are distributed by Reuters.

—Donna Miller

Consumer Price Index

The price of a good can go up for many reasons: an increase in production costs, an increase in demand, or inflation, among others. When the overall price level rises, then the economy has entered a period of inflation. The Consumer Price Index (CPI) measures the overall price level of goods. Specifically, the CPI reports a weighted average of the prices of a fixed set of goods and services over time. In addition to measuring inflation, the CPI is used to adjust prices for comparisons over time, change tax brackets, and determine cost-of-living adjustments to wages, pensions, and government payments like food stamps and Social Security.

Since 1913 the Bureau of Labor Statistics (BLS) in the Department of Labor has calculated the CPI. At the beginning of each month hundreds of BLS economic assistants collect prices in more than 80 urban areas. Their gathering of prices of the same goods and services is called a *market basket*. Items like pens, apples, computers, long distance telephone charges, postage stamps, dry cleaning, movie tickets, gasoline, rental fees—almost anything

consumers buy is in the basket. Having the market basket's contents and quantities fixed allows only the prices to change over time.

The national census and surveys of consumer spending patterns determine in what cities and stores BLS assistants shop, what they buy, and how important each item is to consumers. Individual items and services are put into 200 categories, for example, men's shirts, bedroom furniture, ice cream, and college tuition. Sales taxes and user fees such as water bills or car registration fees are the only taxes included. Items are added or dropped every two years based on survey results.

Categories are then sorted into eight major groups: food and beverages, housing (includes utilities and heat), apparel, transportation (includes gasoline), medical care, recreation, education, and communication, as well as other (for example, tobacco, funeral expenses, haircuts). Groups are weighted to reflect their proportion of household spending. This way a doubling in the price of gasoline will count more than the doubling of the price of salt because more of a consumer's budget goes to gasoline than salt. Group weightings are adjusted every two years based on the survey data.

The CPI is calculated by computing a geometric mean within each category, like beef or

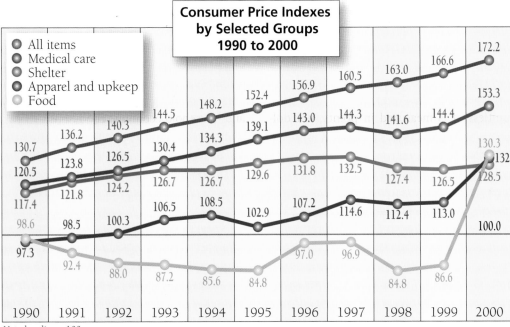

Consumer Price Indexes by Selected Groups 1990 to 2000

- All items
- Medical care
- Shelter
- Apparel and upkeep
- Food

	1990	1991	1992	1993	1994	1995	1996	1997	1998	1999	2000
Medical care	130.7	136.2	140.3	144.5	148.2	152.4	156.9	160.5	163.0	166.6	172.2
Shelter	120.5	123.8	126.5	130.4	134.3	139.1	143.0	144.3	141.6	144.4	153.3
All items	117.4	121.8	124.2	126.7	126.7	129.6	131.8	132.5	127.4	126.5	130.3 / 132 / 128.5
Food	98.6	98.5	100.3	106.5	108.5	102.9	107.2	114.6	112.4	113.0	100.0
Apparel and upkeep	97.3	92.4	88.0	87.2	85.6	84.8	97.0	96.9	84.8	86.6	

Note: baseline = 100.
Source: Bureau of Labor Statistics, *Monthly Labor Review and Handbook of Labor Statistics,* periodic.

U.S. Consumer Price Indexes for Selected Items and Groups 1990 to 2000

	1990	1995	1996	1997	1998	1999	2000
Household furnishings							
Bedroom furniture	118.5	136.4	139.3	141.5	141.3	141.0	138.4
Television	74.6	68.1	64.5	61.7	59.2	54.9	49.9
Video products other than television	91.5	70.3	66.3	63.4	NA	92.1	88.6
Audio products	93.2	92.1	90.7	88.9	85.2	81.7	80.2
Apparel							
Men's and boys'	120.4	126.2	127.7	130.1	131.8	131.1	129.7
Women's and girls'	122.6	126.9	124.7	126.1	126.0	123.3	121.5
Infants' and toddlers'	125.8	127.2	129.7	129.0	126.1	129.0	130.6
Footwear	117.4	125.4	126.6	127.6	128.0	125.7	123.8
Transportation							
New cars	121.0	139.0	141.4	141.7	140.7	139.6	139.6
Used cars	117.6	156.5	157.0	151.1	150.6	152.0	155.8
Airline fares	148.4	189.7	192.5	199.2	205.3	218.8	239.4
Medical Care							
Prescription drugs	181.7	235.0	242.9	249.3	258.6	273.4	285.4
Physicians' services	160.8	208.8	216.4	222.9	229.5	236.0	244.7
Dental services	155.8	206.8	216.5	226.6	236.2	247.2	258.5
Recreation							
Sporting goods, equipment	114.9	123.5	123.4	122.6	121.9	120.3	119.0
Sport vehicles, including bicycles	115.3	125.3	125.7	124.5	125.3	128.7	130.9
Pet supplies and expenses	124.6	132.3	139.0	142.7	143.5	144.5	144.3
Education							
School books and supplies	171.3	214.4	226.9	238.4	250.8	261.7	279.9
Elementary and high school tuition	182.8	259.2	272.8	288.1	307.9	327.3	349.9
College tuition	175.0	264.8	279.8	294.1	306.5	318.7	331.9

NA = Not available.

Note: baseline = 100.

Source: U.S. Bureau of Labor Statistics, *Monthly Labor Review* and *CPI Detailed Report,* 2001.

men's athletic socks, and then a weighted average of the eight groups. As an index the CPI is unitless—it is measured in points, not dollars. The index has meaning only as compared with itself over time. The CPI was set to 100 in the base year of 1984. The month-to-month or year-to-year percentage change in the CPI is the inflation rate.

Estimate errors, called biases, occur in most economic measures. The CPI has three biases: substitution, quality, and outlet. The substitution bias is the result of the fixed content of the market basket; but shoppers' buying habits are flexible. When the price of a good rises, shoppers may buy less of it or substitute another, cheaper good for it. Because consumers are not paying the higher price, they are not experiencing the inflation

measured by the CPI. The CPI corrects for some substitution within categories. For example, if the price of Granny Smith apples increases, the BLS shoppers will record the price of an apple that has not increased in price, like the Golden Delicious. However, some consumers may buy pears instead. Accounting for all possible substitutions shoppers may make would be impossible, thus the CPI overestimates the actual inflation rate.

Quality bias occurs because some price increases reflect product changes or the addition of new features, not just inflation. For example, cars today cost more than cars of 40 years ago. However, cars today are also safer and more fuel efficient and have more standard features. Although difficult, the BLS attempts to correct for this bias by subtracting the value of quality changes from prices. Nevertheless, this bias tends to overestimate inflation.

The outlet bias results from the location of BLS economic assistants in gathering their prices. More and more consumers use large food warehouses for grocery shopping. Prices at those stores are often lower than prices at grocery stores. Accordingly, the measured prices may be higher than what consumers actually are paying. Consumers find ways to avoid the higher prices used to compute the CPI. Overall, the biases in the CPI tend to overstate inflation.

Overestimates of inflation can mean overpayment by government and businesses. Changes in the CPI are used to adjust wages and payments in order to keep purchasing power constant. Purchasing power, or real income, decreases when prices go up and income stays the same. Government payments to more than 80 million people are adjusted every year for inflation. An additional two million worker paychecks covered by union contracts are also adjusted using the CPI. A 1 to 2 percent overadjustment of wages may not mean much for an individual retiree or worker but could mean millions of dollars to government and businesses.

The CPI does not work for all individuals or even all groups. If someone spends money differently from the group weightings, then that person's experienced inflation rate will differ from the overall rate. Social Security recipients, for example, have their checks adjusted for inflation, but they devote a higher proportion of their income to medical expenses. Medical prices are rising faster than other prices; thus even an adjustment for inflation will not allow the average Social Security recipient to buy the same amount of goods. The CPI is determined by prices in urban areas; thus a family living in a rural area may experience a different inflation rate. Each month the CPI is reported along with a breakdown for regions and urban areas in the United States. Specific group increases are also announced, for example, indicating how important an increase in housing or fuel prices was in the total CPI change.

Other price indexes are available. The Producer Price Index includes wholesale and raw material prices. The GDP Deflator, which includes military and investment spending used to adjust the Gross Domestic Product (GDP) for inflation, is also available. In addition, internationally most national statistical agencies calculate their own consumer price indices; in the United Kingdom the index is known as the Retail Price Index. Even with their biases, such indices remains the best index for explaining how changes in price levels affect consumers.

Cars are more expensive than they were 40 years ago; however, thanks to developments such as the safety glass being tested here, cars are also safer. In calculating the CPI, analysts attempt to account for technological improvements that increase the value of goods.

Further Reading
Bureau of Labor Statistics
www.bls.gov/CPI
The BLS Consumer Price Indexes (CPI) program produces monthly data on changes in the prices paid by urban consumers for a representative basket of goods and services.
International Labour Organization
www.ilo.org/public/english/bureau/stat/guides/cpi
The ILO, a specialized agency of the United Nations, maintains a Consumer Price Index Manual, available online.

—*Donna Miller*

Corporate Governance

Corporate governance is the delicate process of aligning the interests of owners and management. A great deal is at stake, including jobs, investor confidence, and spectacular sums of money. The corruption and scandals of the first years of the twenty-first century illustrated how this process has failed at the cost of investor mistrust, bank-ruptcies, and the criminal indictment of managers who gave in to temptation.

A corporation is a stockholder-owned business that has rights and responsibilities as if it were a person. These include the abil-ity to sign contracts, legal protections, and the requirement to pay taxes. A corporation may also be sued or face criminal charges for wrongdoing. Corporations maximize the profits of shareholders by hiring specialists to make business decisions; the healthy operation of a corporation requires a balance between trust and accountability.

Stockholders, Boards, and Managers

The corporate governance structure involves three different groups: stockholders, the board of directors, and management. Anyone can become an owner of a publicly traded corporation by purchasing one or more shares of stock. These shares grant the owner a portion of any profits generated by the company and, in most cases, voting rights to retain or fire management.

Owning stock in large public corpora-tions presents several problems. First, most people own stock through mutual funds that pool money from many investors to hire expert management at low costs. This has the benefit of maximizing long-term results through diversification (the purchase of stocks of many companies). The downside of this strategy is that mutual funds often own

Billionaire investor Warren Buffett makes an appearance at a Dairy Queen diner in Omaha, Nebraska, to chat with shareholders of his company, Berkshire Hathaway. Buffett is well known as an advocate of good corporate governance and shareholder activism.

Board of Directors' Practices

	Good governance	*Poor governance*
Origin of the board	Majority of board from outside corporation	Minority of board from outside corporation
Board's ties to management	Independent; no ties to management	Financial ties to management
Stock ownership by the board	Board members are significant shareholders	Board members hold little or no stock in corporation
Compensation of the board	Significant portion of compensation is stock-related	Compensated only with cash
Formal evaluations of the board	Yes	No
Board response to investor requests for information on governance issues	Responsive	Unresponsive

tens of billions of dollars worth of stocks and regularly buy and sell them; thus many investors are not aware of what stock they own. Also, few investors have a detailed knowledge of the industries they are invested in. This hampers their ability to objectively evaluate the performance of the managers hired to run each company. The fact that investors must rely on the honesty of corporate accounting statements makes this task even more challenging.

Boards of directors were developed to alleviate these problems and ensure that management acts in the best interest of the owners. Boards have several functions, including evaluating management, overseeing the business decisions of the company, and providing advice and counsel to management.

The average board of directors in the United States has 15 members, typically with business backgrounds. Members spend about two weeks throughout the year meeting with management. Sitting on a board of directors is attractive because the pay ranges from $10,000 to $50,000 per year for a small commitment of time.

Management's function is to make the business decisions for the owners. Stockholders rely on the board of directors to select specialists who will maximize profits and run the corporation responsibly. The leading manager is often referred to as the chief executive officer, or CEO. The CEO is selected by the board and approved by a vote of the stockholders. Most corporations also hold an annual vote where members of management must win majority approval to continue in their positions.

Economists and businesspeople have always been concerned about the relationship between ownership and management. Stockholders are risking their money and must trust management to operate with integrity. The fundamental problem is separation of ownership from control, which exists when no single shareholder or group of shareholders owns enough shares of stock to control management. Without this separation, managers may pursue their own objectives, including personal wealth or fame, rather than serve the stockholders.

Theory versus Practice

In theory, the relationship between management and ownership should work well for several reasons. First, competition in the marketplace should bankrupt inefficient companies. Second, corporations often link management pay to the profits of the company. Third, institutional investors, including mutual funds and pension systems, often purchase large blocks of shares and have both the expertise and a strong incentive to monitor management. Nevertheless, experts assert that corporate governance has grown dysfunctional. This situation is illustrated by contrasting the functions of the boards with the way they actually operate.

The primary purpose of a board of directors is to oversee management. However, most American boards are chaired, or led, by the CEO of the company. This creates a conflict of

3. Salary; Signing Bonus; Loan. (a) Executive shall receive a salary of $500,000 per annum during the first three (3) years of the Term. Executive's salary shall be reviewed at least annually and may be increased but not decreased. . . .
(b) Within 10 days from the date of commencement of Executive's employment with the Company, the Company shall pay to Executive a $10 million signing bonus, payable in cash. . . .
(c) The Company shall make available a full recourse unsecured loan facility to Executive at the commencement of Executive's employment with the Company in an aggregate principal amount not to exceed $5 million in order to allow Executive to purchase shares of the Company's common stock. . . .

4. Annual Bonus. For each year of the Term, Executive will be eligible for an annual bonus which will be determined by the Board of Directors, but which shall not be less than $500,000 for any year during the Term. The bonus shall be reviewed at least annually by the Board of Directors and may be increased but not decreased.

5. Stock Options. Subject to Board approval, Executive shall be granted stock options (the "Two Million Options") to purchase an aggregate of Two Million (2,000,000) shares of common stock of the Company. . . .

7. Benefits. Executive shall be entitled to receive the following benefits:
(a) Health care coverage equivalent to that provided to the Company's other executive officers.
(b) Reimbursement of reasonable living expenses for temporary housing in the Los Angeles area until permanent accommodations are arranged but not later than December 31, 1999, and reimbursement of reasonable relocation expenses.
(c) Monthly First Class airfare to Los Angeles for members of Executive's immediate family (spouse, mother and all children including the child of his wife, Patricia).
(d) Private aircraft, if available, or First Class airfare and limousine service to/from residence and/or office in connection with all company travel and for appropriate trips to New Jersey until permanent living arrangements are made in Los Angeles as required. . . .
(e) Four (4) weeks paid vacation each year during the Term.

Source: The Corporate Library, http://www.thecorporatelibrary.com (January 1, 2003).

dation of the chair of the board. As the chair is also the CEO in most corporations, management is selecting the members of the boards, not the owners.

Corporate boards are also lax in protecting the interests of the owners because board members receive their compensation in spite of the performance of the company; thus they have little direct incentive to provide strict supervision. In addition, many directors serve on multiple boards and have full-time jobs of their own. Thus, they may lack the inclination or the time to aggressively defend the interests of owners.

The role of information further weakens the position of board members. Their position requires them to have accurate and timely data about company operations. This information is provided by management, making the board dependent on the very people it is supposed to monitor and giving management a means to downplay or conceal potential or actual problems. Taken together, these conditions make corporate governance problematic at best.

The Compensation Issue

One of the functions of the board of directors is to evaluate and recommend the compensation for management. Since many members of the board are picked by the CEO, conflict of interest arises.

Critics point to a variety of evidence that executive compensation (salary plus other incentives) is out of line with performance. For example, an ERI/SWSJ study about CEO pay in relation to corporate profits and stock performance showed that pay increased during a year of poor performance: overall profits dropped 35 percent and stock value dropped 13 percent, but CEO pay increased by 7 percent. A *BusinessWeek* survey provided further information that executive compensation has escalated dramatically. In 1980 the average CEO earned roughly 42 times more that the average worker. By 2006 this figure had increased to an average of 364 times more. The average compensation package is $10.8 million per year for the CEOs of the largest American firms.

Shareholders' rights activist Nell Minnow cites Robert Annunziata's contract with Global Crossing as an example of bad corporate governance because his salary and perks are not tied to performance. CEO contracts are public documents, and Minnow has posted many on www.corporatelibrary.com.

interest by placing the CEO in charge of evaluating his own performance.

The process of selecting board members often exacerbates this situation. In theory, selection is done democratically through the creation of a nominating committee to make selections when needed. The full board then votes on these recommendations, with a subsequent vote by stockholders. In practice, the majority of board openings are filled by the recommen-

During the 1990s, compensation committees increasingly relied on stock options as a way to retain talented managers. Stock options grant employees the right to purchase shares of company stock for a set price in a set period of time, usually several years. The price is often set at or above the current price of the stock. These options give employees an incentive to work hard because improving company performance will increase the price of the stock and raise the value of the options. Stock options were especially popular during the dot-com boom of the 1990s, when many companies were underfunded but needed to attract top talent to turn a profit. In essence, stock options offered employees tremendous wealth if the company succeeded.

Stock options also give management an incentive to take actions that increase the value of the stock. For example, if a CEO has been granted one million options to buy stock at $20 and the price of the stock increases to $30, she could realize $10 million if she exercised the options. Managers lose nothing if the stock price falls, as they are not required to exercise the option. As options became more common and increasingly generous, the temptation intensified for CEOs to use less-than-legitimate means to drive up the price of their company's stock.

Another important question about stock options is how they are reported in financial documents. Accountants have a difficult time identifying the cost of stock options because they may or may not be used. Formerly, accounting standards did not require companies to report the value of their options. This reduced the projected future expenses of these companies and made them appear more prosperous. The legislative response to the accounting scandals of 2001–2002 led to changes in how options are reported.

Executive compensation became a major issue in the recession of 2008–2009, when it was revealed that executives at companies receiving government bailout funds, such as insurance giant AIG, were receiving millions of dollars in bonuses. The government

Ratio of CEO to Average Worker Pay 1965 to 2006	
1965	26
1980	42
1990	107
2000	525
2006	364

Source: Institute for Policy Studies—United for a Fair Economy.

The average CEO went from earning 26 times more than the average worker to earning 364 times more.

In March 2002 six former attorneys for Enron are sworn in before testifying to the House Energy and Commerce Committee about the collapse of the former energy giant.

Merrill Lynch and Bank of America

The global financial services firm Merrill Lynch was acquired by Bank of America in September 2008 after losses stemming from the subprime mortgage crisis brought the firm to the brink of bankruptcy. Its downfall demonstrates failures of sound corporate governance, and even its acquisition by Bank of America was rife with controversy.

Under chief executive officer Stanley O'Neal, who rose to the position in 2002, Merrill Lynch invested aggressively in collateralized debt obligations (CDOs) based on subprime mortgages in search of the potentially enormous profits produced by such investments and seemingly blind to the potential risk. When the subprime market collapsed in the summer of 2007, O'Neal at first understated the firm's losses, saying it would take a hit for $4.5 billion. Only weeks later the firm finally announced the highest quarterly loss in its history—$7.9 billion—and a continuing $20 billion exposure to the collateralized debt sector. O'Neal resigned in 2007.

O'Neal's successor as CEO, John Thain, fared little better in the corporate governance stakes. It was revealed that, despite continuing large losses by the company, he spent $1.2 million of company money renovating his new office; he also paid up to $4 billion in bonuses to Merrill Lynch employees in advance of the firm's takeover by Bank of America.

In April 2009, it came to light that Bank of America officials underestimated the extent of losses at Merrill Lynch to its shareholders in order to push through the takeover; because of these losses, Bank of America was forced to accept U.S. government financial rescue funds. Kenneth D. Lewis, chairman and CEO of Bank of America, was forced to step down as chairman as a result.

stepped in to limit executive pay in those companies that received government assistance to avoid bankruptcy.

Corporate Scandals

The trends of weak corporate governance and the spread of stock options coincided with changes in the investment banking and accounting industries. Banking and accounting firms audit corporate balance sheets and provide investors with outside assessments of corporate performance. During the 1990s many of these companies merged and started providing both accounting and consulting services, creating incentives to curry management's favor through friendly accounting evaluations in hopes of gaining consulting business. In some cases, the so-called outside assessments were adjusted according to the wishes of management.

The temptation to inflate stock prices, combined with weak corporate governance and reduced accounting rigor, culminated in a series of corporate scandals, bankruptcies, and a crisis in confidence in corporate America during 2002. Executives from several major corporations, including Enron, Adelphia (see sidebar), and WorldCom, were accused of crimes ranging from embezzlement to fraud and racketeering. These accusations and indictments contributed to a pronounced slump in the stock market as investors worldwide lost confidence in management and corporate leadership.

The scandals of 2002 typically featured something called off-balance-sheet loans—corporations either directly lending officers money or guaranteeing their loans to banks. These sums, which often ranged into the tens of millions of dollars, were lent without the knowledge of the stockholders.

In the economic downturn that began in 2008, the focus was on risk management. Shareholders questioned the effectiveness of board oversight of risky lending at financial institutions and risky investment management by other companies.

Stockholders are also taking an active interest in corporate reform. Large investors, including pension boards and mutual funds, are pressuring corporations to explicitly include stock options on their balance sheets. Many institutions, because of their large investments, have taken the position that they are not just stockholders but stakeholders, or active participants, in corporate decisions.

Businesspeople must take risks to generate profits, and they risk losing out to competition if supervision and controls are too stringent. Policy makers will attempt to find a balance that restores investor confidence while minimizing economic losses from regulation. This illustrates the core conundrum of capitalism: how to best focus greed toward productive ends while limiting its excesses.

Further Reading
Corporate Governance
www.corpgov.net
Web site lists links to resources (online library, courses, conferences, and networks).
Global Corporate Governance Forum
www.gcgf.org
The World Bank's multinational trust to foster academic research, improve policy, and finance corporate governance initiatives.

—*David Long*

Corporate Social Responsibility

Accompanying U.S. industrial development in the 1900s was a growing anxiety about the harmful effects of some business practices. Public concern throughout the century produced a laundry list of business infractions, many too serious to be ignored. Corporations responded to public pressure and government interventions with an increasing sense of social responsibility. Development of corporate social responsibility followed an uneven track throughout the twentieth century.

In the late 1800s and early 1900s, when the labor supply was plentiful, powerful industry owners realized large profits by paying workers poorly and not spending money to make workplaces safe. In this era, the general American view of businessmen was highly negative. Businessmen appeared to be interested only in profits for themselves and had little concern for the welfare of workers. One exception was businessman George Pullman. He proactively addressed the needs of his industrial workers (who built Pullman Palace railway cars) by establishing Pullman Town, just south of Chicago, between the 1870s and 1880s. This "company town" was intended to control the workers by forcing them to be moral and upright citizens, but Pullman also furnished housing, schools, and parks (which other company towns did not), and stores (which other company towns did, but with higher

Socially responsible companies are ranked using a variety of criteria, including environmental responsibility, diversity in the workplace, and the quality of employee, customer, and community relations.

Top 100 Corporate Citizens of 2008: Rated by *Corporate Responsibility Officer*	

Rank Company	Rank Company	Rank Company	Rank Company
1. Intel	26. Allegheny Energy	51. Motorola	76. Hess
2. Eaton	27. FPL Group	52. Freeport-McMoran	77. Gilead Sciences
3. Nike	28. Marathon Oil	53. Seagate Technology	78. Integrys Energy Group
4. Deere & Co.	29. Xcel Energy	54. Fairchild Semiconductor	79. Reliant Energy
5. Genentech	30. Staples	55. Constellation Energy	80. SBA Communications
6. Corning	31. Southern	56. PPL	81. Verizon Communications
7. Humana	32. Exelon	57. General Motors	82. MeadWestvaco
8. Bank of America	33. Raytheon	58. Union Pacific	83. Weyerhauser
9. ITT	34. Goldman Sachs Group	59. Bunge	84. Edison International
10. PG&E	35. Starbucks	60. Black & Decker	85. Alliant Techsystems
11. Dominion Resources	36. Ford Motor	61. Gap	86. Cypress Semiconductor
12. State Street	37. PNC Financial Serv. Grp.	62. Cummins	87. El Paso
13. Dow Chemical	38. Applied Materials	63. Citigroup	88. Monsanto
14. Cisco Systems	39. Lockheed Martin	64. Eastman Chemical	89. Merrill Lynch
15. Wisconsin Energy	40. Agilent Technologies	65. Stericycle	90. General Electric
16. Progress Energy	41. Sunoco	66. Corrections Corporation	91. Kraft Foods
17. Entergy	42. Target	67. McKesson	92. Cooper Industries
18. Norfolk Southern	43. Intersil	68. Office Depot	93. Morgan Stanley
19. Sun Microsystems	44. Safeway	69. American Electric Power	94. General Mills
20. Pub. Service Enterprise	45. FirstEnergy	70. Xilinx	95. Coca-Cola
21. IBM	46. J.P. Morgan Chase	71. Guess?	96. Freddie Mac
22. Pepsico	47. Phillips-Van Heusen	72. Goodyear Tire & Rubber	97. Alexander & Baldwin
23. Aetna	48. Colgate-Palmolive	73. Avalonbay Communities	98. Avon Products
24. Baxter International	49. Tiffany	74. Temple-Inland	99. Wyeth
25. Burlington N. Santa Fe	50. Walt Disney	75. Waste Management	100. SPX

Source: Corporate Responsibility Officer magazine

prices). However, his goal of avoiding strikes was defeated in 1894 when his workers rebelled against not only their reduced pay but also the interference of the corporation in their daily lives.

The concept of corporate responsibility to workers emerged again in the 1910s and 1920s with the development of "business welfare capitalism." Hundreds of firms established social support systems for their workers, including pensions, profit-sharing plans, health care, adult education, and so on. Many of these programs extolled the virtues of American society (and thus this movement was also known as the Americanization movement) and featured experiments in democratic governance in the workplace. Henry Ford had been a major contributor to this movement in the mid-1910s when he raised wages and established the so-called $5 day. As had Pullman, Ford interfered heavily in the everyday affairs of his workers. To earn the $5, workers had to work much harder than before and allow Ford's "social workers" access to their homes to confirm that they were living moral lives.

At the same time, American business leaders began to establish programs to encourage a greater sense of business responsibility to society. This included expanding business education in universities and colleges and having executives join local philanthropic and service organizations (for example, the Rotary and Kiwanis clubs). These movements were clear attempts to move away from the negative stereotype of businessmen that had developed in the late nineteenth century.

Much of the progress made in the 1920s toward more socially responsible business practices was undermined by the financial strains of the Great Depression. The Depression also led Americans to view business less favorably and built sympathy for unions. The New Deal established the Fair Labor Standards Act to force businesses to pay higher wages (not all workers were covered; women and tenant farmers were omitted initially).

In the boom years of the 1950s corporate responsibility to workers and society emerged again as a coherent movement. Invoking "duty to the employee," corporations expanded the older welfare capitalism programs of the 1920s. In addition to pensions, profit sharing, and improved health plans, employers offered programs for spouses and children of the male workers. Civic programs, abandoned in the Depression, also reemerged to reflect a new sense of "duty to society." These measures, generous as they may have been, also had a clear economic motive: to engender employee and consumer loyalty to the firm.

Broadening Responsibility

For most of the twentieth century, corporations had little or no inclination to act for the public good, as opposed to the good of their employees. The modern environmental movement, greatly inspired by Rachel Carson's book *Silent Spring* (1962), emerged in the 1960s and 1970s to challenge corporate behavior on a broad public level. Environmentalists argued that certain kinds of consumption and waste production are disproportionately harmful and that some industries acted recklessly, promoting and profiting from practices that were essentially destroying ecological systems.

From the environmental movement, pressure grew on corporations to take social responsibility for the condition of the Earth, the air, the water, and life itself. Activists devoted to land issues questioned mining practices and land pollution and pushed for recycling to slow landfill development and

Web Resources on Corporate Social Responsibility

www.worldcsr.com/pages is a collection of links to Web sites of the leading international organizations concerned with corporate social responsibility.

www.csrforum.com, the Corporate Social Responsibility Forum, promotes responsible business practices.

www.bsr.org is the Web site of a global nonprofit organization that offers resources to its member companies to promote ethical values and responsible business practices.

www.csrwire.com is a newswire service that provides press releases and reports that promote corporate social responsibility.

www.csramericas.org is the Web site of a consortium of North and South American companies that implement corporate social responsibility programs and initiatives.

resource depletion. Others raised concerns about the dangers of certain kinds of energy production and hazardous waste. Scientists were enlisted to study air quality, to evaluate ozone depletion, global warming, and the levels and effects of air pollution. In nearly every instance, corporate practices were called into question and industries were asked to be accountable.

At about the same time, profound social changes forced corporations to reconsider issues of equity in the workplace. Minorities and women argued that because of discriminatory practices, they were being paid less for equal work and were overlooked for promotions that went to less-qualified white males. Again, interest groups put business under fire.

Industry, facing mounting public pressure but heavily invested in the status quo, clung to established practices. Corporate powers argued that equity problems were overstated and that addressing environmental issues would compromise profitability. The impasse between activist insistence and industrial resistance forced the government to take action in the public interest.

Between 1969 and 1972, some of the most important business-related social legislation in U.S. history was passed. Four regulatory agencies were established, all greatly affecting American business: the Environmental Protection Agency (EPA), the Occupational Safety and Health Administration (OSHA), the Equal Employment Opportunity Commission (EEOC), and the Consumer Product Safety Commission (CPSC). The majority of businesses were caught unawares by the social legislation of the 1960s, for example, the Civil Rights Act of 1964. Many businesses established Political Action Committees (PACs) to combat expansion of these programs, but met with little success.

The election of Ronald Reagan to the presidency in 1980 shifted Washington's agenda. With increased concern for corporate independence and profits, the federal government vowed to intrude less in business affairs. Several times, the administration attempted to repeal the social legislation of the previous decade.

Although the 1980s tend to be remembered as a pro-business, pro-greed era, a watershed in the history of corporate social responsibility occurred in 1982, after seven people were killed by cyanide-laced Tylenol capsules. Johnson & Johnson, producers of the over-the-counter pain reliever, reacted quickly, making the public aware of the tampering and recalling millions of bottles of the drug at a cost of more than $100 million. At the time, industry experts believed that Johnson & Johnson was doomed, but the company's swift and forthright handling of the crisis improved the company's reputation rather than destroying it.

On March 24, 1989, an Exxon oil tanker ran aground in the icy waters of Alaska's Prince William Sound, spilling 11 million gallons of crude oil along more than one thousand miles of previously pristine shoreline. The world watched vivid and disturbing broadcasts of Exxon workers and volunteers swabbing gummy black oil from the wings of gasping sea birds, while Exxon executives appeared to be reluctant to take responsibility for the disaster. That oil spill, as well as the earlier toxic discoveries at Love Canal in the early 1970s and the Three Mile Island nuclear accident in 1979, renewed public outrage at

In 1986 Johnson & Johnson president David Clare testifies before a U.S. Senate hearing about tamperproof packaging. Most analysts believe that Johnson & Johnson's forthright handling of the product-tampering tragedy in 1982 saved the company from ruin.

The Domini 400 Social^SM Index (DSI) is a benchmark that gauges the stock market performance of shares most socially responsible investors will buy. The DSI compares favorably with the traditonal Standard and Poor's 500.

Socially Responsible Investing: Domini 400 Social^SM Index (DSI) vs. Standard and Poor's 500
(total return as of 2008)

	DSI 400	S&P 500
One Year	-34.94%	-37.00
Three Year *	-8.57%	-8.36%
Five Year *	-2.79%	-2.19%
Ten Year *	-1.78%	-1.38%

* Annualized returns.
Source: KLD Research & Analytics

the lack of corporate concern for people and the environment.

Responsibility versus Profit?

Throughout the twentieth century, many businesses came to realize that irresponsible corporate behavior was not only publicly unacceptable but also economically imprudent. The high cost of fighting government regulation together with the damaging effects of public criticism adversely affected profits. Honest and ethical business leaders in the United States and throughout the world sought to distance themselves from scandalous business activity. In developing a proactive stance on the public issues that are part of corporate concern, these business leaders paved the way for voluntary corporate social responsibility.

The earliest form of a voluntary corporate citizenry was philanthropic. What began as donations to charity expanded to include extensive involvement in workers' communities. Most major corporations added a section to their annual reports detailing their community involvement, including discussions of their involvement in education and literacy, their support of the arts, their promotion of diversity, and the volunteer activities of their employees.

Globalization provided enormous opportunities for industry from the late twentieth century. Corporations formed conglomerates, which supplied a number of new jobs and brought additional wealth to the countries where they operated. With worldwide operations and impact, businesses face broader eth-

ical challenges and need to set a new agenda for corporate responsibility.

Corporate social responsibility, in its broadest sense, implies that corporations have stakeholder interest at a level equal to shareholder interest. In other words, profits should not occur at the expense of anyone or anything affected by the way a corporation conducts its business. Stakeholders include employees, customers, suppliers, community organizations, subsidiaries and affiliates, joint venture partners, local neighborhoods, and the environment. Common wisdom says that when companies foster mutually beneficial relationships with stakeholders, they create sustainable communities that, in turn, will be supportive of business. When stakeholders are happy and live well, they form healthy communities that generate stable economies. All this is good for business in the long run.

Companies today realize the benefits of this kind of responsibility. Research in the United States and Canada has shown that over time the most socially responsible companies become the most profitable. Furthermore, they are more likely to have their stock bought by investors. Most major families of mutual funds now have a category for socially responsible investing (SRI). These SRI funds are performing as well and sometimes better than the average mutual fund; as of 2007, $2.7 trillion had been invested in U.S. funds that adhered to a socially responsible investment ethic. In Europe, there was more than $3.6 trillion under SRI management.

Further Reading
Business for Social Responsibility
www.bsr.org
Web site of a nonprofit organization that provides resources and news on business ethics and ethical companies.
CSRWire
www.csrwire.com
A source of news, reports, and information.
Social Investment Forum
www.socialinvest.org
SIF is the U.S. nonprofit association for professionals, firms, and organizations dedicated to promoting socially responsible investing (SRI).

—Karen Ehrle

Corporation

In law, a corporation is an organization that is formed by a group of people for the purpose of carrying out certain specified activities and that is legally endowed with certain rights and duties. Corporations take various forms. A corporation may, for example, be a religious body (the word *incorporate* comes from the Roman Catholic church's medieval definition of itself as a "corpus") or it may be a municipal body. In the United States, government entities below the level of a state, for example, cities and counties, are considered to be corporations; the federal government itself has established corporations like the Community Credit Corporation and the Federal Deposit Insurance Corporation. A corporation may also be a charitable, nonprofit organization, or it may be what is known as a professional corporation, which can have only one stockholder (a licensed professional, like a doctor or engineer).

Most commonly, however, the corporation is thought of as a private association organized for the purpose of making a profit—a business. Legally, in the United States, a corporation is considered to be a person, a definition codified in the important Supreme Court decision of 1886, *Santa Clara County v. Southern Pacific Railroad*. In this case the Court ruled that, as a person, a corporation had the same rights as human individuals under the 1st Amendment and, especially, under the 14th Amendment, which states that "no state shall deprive any person of life, liberty, or property, without due process of law." As a person, a corporation can buy, sell, and own property, bring lawsuits, and enter into contracts. It also pays taxes and it can be prosecuted for crimes.

Unlike a person, a corporation can exist indefinitely. As Chief Justice John Marshall wrote in 1819, "a perpetual succession of individuals are capable of acting for the promotion of the particular object, like one immortal being." One of the chief advantages of a corporation is that it protects its owners (the shareholders) from unlimited, personal liability. In most instances, if a corporation cannot pay its debts, its assets may be seized and sold. However, the personal assets of the shareholders may not.

Historians trace the origin of corporations to antiquity, but their modern history is usually said to begin in the sixteenth century. Some of the best-known examples of early corporations were British overseas trading companies, including the Massachusetts Bay Company and the Hudson's Bay Company; both were joint-stock companies and, as such, are considered to be forerunners of the modern corporation.

Starting a Corporation

In the United States before the Industrial Revolution, corporations were individually granted by the special act of a state legislature. Eventually, state legislatures were empowered to authorize incorporation by general law, which enables a group of individuals to organize a corporation under "articles of incorporation," a document that is submitted for approval to a specific official, normally the state's secretary of state.

A corporation gains its initial financing from the sale of stock (shares). Small corporations are often owned by family or friends, or both, and their shares in stock are not publicly sold (a closed corporation). When very large financing is needed and a corporation's shares are publicly sold, the raising of capital is commonly the task of a promoter. Publicly sold companies often seek to incorporate in a state that has liberal incorporation laws—that is, with regulations less stringent in protecting investors' interests.

Corporations usually issue common or preferred shares. Holders of common stock are usually entitled to vote at the corporation's yearly meeting and receive dividends when the company declares them. Holders of preferred stock normally do not have voting rights but have precedence over owners of common stock in claiming dividends and assets. They also receive an annual dividend payment regardless of the corporation's profitability.

In addition to selling shares to raise capital, a corporation can be financed through borrowing. Corporations that have successfully conducted business for a while also have retained earnings that can be used as a source of financing for further business ventures.

Rupert Murdoch, chairman of News Corporation, addresses the company's annual general meeting.

Corporate Structure

As a rule, management of a corporation is divided into three groups: directors, officers, and shareholders. The directors are elected by the shareholders; they are charged with developing the corporation's policies and managing its affairs. Directors are also

Corporations by Size and Industry: By Receipts Class
2005
(Number in thousands; receipts in billion dollars)

Industry		Total	Under $1 mil.[1]	$1–$4.9 million	$5–$9.9 million	$10–$49.9 million	$50 mil. or more
Agriculture, forestry, fishing, and hunting	Number	142	124	15	1	1	<500
	Total receipts	126	18	30	10	23	44
Mining	Number	33	25	6	1	1	<500
	Total receipts	280	4	12	8	22	234
Utilities	Number	8	7	1	1	<500	<500
	Total receipts	604	1	1	1	<500	599
Construction	Number	752	573	137	21	18	3
	Total receipts	1,427	145	299	150	345	488
Manufacturing	Number	278	165	70	18	18	7
	Total receipts	6,506	45	161	128	373	5,789
Wholesale and retail trade	Number	993	671	219	44	46	12
	Total receipts	6,652	176	500	306	982	4,688
Transportation and warehousing	Number	187	149	27	6	4	1
	Total receipts	659	28	60	40	81	450
Information	Number	123	103	14	2	2	1
	Total receipts	887	15	30	15	47	780
Finance and insurance	Number	243	197	29	6	7	3
	Total receipts	3,302	38	63	42	152	3,007
Real estate, rental, and leasing	Number	642	609	28	3	3	<500
	Total receipts	268	61	58	18	37	94
Professional, scientific, and technical services	Number	786	688	81	9	7	2
	Total receipts	814	123	159	66	135	332
Educational services	Number	45	42	3	<500	<500	<500
	Total receipts	33	7	6	1	3	16
Health care and social services	Number	381	308	62	5	5	1
	Total receipts	515	92	123	31	88	181
Arts, entertainment, and recreation	Number	116	106	9	1	1	<500
	Total receipts	80	17	18	6	11	28
Accommodation and food services	Number	287	238	43	4	2	<500
	Total receipts	396	70	83	26	33	185
Other services	Number	345	314	28	2	1	<500
	Total receipts	184	68	52	12	22	29
Total[2]	Number	5,261	4,319	772	124	116	30
	Receipts	22,733	908	1,655	860	2,354	16,944

[1] Includes businesses without receipts. [2] Includes businesses not allocable to individual industries.
Notes: <500 = fewer than 500 returns. Totals do not include these returns.
Source: U.S. Internal Revenue Service, *Statistics of Income*, various publications, and unpublished data.

responsible for deciding when to declare dividends. Directors do not, however, conduct the day-to-day operations of the corporation, a job that falls to the officers (although in most U.S. states, the corporation's president is required to be one of the directors).

The officers of the corporation usually include the chief executive officer, the chief financial officer, and the treasurer. Although shareholders commonly have the right to vote at company meetings, in some cases voting rights are limited or nonexistent. In practice, most shareholder voting is done by proxy (the shareholder designates in writing someone to vote in his or her place).

Although Marshall described a corporation as "immortal," its lifetime can be limited for several reasons. Some corporations are intended from the beginning to have a limited lifetime—when the term laid out in the

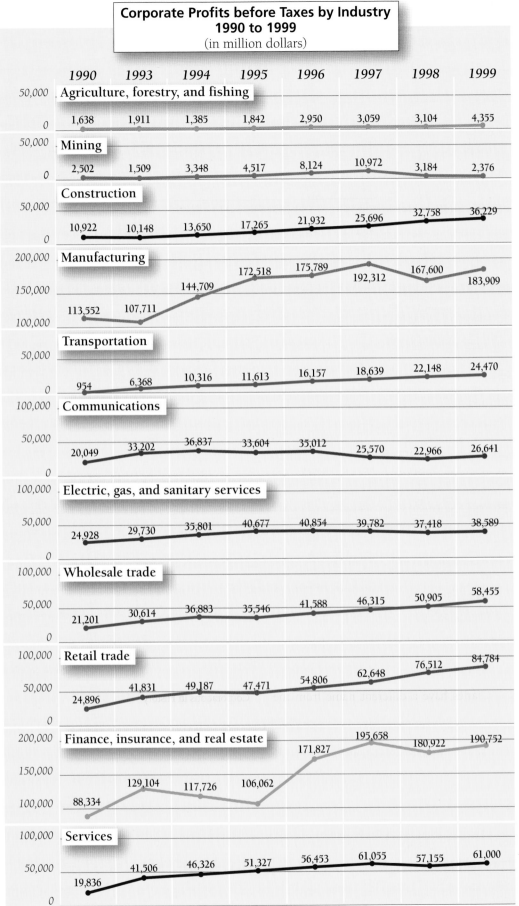

Corporate Profits before Taxes by Industry 1990 to 1999
(in million dollars)

	1990	1993	1994	1995	1996	1997	1998	1999
Agriculture, forestry, and fishing	1,638	1,911	1,385	1,842	2,950	3,059	3,104	4,355
Mining	2,502	1,509	3,348	4,517	8,124	10,972	3,184	2,376
Construction	10,922	10,148	13,650	17,265	21,932	25,696	32,758	36,229
Manufacturing	113,552	107,711	144,709	172,518	175,789	192,312	167,600	183,909
Transportation	954	6,368	10,316	11,613	16,157	18,639	22,148	24,470
Communications	20,049	33,202	36,837	33,604	35,012	25,570	22,966	26,641
Electric, gas, and sanitary services	24,928	29,730	35,801	40,677	40,854	39,782	37,418	38,589
Wholesale trade	21,201	30,614	36,883	35,546	41,588	46,315	50,905	58,455
Retail trade	24,896	41,831	49,187	47,471	54,806	62,648	76,512	84,784
Finance, insurance, and real estate	88,334	129,104	117,726	106,062	171,827	195,658	180,922	190,752
Services	19,836	41,506	46,326	51,327	56,453	61,055	57,155	61,000

Source: U.S. Bureau of Economic Analysis, *National Income and Product Accounts of the United States, 1929–97*, and *Survey of Current Business,* Washington, D.C., July 2001.

articles of incorporation is reached, the company's dissolution is automatic. A corporation may also be dissolved by a vote of the shareholders (a voluntary dissolution); another form of voluntary dissolution occurs when the corporation is merged into another (as opposed to a consolidation, in which each of the combining companies continues to exist).

A dissolution can also be involuntary—a minority of the shareholders, if they believe the company is being mismanaged, can bring a lawsuit seeking the termination of the corporation. Another kind of involuntary dissolution occurs when a bankrupt company is sued by its creditors or when the state acts to dissolve the corporation in response to corporate misconduct or a failure to pay taxes. When a corporation is dissolved, it gathers its assets, pays its debts (as best it can), and distributes its remaining resources to the shareholders.

Multinationals

Perhaps the most significant development for the corporate form is the rise of the international, or multinational, corporation. Beginning in the late nineteenth century, faster transportation and a desire to expand markets—combined with companies' needs for items found overseas, like oil and minerals—permitted, or even compelled, companies to expand beyond the borders of the nations in which they were founded.

Multinational corporations normally have a parent company, located in the country of the firm's origin, and various subsidiaries in other nations. Sometimes these subsidiaries have a different name from the parent company, and the amount of direct control exercised by the parent can vary. When a corporation becomes a multinational, its goals and strategies no longer apply to one country but become regional or global.

At the beginning of the twenty-first century, there were more than 63,000 multinational corporations, employing 90 million people and producing 25 percent of the world's gross product. Analysts often point out that the annual sales of some of the biggest multinationals may exceed the gross domestic product of many individual countries.

Public Opinion of Corporations

Surveys indicate that the U.S. public is of two minds about corporations and corporate power. A poll taken by *BusinessWeek* magazine showed that although two-thirds of respondents praised U.S. corporations for making good products and being globally competitive, no fewer than three-quarters of them said that big business had gained too much power over their lives. Several factors were cited for the unpopularity of corporations, including a declining standard of customer service, the failure of wages and benefits to keep pace with productivity increases, burnout and mandatory overtime among employees, and, perhaps most of all, excessive executive pay.

The bankruptcies of the Enron Corporation (2001) and WorldCom (2002) and subsequent revelations of widespread unethical business practices served only to heighten the suspicion of corporations among the U.S. public. Revelations about executive compensation and perks at financial institutions receiving government bailout money in 2009 strengthened negative public perceptions. Taking a long-term view, however, some analysts pointed out that, although corporations have a generally unenviable image, the U.S. public's good opinion of corporations has waxed and waned throughout history.

Further Research
Corporations in History
history.wisc.edu/dunlavy/i_corporations.htm
A research database of corporate charters established by a professor at the University of Wisconsin-Madison.
International Labour Organisation
actrav.itcilo.org/actrav-english/telearn/global/ilo/multinat/multinat.htm
ILOs database on multinationals.
Legal Information Institute
topics.law.cornell.edu/wex/corporations
From Cornell Law School, information about the legal framework for corporations, including links to original source material.

—*Joseph Gustaitis*

Deregulation

During the last quarter of the twentieth century, the United States and other nations of the world moved to reduce government influence on their economies. This was accomplished in several ways—by turning government enterprises over to private companies and by reducing or rethinking prior commitments to government regulation.

That trend toward deregulation is often associated with the rise to power of two conservatives—Margaret Thatcher, who became prime minister of England in 1979, and Ronald Reagan, who was elected president of the United States in 1980. In fact, however, the trend began in 1977, when Democratic president Jimmy Carter asked Alfred Kahn, a Cornell University professor, to head the Civil Aeronautics Board (CAB), which regulated airlines.

Conservative Republicans had long opposed regulation, taking their lead from free-market economists like Milton Friedman, Friedrich von Hayek, and George Stigler at the University of Chicago. Kahn was not part of that conservative school. He was a liberal, and a follower of Thorstein Veblen, the satirical writer and economist whose work *The Theory of the Leisure Class* (1899) was sharply skeptical about the ability of the free market to deliver the greatest happiness to the most people.

Kahn was also a realist. What he found in Washington was a growing political consensus that airline regulation had failed. The CAB had been established during the 1930s, near the beginning of the Great Depression, and was supposed to ensure reliable service and low rates for airline customers. By 1977, however, many analysts had concluded that regulation was not benefiting consumers; rather, it was protecting inefficient and poorly run airlines. Support for deregulating the airlines was growing even among liberal Democrats, including Senator Ted Kennedy of Massachusetts, who was being advised on regulatory matters by Stephen Breyer, a lawyer who later was named to the U.S. Supreme Court. "The CAB was supposed to be protecting the public," Breyer said. "But regulation was leading to higher prices. [The CAB] spent 95 percent of its time keeping prices from being too low instead of pushing them to get lowered."

At first, Kahn moved slowly to lift the regulations on airline schedules and fares. He concluded, however, that gradual deregulation did not work, and he moved to eliminate airline regulation altogether. The result was an upheaval in the industry; in the aftermath, companies like Pan American Airlines and Eastern Airlines went out of business. Prices fell, however, and competition increased. America became a nation of fliers, with the number of passengers more than doubling in the next two decades.

Over the course of the next quarter-century, deregulation spread to the trucking industry, the telecommunications industry, the health care industry, the electric power industry, and many others. Regulations were removed, competition was encouraged, and the reach of what eighteenth-century economist Adam Smith called the "invisible hand" of the free market extended further than ever.

President Jimmy Carter signs legislation deregulating the airline industry.

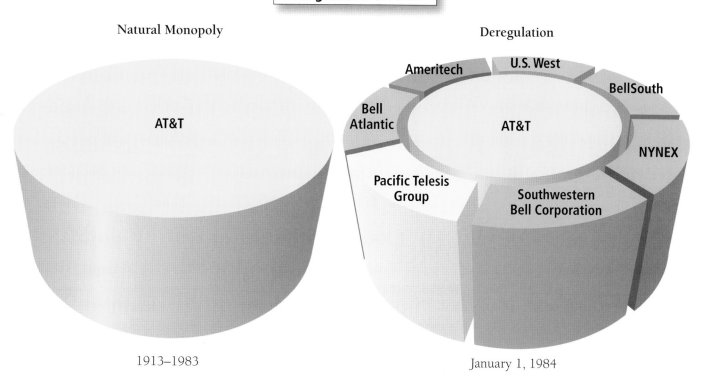

Natural Monopoly

AT&T

1913–1983

Deregulation

Ameritech U.S. West

Bell
Atlantic BellSouth

AT&T

NYNEX

Pacific Telesis
Group

Southwestern
Bell Corporation

January 1, 1984

The shape of AT&T, before and after the company breakup.

The deregulatory movement in the United States was influential elsewhere, as several nations moved to sell off government-owned businesses and reduce the burden of government regulation. The collapse of the Soviet Union in the late 1980s eliminated communism as an alternative model for government's role in the economy. The failure of the Japanese economy in the 1990s, as well as the Asian economic crisis of 1997, undercut any idea that the Asian model of economic development, in which governments helped to guide business investment, might be superior to the capitalism of the United States. By the end of the twentieth century, except in isolated areas remaining committed to collectivist ideologies, only one model for a successful economy remained: the market economy with limited government intervention.

A Legacy of the Progressive Era

Government regulation of the economy in the United States dates to the end of the nineteenth century, when a progressive Congress established the Interstate Commerce Commission to regulate the railroads. In the Great Depression and the years that followed, government regulation was expanded to the airlines, telephone companies, and other areas. Economists focused their attention on the failures of the marketplace. Whenever a market failure was found, a government regulatory solution was proposed.

By the 1970s, however, a growing group of economists had concluded that, although the free market sometimes failed to serve society's needs, so, too, did government regulation. In many cases, as in the case of the CAB, a regulated industry would "capture" the regulator with skillful lobbying; then it would use the regulatory regime to its own advantage, rather than to the advantage of consumers. Nobel Prize–winning economist George Stigler was one of the first to explain this sad cycle, but he persuaded others. Liberals, including Alfred Kahn and Stephen Breyer, joined their conservative brethren in opposing regulation.

Economist Lawrence Summers (former treasury secretary under President Bill Clinton and President Barack Obama's chief economic advisor) told Daniel Yergin the story of his own conversion, included in Yergin's book on the global trend toward deregulation, *The Commanding Heights*

AT&T lost its monopoly of the telephone system in the United States after a ten-year legal battle.

(1998). Summers said his parents, both distinguished economists and supporters of President Franklin Roosevelt's New Deal, always had spoken of free-market economist Milton Friedman with disdain. "He was the devil figure in my youth," Summers said. "Only with time have I come to have large amounts of grudging respect. And, with time, increasingly ungrudging respect." Summers was a key figure in the deregulation of the financial services industry, including the abolition of the Glass-Steagall Act that had formerly separated the operations of investment banks and commercial banks, during the Clinton administration.

Deregulation of the Telephone Industry

Many of the regulatory plans of the early part of the century were justified under the theory of "natural monopoly." The telephone system run by AT&T, also known as

"Ma Bell" in its heyday, was the prime example. Building telephone lines to every home and business in the country was expensive. If many companies were allowed to compete in building those facilities, they might engage in costly duplication, with little hope of ever recouping their investment. Instead, industry executives and economists argued in unison that AT&T should be seen as a benign and necessary monopoly, should be protected from competition, and should be regulated to ensure that it would serve the public interest.

AT&T jealously guarded its monopoly, arguing that competition would undercut both service and prices. An upstart entrepreneur by the name of William McGowan launched an attack on the phone company in the 1960s, however, starting a firm called Microwave Communications, Inc.—later MCI—to compete with AT&T in providing long distance telephone services. In 1974 the Justice Department filed an antitrust suit against AT&T. The court case lasted for nearly a decade and ultimately led to the breakup of AT&T into a long distance company (that would have to compete with the likes of MCI) and multiple regional companies—known as the "baby bells"—to provide local service.

Deregulation of the telephone system took another step forward in 1996, when Congress passed legislation to open phone service to further competition. During the debate over the 1996 law, proponents argued that technology had eliminated the need for regulation. Even if telephone companies had a monopoly on local phone lines, the proponents of deregulation argued, they would face stiff competition in the future from cable companies, wireless companies, and satellite companies. That competition would ensure that Adam Smith's invisible hand did its work, keeping prices down and quality up.

A similar argument was made by the Microsoft Corporation as it battled a U.S. government effort to dismantle its monopoly. Concerns about monopoly were misplaced in the new world of technology, Microsoft's lawyers argued, because the rapid pace of technological innovation ensured that any monopoly would be temporary, soon toppled by new and more powerful technologies.

Electricity Deregulation in the 1990s

In the late 1990s, the electricity industry became the focus of deregulation efforts. A number of states passed laws to allow businesses and consumers to choose from a variety of electricity suppliers, much as they chose among long distance phone carriers. A television advertisement in Pennsylvania captured the moment. It showed a young couple in a romantic apartment in Paris. The man was desperately trying to convince the woman to stay with him and build a new life in the City of Love. The woman appeared willing, except for one troubling detail. Would she be able to choose her electricity supplier? "Whoa," the man said,

taken aback. "Where do you think you are, Pennsylvania?"

Like the telephone industry, the electricity business had long been deemed a natural monopoly. Companies had to make large investments up front to build generating plants and install electrical wires. In return, they wanted the government to protect them from competition and guarantee them a healthy profit. So local utility commissions developed a system of cost plus pricing. Utilities were allowed to charge prices to consumers that enabled them to recover all their costs, and then make a reasonable profit on top.

Over time, however, that system encouraged companies to make huge mistakes, and it forced consumers to pay for the mistakes. Utilities that invested in costly nuclear plants in the 1960s and 1970s, for instance, were allowed to charge their customers high rates throughout the 1970s and 1980s, even though the plants sometimes turned out to be unnecessary. Electricity rates varied widely. By the 1990s an electricity user in Pittsburgh was paying rates that were nearly double those paid just 50 miles away in Uniontown, Pennsylvania. Consumers in New York state, which had the most expensive electricity in the nation, were paying on average three times as much

Portland, Maine, at night. Electricity in Maine was deregulated in 2000.

Airline security personnel load baggage onto an X-ray machine at Boston's Logan Airport. In the wake of the 2001 terrorist attacks, the U.S government stepped in to federalize airport security.

as consumers in the state of Washington, which benefited from cheap hydropower generated by government-built dams.

The idea behind deregulation was to open up the electricity system, allowing power consumers in Pittsburgh to buy the same cheap power available in Uniontown. Over time, the theory went, consumers would get the lowest possible prices, and inefficient power-generating plants would be shut down.

Electricity deregulation ran into trouble in 2000, however, when California's deregulation plan caused a crisis that bankrupted some of the state's utilities and forced residents to suffer rolling brown-outs and blackouts. The California experience was a reminder that deregulation is no panacea— particularly if done in a haphazard or poorly thought-out manner. California had deregu-

lated energy suppliers, requiring utilities to buy electricity from multiple suppliers at variable rates. But the state continued to cap the rates paid by consumers. When supplies got tight, the state's utilities found themselves stuck with ever-higher prices for wholesale energy but unable to cover their costs by raising prices to consumers.

Meanwhile, state and local governments joined the deregulation trend, turning over more and more public services to private companies. Garbage collection services, public transportation services, welfare offices, prisons, and even police forces were contracted to profit-making companies. Even some public schools were taken over by private companies. The idea was that the power of the marketplace could cure many of the problems created by government bureaucracies.

The steady march toward deregulation, privatization, and reliance on the marketplace contributed to the unprecedented prosperity of the last decade of the twentieth century and the start of the twenty-first century. However, signs that the trend might have run its course were evident by the end of the first decade of the new century. The terrorist attacks on New York City and Washington, D.C., on September 11, 2001, prompted many to begin rethinking the role of government in the economy. Congress quickly authorized the federal government to take over the airlines security system, and plans for privatization of government services in many communities were put on hold. The banking crisis of 2008–2009 led to calls for enhanced regulation of the financial services industry: deregulation of the industry during the Clinton administration, say some commentators, laid the groundwork for the crisis.

Further Research

"Thirty-Year Deregulation Era Dies a Sudden Death"
www.msnbc.msn.com/id/26774653

A comprehensive article from *BusinessWeek* magazine discusses the history of modern deregulation in a variety of industries and presents the background to later calls for reregulation.

—*Alan Murray*

Economic Growth

Economic growth is a measure of a nation's progress and wealth, and it determines the standard of living of its citizens. For these reasons, growth is important when judging the performance of an economy and is at the center of both economic debates and political events across the world.

Economic growth is defined as an increase in an economy's ability to produce goods and services and is commonly measured by gross domestic product (GDP), the value of the total amount of goods and services produced by the economy during a specific period. A nation with a growing GDP is producing more goods and services than in the previous year and thus is experiencing economic growth. Such growth is associated with stable or increasing employment, rising wages, political stability, and a rising standard of living. A nation with shrinking GDP likely has the opposite conditions.

Economists do not have a complete understanding of economic growth. They do agree that the central underlying idea is productivity, which is defined as the amount of goods and services that can be produced for each unit of time. Adam Smith, the founder of modern economics, developed the concept of economic growth in a famous passage from his landmark 1776 work *The Wealth of Nations* in which he discussed the example of a pin factory. Smith theorized that, working alone, one person could make no more than 20 pins in one day of work. Smith then explained how the manufacturer could increase output by introducing better tools and by training workers to do specific tasks, a process called specialization of labor or division of labor. The result of Smith's hypothetical example was an increase in daily production from 20 pins per person working alone to 48,000 produced by 10 workers.

The division of labor results in numerous benefits. Consumers gain as production increases and prices decrease with the increase in supply. The entrepreneur benefits from increased sales, while the workers can earn raises because of their increased contribution to profits.

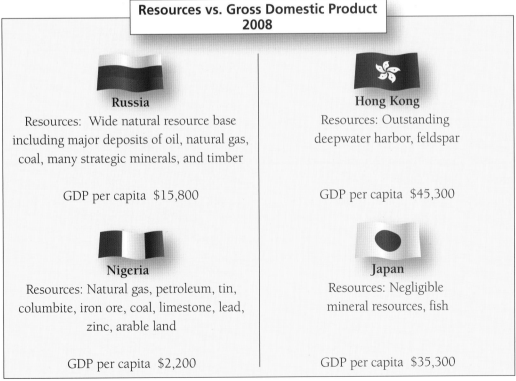

Resources vs. Gross Domestic Product 2008

Russia
Resources: Wide natural resource base including major deposits of oil, natural gas, coal, many strategic minerals, and timber

GDP per capita $15,800

Hong Kong
Resources: Outstanding deepwater harbor, feldspar

GDP per capita $45,300

Nigeria
Resources: Natural gas, petroleum, tin, columbite, iron ore, coal, limestone, lead, zinc, arable land

GDP per capita $2,200

Japan
Resources: Negligible mineral resources, fish

GDP per capita $35,300

Source: Central Intelligence Agency, *CIA Factbook*, Washington, D.C.

Encouraging Economic Growth

Smith's work contributed to the understanding of how to create growth. Economists generally agree that the key elements are physical and human capital, investment, infrastructure, and private property rights.

The first two are prominent in the pin factory example. Physical capital is defined as tools used to produce and distribute goods and services. Human capital refers to the skills and experience of workers in production. Clearly, as both physical and human capital become more abundant, production will increase and economic growth will be encouraged.

Investment is the use of resources today so that they will enable greater production in the future. For example, when an entrepreneur builds a new factory or buys new equipment, she is contributing to economic growth in the future. The key to investment is savings: if investors are confident in the future, they will delay current spending to invest, in hopes of greater returns later. Thus, both savings and investment encourage growth.

Infrastructure encompasses a country's transportation, education, communication, and financial systems. Because these reduce the cost of doing business, they encourage economic growth. For example, an excellent highway system lowers transportation costs, thereby increasing profit opportunities and encouraging businesses to take risks. Each part of infrastructure is an example in how investing now can result in economic growth in the future.

A common misperception is that natural resources, for example coal, iron, and steel, play a prominent part in economic growth. Economists have found that they are not very important. For example, both Russia and Nigeria are rich in natural resources, including oil and gas, which can be very profitable to sell. Hong Kong and Japan, by contrast, are endowed with few natural resources. Yet Hong Kong and Japan have far higher GDP per capita (the average amount of economic production per person in a nation). Hong Kong and Japan are far more economically

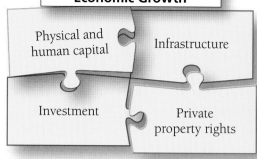

Key Elements in Creating Economic Growth

Physical and human capital

Infrastructure

Investment

Private property rights

productive than Russia and Nigeria. Infrastructure, especially access to education, has contributed to Hong Kong and Japan's GDP.

Another part of the answer to the puzzle of economic growth lies in a nation's treatment of property rights. Property rights allow individuals to control and reap benefits from things of value that they own. This includes the right to freedom of choice concerning management of the property, including selling it, buying more, and so on. Economics is based on the idea that individuals are motivated by greed and will therefore manage their property to maximize their self-interest, in other words, profits. In theory, private property creates an incentive to succeed economically.

Private property rights are almost universally weak in poor countries, including Russia and Nigeria. In countries with weak property rights, generally a rich minority dominates the government and the judicial system. Those in power tend to ignore the property rights of the poor majority and manipulate the police and legal system through corruption. One immediate result is that the poor lack incentives to work hard, because any property they earn is subject to confiscation by others. A result is that the country remains poor.

Governments and Economic Growth

As a way to best support economic growth, Adam Smith argued for the concept of laissez-faire, a policy of minimizing government interference in the economy. Nevertheless, the worldwide trend since the late 1800s has been one of increasing government involvement in economic activity.

Economic growth, rarely reliable and predictable, occurs during a process called the business cycle. The business cycle has periods of growth, or expansion, and slower or even negative growth, called contraction. Governments have developed several tools to help stabilize the business cycle and encourage sustainable economic growth. The most important of these are the central banks; in the United States, the central banks are called the Federal Reserve System.

Central banks promote economic stability by implementing a monetary policy. Such policy involves controlling the money supply and changing interest rates to promote or reduce economic activity. Thus, the central banks can speed or slow economic growth and reduce the severity of swings in the business cycle.

Governments can also use fiscal policy, or government spending, as a tool for managing economic growth. John Maynard Keynes advocated government spending as a solution to the Great Depression, arguing that it could regulate the business cycle. For example, if a nation is entering a recession, the government may increase spending or cut taxes to reduce unemployment and increase funds in the hands of individuals; such funds would be available for spending.

Problems with Growth

Economic growth is not without its negatives. It can cause inflation and does not occur without social cost. Inflation is a rise in prices caused by an increase in the money supply. These changes are positively associated with economic growth, meaning that as the economy expands, the money supply as well as prices will rise. However, uncontrolled inflation is very unhealthy for an economy. As prices increase, consumers have an incentive to spend their money immediately—rather than save—before the goods they desire become even more expensive. Consumers also tend to demand higher wages to preserve their purchasing power. Both acts serve to exacerbate the inflation.

Countries with the Highest and Lowest Gross National Income per Capita 2001

	Highest GNI per Capita			Lowest GNI per Capita
1.	Luxembourg		1.	Ethiopia
2.	Liechtenstein		2.	Burundi
3.	Switzerland		3.	Sierra Leone
4.	Japan		4.	Guinea-Bissau
5.	Norway		5.	Tajikistan
6.	Bermuda		6.	Niger
7.	United States		7.	Malawi
8.	Denmark		8.	Eritrea
9.	Cayman Islands		9.	Chad
10.	Iceland		10.	Mozambique

Source: World Bank, GNI Per Capita 2001, http://www.worldbank.org/data/databytopic/GNIPC.pdf (January 7, 2002).

Critics point out that economic growth is not always completely positive; for example, the construction of more factories can mean more jobs but also more pollution.

The accepted medicine for inflation is for the central bank to raise interest rates, slowing the economy and reducing the inflation. Thus, the only cure for serious inflation is to send the nation into a recession, deliberately increasing unemployment. This very unpopular policy is the reason for many central banks being independent of political control.

The other drawback of economic growth is social cost: growth can be very disruptive. The quest for higher business profits through increasing productivity and creating new goods and services is the basis of capitalism. The cost of this system is that the new and improved products result in the displacement of established producers, often resulting in the bankruptcy of companies and unemployment for their workers.

The manufacturing sector of the U.S. economy provides a clear example. The trend since World War II has been a decline in highly paid factory jobs as companies relocate abroad to take advantage of cheaper labor

Overall employment in the United States has increased, as manufacturing jobs have been replaced by service jobs.

costs. Many industries once dominated by American manufacturers, including the manufacture of television sets, steel, and textiles, have mostly disappeared in the United States.

One result of this trend has been pressure on the American middle class. Earning higher wages requires more education than it did in the 1950s, while more households earn dual income (both husband and wife working) to preserve spending power. Overall employment in the United States, however, has actually increased despite the loss of jobs in some industries, though the jobs being created tend to be lower-paid service-sector jobs.

Accordingly, many critics charge that economic growth is misrepresented as a measure of progress. They assert that definite costs are associated with growth and that those costs are not included in the standard measure of GDP. For example, economic growth often results in increased pollution as more factories are built. More pollution can lead to increased illness, destruction of natural resources, and other harmful effects.

Critics contend that the GDP is a flawed measure because it incorporates neither these negatives nor any quality-of-life measurements.

They suggest that additional measures, including poverty rates, pollution, and wealth distribution, be used to accurately measure the economic progress of a nation.

One result of these critiques is that measurement of economic growth is increasingly controversial. Ideas about balancing growth with environmental concerns, equity, and other factors are becoming more accepted. The increased scrutiny of growth by both academics and politicians has resulted in the world's economies being more stable, better understood, and less prone to destructive boom and bust cycles.

Further Research

American Economics Association—Resources for Economists on the Internet
www.aeaweb.org/rfe/
Site sponsored by the American Economics Association and compiled by faculty at SUNY Oswego has links to resources on economics.

Center for Economic Policy and Research
www.cepr.net/index.php/economics-seminar-series
This online lecture series includes two talks about economic growth by respected economists.

World Bank
www.worldbank.org
Home page of the World Bank, a valuable source of international economic indicators.

—David Long

Environmentalism

Environmentalism is a political ideology founded on four propositions. First, the quality of human life is linked to the condition of the physical environment, which is, therefore, much more than an economic resource. Second, human beings are uniquely able to determine the quality of the environment; third, since the beginning of the industrial age, human behavior has damaged the environment in ways that could prove catastrophic in the absence of far-reaching changes. Finally, environmental protection should be the guiding principle of government, corporate, and consumer behavior.

Environmentalist Issues

Most environmentalists share four main concerns: human population growth, the production and consumption of energy, the pollution produced by continuing industrialization, and the effect of human activities on plant and animal life. Environmentalists usually trace their concern about human population to the English political economist Thomas Malthus. In 1798 Malthus published "An Essay on the Principle of Population" that attempted to show that population increased at a faster rate than improvements in agricultural productivity. Malthus predicted an impoverished future in which increasing population would bring about famine and disease. Malthus's predictions were confounded by subsequent advances in science, agriculture, industry, and medicine. These advances, combined with economic growth and changes in public health policy, have extended the human life span and made

possible vast population increases without mass starvation. In 1968 biologist Paul Ehrlich stated a neo-Malthusian warning in *The Population Bomb*, claiming that devastating environmental consequences could be avoided only by urgent measures to slow or reverse population growth.

In developed countries, population is now growing very slowly and, in some cases, is declining. Reasons include: wealthier and better-educated families tend to have fewer children; birth control has become more effective and widespread; and women have secured greater reproductive rights and a permanent place in the workforce. Population is now expanding most rapidly in poorer countries, where economic development is increasing life expectancy while cultural factors often inhibit the social changes that decrease family size. Richer countries, however, still produce and consume the vast majority of the world's resources.

Environmentalists are also concerned about the rate at which humans are consuming the Earth's energy resources. Environmentalists argue that modern economic theory is based on the assumption of infinite economic growth, which is unattainable in a world of finite resources.

For example, entire economies and societies are now dependent on hydrocarbon fuels. These resources, which can be extracted only through environmentally harmful mining and drilling operations, are nonrenewable and, environmentalists claim, must eventually run out. The Arab–Israeli War of 1973 and the Iranian revolution of 1978 both resulted in oil price increases that triggered worldwide recessions. Environmentalists claim these violent

---

Key Principles of Environmentalism

- The physical environment is much more than an economic resource.
- Human beings are uniquely able to determine the quality of their environment.
- Human behavior has damaged the environment in ways that could prove catastrophic.
- Environmental protection should be the guiding principle of governmental, corporate, and consumer behavior.

upheavals show the vulnerability of the fuel supply and point to the dangerous impact of resource scarcity on international relations, sometimes suggesting that the Persian Gulf War of 1991 was a preview of more resource wars to come.

Environmentalists' third concern is the pollution generated by human consumption of resources. The scientific evidence concerning the relationship between human-generated atmospheric pollution and global warming remains subject to political as much as scientific debate. Environmentalists say that we may be putting enough carbon dioxide, methane, and nitrous oxide into the atmosphere to cause a rise in the Earth's temperature. Such a rise could cause harmful environmental changes, including flood, drought, hurricane, the spread of disease, and new threats to agriculture from insects.

Environmentalists also claim that atmospheric pollution is depleting the ozone layer, the part of Earth's atmosphere that shields the planet from the sun's cancer-causing ultraviolet rays. Chemicals called chlorofluorocarbons (CFCs), used in refrigeration and air conditioning systems and in aerosol sprays, release chlorine into the atmosphere, breaking down ozone and permitting the entry of more dangerous radiation. Acid rain, which is caused when oxides of sulfur and nitrogen react with moisture in the atmosphere to form sulfuric acid and nitric acid, is also a problem. Acid rain sometimes affects forests and lakes far from the sources of the pollution.

Industrial activity also pollutes the world's water supply. The oceans have been used for the disposal of both industrial waste and raw sewage and have been contaminated by oil spills. Some rivers and lakes have been polluted by industrial effluents and also by runoff water containing pesticides used on nearby agricultural lands.

Environmentalists' fourth concern is that Earth's ecosystems are being damaged by human activity. An ecosystem is a locale, or habitat, in which organisms and their environment function interdependently as an integrated whole. Ecosystems generally benefit from biodiversity—a great variety and large number of different plants and animals.

The oil fields of Kuwait were set on fire by fleeing Iraqi soldiers at the close of the 1991 Gulf War.

Environmentalists argue that humans have reduced biodiversity by destroying habitats through practices like slash-and-burn clearing. Because ecosystems are interdependent, such practices pose unpredictable hazards for humans. Environmentalists also maintain that we have a moral obligation to protect endangered species from extinction, especially when we are the predator, as in the case of whales.

Environmentalists act on the conviction that Earth cannot sustain ever-increasing numbers of human beings because it cannot provide infinite resources nor continue to absorb waste endlessly. Humans cannot forever push aside the plants and animals with whom they have no option but to share the planet.

The Environmental Agenda

Environmentalists seek to change the actions of governments, corporations, and consumers to achieve sustainability, a rate of economic growth that is compatible with planetary welfare and the needs of future generations. As environmental hazards are rarely confined within national borders, environmental groups have increasingly directed their lobbying at international organizations, the United Nations or the World Trade Organization among them.

Environmentalists argue for environmentally friendly technologies, for energy conservation, and for energy derived from renewable wind, solar, and geothermal resources. They support recycling as a method of conserving resources, and they encourage consumers to boycott environmentally harmful products. They also advocate planned population growth and technology transfers to help developing countries manage the environmental consequences of expanding economies.

Historical Development of Environmentalism

Systematic thinking about the impact of humans on their environment began in the nineteenth century in Great Britain. In the United States, Ralph Waldo Emerson and Henry David Thoreau wrote early protests against environmental degradation. In 1864 George Perkins Marsh published *Man and Nature; or, Physical Geography as Modified by Human Action,* a pioneering study of the negative effect of agriculture on the environment.

Environmental issues did not enter American national politics until early in the twentieth century, when President Theodore Roosevelt created the national park and forest systems and established national wildlife refuges. During the Depression, President Franklin D. Roosevelt formed the Civilian Conservation Corps to create jobs through environmental projects like land reclamation.

The modern environmental movement is a product of the post–World War II affluent society. As countries become richer, people devote less time and resources to acquiring material basics—food and housing—and become more interested in quality-of-life issues. Environmentalism as we know it can be dated from the publication in 1962 of Rachel Carson's *Silent Spring.* Carson pointed out the dangers posed to humans and wildlife by the use of DDT and similar pesticides. The book inspired a generation of activists who, during the 1960s, pressured the U.S. government into passing new environmental legislation and creating new enforcement bodies, for example, the Environmental Protection Agency. Environmental issues entered the world stage when the United Nations sponsored the first international conference on the environment in Stockholm in 1971, and the Club of Rome, a global think tank, published its report *Limits to Growth* in 1972.

Several destructive incidents have since spurred public demand for more environmental action on the part of governments. The near meltdown at Three Mile Island nuclear plant in Pennsylvania in 1979, followed in 1986 by the explosion at the Chernobyl nuclear plant in the Ukraine, raised fundamental doubts about whether nuclear power could be used safely. Damaging oil spills from the *Amoco Cadiz* in 1979 and the *Exxon Valdez* in 1989

Environmentalism Time Line

1798
Thomas Malthus publishes "An Essay on the Principle of Population," predicting an impoverished future.

1864
George Perkins Marsh publishes *Man and Nature; or, Physical Geography as Modified by Human Action*, a study of the negative environmental impact of agriculture.

1905
President Theodore Roosevelt creates the Forest Service and establishes national park and forest systems.

1933
President Franklin D. Roosevelt creates the Civilian Conservation Corps to create jobs through environmental projects.

1962
Rachel Carson's *Silent Spring* alerts public to the dangers of DDT and other pesticides.

1968
Biologist Paul Ehrlich urges measures to slow or reverse population growth in *The Population Bomb*.

1970
The Environmental Protection Agency is created by the Nixon administration.

1971
The United Nations Conference on the Human Environment is held in Stockholm.

1979
A near meltdown at Three Mile Island nuclear plant in Pennsylvania boosts opposition to nuclear power plants.

1984
Industrial accident at Union Carbide plant in Bhopal, India, kills more than 3,000 people.

1986
The explosion at the Chernobyl nuclear plant in the Ukraine releases huge amounts of radioactive material into the atmosphere.

1989
The *Exxon Valdez* runs aground and creates the largest oil spill in U.S. history to that point.

1991
Free Market Environmentalism by Terry L. Andersen and Donald R. Leal argues that the free enterprise system offers the best prospects for environmental protection.

1992
United Nations Conference on Environment and Development (also called the Earth Summit or the Rio Summit).

2005
Kyoto protocol on greenhouse gas emissions comes into force.

Plastic bottles at a recycling plant.

Liberal environmentalists generally constitute the movement's mainstream. They lobby politicians for a regulatory framework of environmental standards, and they try to promote environmentally sensitive behavior by businesses and consumers. Some political parties are more open to their ideas than others, but most major parties in the democratic world now incorporate aspects of liberal environmentalism in their platforms.

Greens are radicals, sponsoring their own political parties to promote a distinct political philosophy. Greens fundamentally reject industrial society and criticize mainstream environmentalists for merely seeking less harmful ways of exploiting nature for human purposes. Greens draw their ideas from an eclectic range of sources, including Eastern philosophies, anarchist writings like Pyotr Kropotkin's *Mutual Aid* (1902), and unorthodox economic theories like those found in E. F. Schumacher's *Small Is Beautiful* (1973). Greens work for an alternative society organized on the basis of small-scale communities, participatory democracy, disengagement from the world economy and from military alliances, low energy consumption, simplified technology, organic agriculture, and an end to the human exploitation of animals. However, as the Green parties have secured greater electoral success, especially in Germany, they have tended to moderate their stances and to more closely resemble liberal environmental groups.

Market-oriented environmentalists are at odds with both the Greens and the liberal mainstream. Their case, set out in books like *Free Market Environmentalism* (1991) by Terry L. Andersen and Donald R. Leal, is that private property, free enterprise, and economic growth offer the best prospect for environmental protection. Clearly defined private property rights prevent the so-called tragedy of the commons, whereby resources held in common are depleted because no one's self-interest is served by conserving them. According to Andersen and Leal, the price mechanism promotes conservation, and the competitive

attracted widespread attention. In 1984 methyl isocyanate gas leaked from the Union Carbide plant in the Indian city of Bhopal, killing more than 3,000 people in the world's largest industrial accident. Cases of *E.coli* and salmonella contamination, and the bovine spongiform encephalopathy (BSE) or "mad cow" pathogen in beef, have raised doubts about food safety and the safety of modern farming techniques. In addition, innovations in the biological sciences have raised new concerns about genetically modified crops and animals.

The Politics of Environmentalism

Environmentalism enjoys support across the political spectrum. Even within the environmental movement itself, however, disagreements arise about which measures will protect the environment most effectively. Liberal environmentalists, Greens, and free-market environmentalists have proposed different solutions.

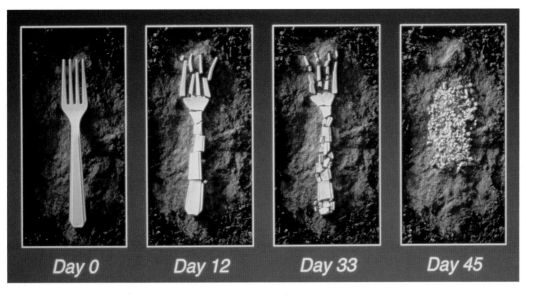

Day 0   Day 12   Day 33   Day 45

Some firms have approached the environmental movement as a business opportunity rather than an obstacle. A demonstration of biodegradable plastic made by Cargill is pictured here.

marketplace generates the economic growth, the technological innovation, and the wealth needed to solve environmental problems. Market-oriented environmentalists criticize mainstream environmentalists for undermining property rights and fostering counter-productive government regulations. This form of environmentalism has sometimes been influential in Republican administrations in the United States.

The successes of the environmental movement can be seen in the prominence now given to environmental questions by politicians, in the quest by corporations for a "green" image, and in a greater environmental awareness among the general public. Yet the movement still faces difficult challenges. Conflicts will arise and trade-offs will need to be made between environmental imperatives and other important issues like property rights, defense requirements, economic growth, and employment. Disputes will occur between environmentalists and their critics—and even among environmentalists themselves—over how to interpret the available science. Perhaps the most important question facing environmentalists is how developed countries can help developing ones to continue on the path of economic development without exacerbating existing environmental pressures. Levels of international cooperation that are often difficult to achieve will be required for success.

Further Research

CSRWire

www.csrwire.com

CSRWire provides news and reports about corporate and social responsibility issues, including environmentalism and clean technology.

Envirolink

www.envirolink.org

EnviroLink is a nonprofit organization dedicated to providing comprehensive, up-to-date environmental information and news.

United Nations Environment Programme

www.unep.org

The mission of UNEP is to provide leadership and encourage partnership in caring for the environment by inspiring, informing, and enabling nations and peoples to improve their quality of life without compromising that of future generations.

—*Peter C. Grosvenor*

Sustainable Design

Some visionaries like industrial designer William McDonough look to a future where profitable companies will reach ultimate levels of social responsibility. McDonough advocates "sustainable design" and has taken the lead by designing an automobile for Ford that "eats" rather than emits pollution, a building with an undulating prairie roof that enticed long-absent bird species to the local community, and another building that recycles its own waste. McDonough's architectural firm also designed Wal-Mart's environment-friendly prototype store, Eco-Mart, in Lawrence, Kansas.

In Switzerland, he developed a plant that manufactures textiles without toxicity, where industrial by-products are used to grow strawberries and the runoff water is clean enough to drink. He proposes the elimination of the concept of waste. All discarded products will be returned to the manufacturer (for example, old television sets sent back to the manufacturer for recycling) and everything else will be returned to the Earth to nourish it. In 1996 McDonough received the Presidential Award for Sustainable Development, America's highest environmental honor.

European Union

The European Union is a result of a process of European economic and political integration that has been ongoing since the end of World War II. Between 1870 and 1945, Europe had been torn apart by wars resulting largely from Franco-German rivalry. At the end of World War II, leading European politicians began to design structures that would forestall the outbreak of similar conflicts and would create a European "third power" between the United States and the Soviet Union. The project was encouraged by the United States because increased economic and political coordination would hasten postwar West European economic recovery, thereby bolstering resistance to the further expansion of communism and normalizing trade and business relations between the United States and Europe.

Two key French political figures, Robert Schuman and Jean Monnet, proposed a European Coal and Steel Community (ECSC), which was established by the Treaty of Paris in 1951. Although it also included Belgium, Luxembourg, Italy, and the Netherlands, the central aim of the ECSC was to put the two principal war-related industries of France and West Germany under supranational control.

The six members of the ECSC signed the Treaty of Rome in May 1957, which created the European Economic Community (EEC). The EEC established a tariff-free internal market for agricultural and industrial products. At the same time, the European Atomic Energy Community (EURATOM) was created to coordinate research on the peaceful uses of nuclear energy. The Treaty of Rome also established new and complex European policy-making structures. The Council of Ministers, comprising representatives of the national governments of member states, functions as the executive. Originally, the council made policy on the basis of unanimity. The exclusive right to initiate legislation is invested in an appointed European Commission, and a European Court rules on issues of EEC law.

The European Parliament, initially consisting of delegates from national parliaments, has played largely a consultative role. In 1967, the ECSC, the EEC, and EURATOM were merged into a single bureaucracy called the European Community (EC).

European Union

1951
Treaty of Paris establishes the European Coal and Steel Community (ECSC).

1957
EURATOM established.

1957
Six members of the ECSC sign the Treaty of Rome, creating the European Economic Community (EEC).

1967
The ECSC, the EEC, and EURATOM merge to form the European Community (EC).

1973
Britain joins the EC, along with Denmark and Ireland.

1986
Single European Act removes residual nontariff barriers to trade.

1991
Maastricht Treaty transforms the EC into the European Union (EU).

2002
The euro becomes the common currency in all EU states except Britain, Denmark, and Sweden.

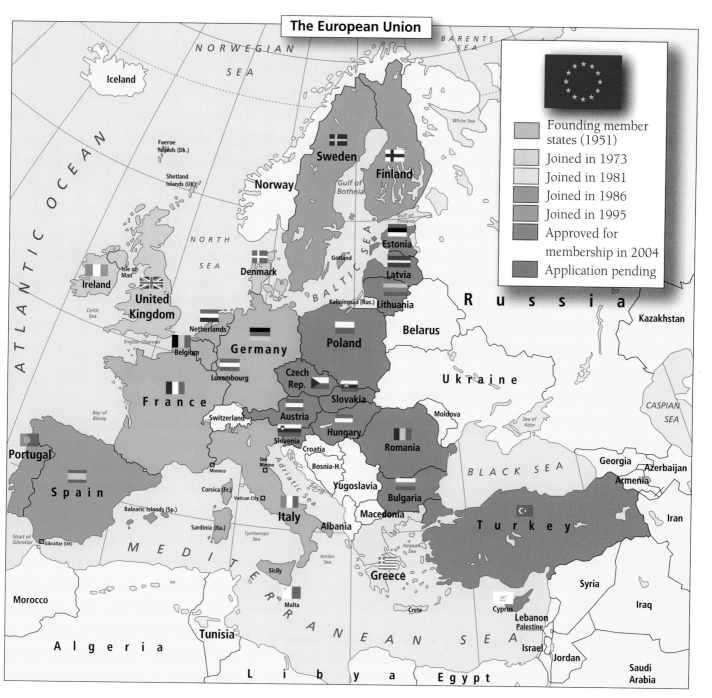

Britain was alarmed at the federalist implications of the Treaty of Rome and, in 1960, took the lead in establishing the European Free Trade Area (EFTA). This created a free market between its member states (Austria, Britain, Denmark, Norway, Portugal, Sweden, and Switzerland), but with no corresponding political structures. However, as British world influence diminished, Britain reconsidered its position and applied for membership in the EEC. Its applications in 1963 and 1967 were vetoed by French president Charles de Gaulle who saw Britain as a potential vehicle for American influence in Europe. Britain eventually joined the EC in 1973, along with Denmark and Ireland. EC membership increased further with the admission of Greece in 1981, and of Spain and Portugal in 1985. Ten additional nations were approved for entry into the EU in 2004: Cyprus, Czech Republic, Estonia, Hungary, Latvia, Lithuania, Malta, Poland, Slovakia, and Slovenia. Bulgaria and Romania joined in 2007. In addition, negotiations are underway with other

A man in Devon, western England, burns a European Union flag during an anti-EU demonstration.

states, including Turkey, Macedonia, and Croatia.

Over the course of the 1980s, French president François Mitterrand and West German chancellor Helmut Kohl pushed for greater European integration. The Single European Act of 1986 aimed to further liberalize the European market by removing residual nontariff barriers to trade and to give the EC greater political coherence by relaxing the unanimity principle and allowing for more majority decision making.

Economic and political integration took a further step forward with the Maastricht Treaty of 1991. Economically, this involved laying the foundations for a European Central Bank and for the eventual adoption of a common European currency. It also specified a "social chapter" of workers' rights. Politically, Maastricht also transformed the EC into the European Union (EU), with new structures for the formation of common foreign and defense policies, and for Europe-wide policies on justice and immigration. In 1995 Austria, Finland, and Sweden were admitted to membership. Further enlargement is expected as countries in post-communist Eastern Europe and the Balkans enter.

Levels of enthusiasm for European integration have varied. For example,

The Euro

The euro (€) is legal tender in 12 of the European Union's 15 member states. The idea of a common European currency has its origins in attempts to harmonize trade relations between the European economic partners by stabilizing exchange rates (i.e., the value of European currencies in relation to one another). To this end, in the early 1970s, the major European economies created the "snake"—an attempt to contain exchange rate fluctuations within set limits. This experiment was destroyed mid-decade by oil price shocks. In 1979 it was replaced with the European Monetary System (EMS) and its constituent Exchange Rate Mechanism (ERM).

During the 1980s, discussion moved from the stabilization of exchange rates to the possibility of a single currency. The Maastricht Treaty (1991) set the goal of an Economic and Monetary Union (EMU) and established strict criteria for member states to participate in a Europe-wide common currency. These included targets for inflation, interest rates, and budget deficits.

On January 1, 2002, the euro replaced the national currencies of Austria, Belgium, Finland, France, Germany, Greece, Ireland, Italy, Luxembourg, the Netherlands, Portugal, and Spain. These countries, along with Cyprus, Malta, Slovenia, and Slovakia, constitute the euro zone. The three EU members not participating in the euro are Britain, Denmark, and Sweden.

Presidents of the European parliaments gather in advance of a European Union meeting in 2009 in Paris, France.

under Prime Minister Margaret Thatcher (1979–1990) the British resisted political integration. Her successor, John Major (1990–1997), negotiated an "opt-out" from the social chapter and from the euro. Denmark rejected the Maastricht Treaty in a national referendum in June 1992, and the treaty was only narrowly accepted by French voters in September of that year. In a second referendum in 1993, the Danes approved the treaty, but only after gaining exemptions. In January 2002 the euro became the common currency in all EU states except Britain, Denmark, and Sweden.

To its federalist supporters, the EU and the euro represent significant steps toward a "United States of Europe" of the kind originally envisaged by Jean Monnet. To its critics, the EU is a bureaucratic "superstate" that threatens the sovereignty and democracy of its member states. Concern about the "democratic deficit" within the EU has led to a strengthening of the European Parliament, which has been directly elected since 1979.

The United States has supported and encouraged European integration. Paradoxically, the EU has become an economic rival. Disputes between the EU and the United States over issues of free trade and protectionism are common, such as when the United States levied tariffs on European luxury goods in 2009 in retaliation for an EU ban on U.S. hormone-treated beef.

Further Research

Europa—Gateway to the European Union

europa.eu/index_en.htm

The EU's home page provides a detailed account of its activities and history, as well as an online library.

—*Peter C. Grosvenor*

Farmers drive their tractors along the Strasbourg–Paris motorway following a demonstration at the European Parliament building in Strasbourg. The farmers protested the European Union's Common Agricultural Policy (CAP), part of a reform package designated to prepare the EU for enlargement into Eastern Europe.

Federal Trade Commission

The Federal Trade Commission (FTC), established by President Woodrow Wilson in 1914, is an independent federal agency. Its mission is to keep U.S. business competition free and fair by ensuring no undue restraints are placed on trade and that businesses abide by the law when competing in the marketplace. The FTC's mission is critical, because the foundation of a market economy requires that consumers be well informed and able to exercise their free choice when purchasing goods and services. For those conditions to exist, the marketplace must be competitive.

The FTC is one of 59 independent federal agencies in the United States; others include the Central Intelligence Agency, the National Science Foundation, and the Postal Service. The FTC has five members, each appointed by the president with the consent

of the Senate for a term of seven years. Not more than three members can be from the same political party. Its chairman is responsible for the administrative management of the FTC. In 2007 the FTC employed approximately 1,100 people and had a budget of about $240 million.

The need for the FTC arose in the late 1800s. Several business owners and financiers were setting out to quash competition within their industries to gain control of the market for their goods. In some instances, this was accomplished by actually buying out the competition, thereby creating a monopoly. In other cases, a group of companies would work together to control their industry by forming a trust. Trusts were formed in the tobacco and oil industries, among others.

Consumers, left without an alternative as the monopoly or trust was without competition, were forced to purchase from a controlled source, regardless of price. Forced into action by a strong public backlash, the federal government responded by passing significant antitrust laws in the late 1800s and early 1900s. These antitrust laws helped foil some attempts to rid industries of competition but failed to defeat others; by 1914 monopolies and trusts still existed in several industries.

The FTC, established by the Federal Trade Commission Act in that year, was part of President Wilson's effort to control the powerful monopolies and trusts of his day. If a single company, or group of companies, could control an entire industry (the timber industry, the steel industry, or the textile industry, for example), the marketplace would not be a free and open one: new companies could not enter the market, consumers would not have options, and, in general, the laws of supply and demand, the bedrock of a capitalist economy, would be abrogated.

The Work of the FTC

The FTC performs several functions and has a variety of tools at its disposal. It is charged with promoting fair competition

Federal Trade Commission: Areas of Consumer Education

Abusive Lending

Advertising

Children's Issues

Diet, Health, and Fitness

Audio (Recorded Information, Public Service Announcements)

Automobiles

Credit

E-Commerce and the Internet

Energy and the Environment

Franchises and Business Opportunities

IDENTITY THEFT

Investments

Privacy

Seniors' Issues

Telemarketing

Telephone Services

Tobacco

Travel

Federal Trade Commission: Bureaus

Bureau of Competition	Bureau of Economics	Bureau of Consumer Protection
• Enforces antitrade laws. • Serves as policy and research resource on competition issues. • Advocates policies to increase competition and improve consumer choice in legislative hearings and court proceedings.	• Studies economic effect of regulations. • Advocates policies to increase competition and improve consumer choice in legislative hearings and court proceedings.	• Protects consumers against unfair, deceptive, or fraudulent practices. • Enforces consumer protection laws and FTC trade regulations. • Provides consumer education. • Advocates policies to increase competition and improve consumer choice in legislative hearings and court proceedings.

through the enforcement of antitrust laws, preventing false and deceptive advertising, investigating how businesses are operating, and keeping Congress and the public informed of developments in all of these areas. It also recommends legislation and regulations based on its findings.

The FTC's law enforcement responsibilities are significant. The Federal Trade Commission Act of 1914 and the Wheeler–Lea Act of 1938 charge the FTC with preventing unfair methods of business competition and false advertising. The Clayton Antitrust Act of 1914 and the Robinson–Patman Act of 1936 require that the FTC enforce provisions regarding price discrimination. The FTC also enforces the Truth in Lending Act, which regulates creditors not covered by other agencies. More recent examples of the FTC's statutory responsibilities are the Federal Cigarette Labeling and Advertising Act of 1966, the Fair Credit Reporting Act, the Consumer Leasing Act, and the Energy Policy Act of 1992.

The FTC conducts investigations of suspected wrongdoing. Letters from consumers, inquiries from Congress, and even media coverage of a consumer-related issue can all trigger investigations by the FTC. It may then enter into a consent order with the offending business, whereby that business agrees to voluntarily comply with the law. Consent orders do not require an admission of guilt. In other cases, the FTC

As a nation, we derive vast economic benefits from competition. These cannot be taken for granted. The benefits, and the competition that yields them, are not immutable. The FTC has a special responsibility and capability to speak for the competitive process and resist measures, especially legislative or regulatory immunity from antitrust scrutiny, that would dissipate the benefits of competition by reducing the role of business rivalry in organizing the economy.

More than a mere collection of laws, the antitrust laws and the pro-competition ethic they embody serve as an organizing principle in our country's economy. Antitrust plays a major role in shaping our markets, institutions, and the relationships among market participants. Indeed, the Supreme Court has called the Sherman Act "a comprehensive charter of economic liberty. . . ." By spurring competition, antitrust contributes to a market system that provides lower prices, encourages greater innovation, and generates faster responses by business to changing consumer needs and desires.

In what sense is antitrust an organizing principle? Whether or not a country should adopt antitrust laws is not, of course, the first consideration for organizing an economy. More fundamental is the choice of an economic system. Should the economy be based on competition through free enterprise and open markets, on command-and-control regulation, or on public or collective ownership? In the United States, we have largely chosen free enterprise and markets.

Free enterprise does not mean a system without rules. Any market economy needs a well-specified structure of property rights, contract law, and other rules of conduct. These rules of the road largely focus on the relative rights of particular parties; they do not, for the most part, address problems in the market that interfere with competition and decrease consumer welfare. . . .

The United States has chosen antitrust law to provide the governing rules for competition in most sectors of the economy. Why antitrust law? Our faith in the market system is firmly grounded in the principle that free enterprise and competition are the best guarantors of commercial freedom, economic efficiency, and consumer welfare. Effective competition is most likely to yield the optimal mix of goods and services at the lowest cost. Antitrust law helps maintain effective competition by prohibiting conduct that unreasonably restricts markets.

—Timothy J. Muris, Chairman, Federal Trade Commission
Comments at the Milton Handler Annual Antitrust Review, 2002

Statutes Enforced or Administered by the FTC

1914 Clayton Antitrust Act
1914 Federal Trade Commission Act
1918 Webb–Pomerene Act
1921 Packers and Stockyards Act
1939 Wool Products Labeling Act
1946 Lanham Trade-Mark Act
1950 Defense Production Act of 1950
1951 Fur Products Labeling Act
1958 Textile Fiber Products Identification Act
1966 Fair Packaging and Labeling Act
1968 Truth in Lending Act
1970 Postal Reorganization Act of 1970
1974 Equal Credit Opportunity Act
1974 Deepwater Port Act of 1974
1975 Fair Credit Billing Act
1975 Magnuson Moss Warranty–Federal Trade Commission Improvements Act
1976 Consumer Leasing Act
1978 Electronic Fund Transfer Act
1978 Petroleum Marketing Practices Act
1980 Fair Debt Collection Practices Act
1980 Deep Seabed Hard Minerals Act
1986 Comprehensive Smokeless Tobacco Health Education Act of 1986
1986 Conservation Service Reform Act of 1986
1988 Fair Credit and Charge Card Disclosure Act
1988 Home Equity Loan Consumer Protection Act
1990 Dolphin Protection Consumer Information Act
1991 Federal Deposit Insurance Corporation Improvement Act of 1991
1992 Energy Policy Act of 1992
1992 Energy Policy and Conservation Act
1993 National Cooperative Research and Production Act of 1993
1994 Telemarketing and Consumer Fraud and Abuse Prevention Act
1994 Violent Crime Control and Law Enforcement Act of 1994
1994 Home Ownership and Equity Protection Act
1994 International Antitrust Enforcement Assistance Act of 1994
1995 Interstate Commerce Commission Termination Act of 1995
1996 Telecommunication Act of 1996
1996 Credit Repair Organizations Act
1998 The Children's Online Privacy Protection Act
1998 Identity Theft Assumption and Deterrence Act of 1998
1999 Gramm–Leach–Bliley Act
2003 Medicare Prescription Drug Improvement and Modernization Act
2004 Standards Development Organization Act
2006 Pandemic and All-Hazards Preparedness Act

across an entire industry, the FTC may begin an administrative rule-making procedure, resulting in industry-wide trade regulation rules. These rules have the full force of the law, and court-ordered civil penalties up to $10,000 can be levied for each violation of an FTC order or trade regulation rule.

In addition to actively enforcing these laws and regulations, the FTC uses public hearings, conferences, and media alerts to educate both industry and the public about its concerns. Industry representatives monitor FTC hearings and conferences closely. Instead of having to catch up to whatever rule changes may occur if lack of competition appears to exist within an industry, industries sometimes voluntarily adopt the FTC's recommendations.

An example of an FTC consumer alert is a 2008 report on "phishing" fraud in the wake of numerous bank failures, mergers, and takeovers that occurred that year. The FTC learned that "phishers"—Internet fraud artists who send spam or pop-up messages in order to acquire personal information (credit card numbers, bank account information, Social Security number, passwords, or other sensitive information) from unsuspecting victims—were taking advantage of consumer confusion. The scam involved emails that looked like they were coming from a financial institution that had recently acquired another one, asking consumers to "update," "validate," or "confirm" their account information. The messages directed consumers to a Web site that looked like the site of the new financial institution or lender but in fact was a bogus site designed to trick people into divulging personal information that can be used in identity theft fraud. The FTC offered advice to consumers to protect against "phishing" and identity theft: never reply to an email or a pop-up message that asks for personal or financial information or follow the links in such messages; also, never respond to similar phone enquiries. The FTC also referred consumers to anti- "phishing" authorities. A similar consumer alert was issued about

may issue cease and desist orders to offenders (essentially, orders to stop what they are doing). If the activity in question reaches

FTC Consumer Alert!

Payday Loans = Costly Cash
Identity Crisis: What To Do If Your Identity Is Stolen
What's Dot and What's Not: Domain Name Registration Scams
What's in Your In-Box? (How to deal with junk e-mail)
Consumer Credit File Privacy: The Real Deal
Profits in Pyramid Schemes: Don't Bet on It!
Virtual Worlds and Kids: Mapping the Risks

Sample headlines of press releases from the FTC. Periodically the FTC issues these consumer alerts to notify consumers about specific problems.

"phishing" on the basis of fraudulent offers of government stimulus payments.

Such public alerts accomplish several objectives. Consumers are alerted to some potential problems identity theft. Meanwhile, fraudsters are put on notice that the FTC is closely monitoring their activities and has noticed this attempt to take advantage of the financial crisis.

Through law enforcement, regulatory, and educational activities, the FTC is a key player in the federal government's efforts to ensure that the U.S. economy remains based on open and competitive markets.

Although the issues and industries the commission has addressed have changed from year to year, its place in the federal regulatory scheme has remained a constant since the early 1900s.

Further Research
Federal Trade Commission
www.ftc.gov
The FTC Web site provides a wealth of information on the agency's activities, as well as consumer protection issues, economics, and competition, both domestic and international..

—John Keckhaver

Steve Baker, a director of the FTC, announces that the FTC shut down a global spam operation in 2008.

Fiscal Policy

Fiscal policy is the collection of government policies related to spending and taxation. The term is usually used in the context of evaluating how government policies affect the whole economy rather than specific program proposals. Fiscal policy is one of the principal ways that government can affect the economic vitality of a country. (The other major economic policy is monetary policy and refers to the activities of central banks to raise or lower interest rates and increase or decrease the supply of money in an economy.)

The two approaches to fiscal policy are called expansionary and contractionary. Expansionary policy has governments spending more money or lowering taxes. Contractionary policy has governments spending less money or increasing taxes. The specific effects that fiscal policy can have in improving or undermining economic strength are hotly debated and are also highly dependent on what else is going on in the economy.

Expansionary policy, whether through increased defense spending, increased spending on infrastructure projects, or other areas, adds more money to the economy. Lower taxes also add money to the economy by allowing individuals to keep and spend more of their income. Increased spending can improve the incomes of many businesses and individuals. Expansionary policies are often advocated during periods of economic slowdown as a way of boosting growth in the country, reducing unemployment, and improving people's income.

Increased government spending also has some negative effects. If spending exceeds revenues, a deficit is incurred in that year. The government must then borrow money to meet its obligations. The government must also pay interest on the borrowed money, which can lead to larger deficits in the future. The amount of money borrowed and the amount that must be paid in interest can become extremely large. As the government borrows more money, interest rates and thus interest payments can go up for everyone. When interest rates are higher, businesses must make higher interest payments on the money they borrow for investments like new buildings and equipment. Not only will investments become more expensive, but also, with higher interest rates, some firms will not make investments at all. Similarly, individuals would also have to pay higher interest when they borrow to buy a house or car. The reduction in investment by businesses and individuals can have very negative economic effects.

In 1998 the U.S. government had its first budget surplus since 1969. For almost 30 years, the federal government had been spending more than it earned and took in in taxes and had accumulated very large debt and accompanying interest payments. By 1992 the publicly held debt was a record $290 billion. During the 1990s a concerted effort was made to reduce the deficit and debt so that interest payments would be lower, and lower interest rates would stimulate business investment. After years of accumulating deficits, the nation's publicly held debt reached a peak in 1997 at $3.772 trillion.

Another factor that plays a role in the economic impact of fiscal policy is inflation.

Expansionary vs. Contractionary Fiscal Policy

goal   action

Increase spending   Increase taxes

Increase money supply   Decrease money supply

Lower taxes   Lower spending

Expansionary Policy   **Contractionary Policy**

If a government's policy is expansionary—adding significant amounts of money to the economy—another result can be rising prices. Thus, when governments spend more to improve immediate income and growth, they can also hurt longer-term economic vitality by causing higher deficits, interest payments, and increased interest rates for everyone. Balancing these negative and positive effects is complicated and very controversial.

Contractionary fiscal policy occurs when government cuts spending. As a result, it spends less on, for example, government contracts and income support. Cutting spending can be controversial: On the one hand, businesses and individuals may suffer from less income; on the other, economic benefits may be realized. When the government spends less money than it earns through taxes and other areas, it can lower deficits or achieve a budget surplus. Consequently, it does not need to increase borrowing and make ever-higher interest payments, and interest rates decline for everyone. Lower interest rates enable businesses to more easily borrow money for their own investment purposes like new buildings, plants, and equipment. Similarly, individuals can more easily borrow money to buy a house or a car. When individuals or firms increase their purchases, businesses need to produce more, which can create jobs and generate more spending. The result can be higher employment and a growing economy.

Many economists think that the U.S. government is poorly suited to manage the economy and thus should not adopt an explicitly expansionary or contractionary approach; instead, these economists maintain, the government should be passive. These economists argue that because government policies can take a long time to be approved by Congress, legislators often miss the right moment to affect the economy in the best way. Poor fiscal timing can damage the economy by pushing money into the economy at exactly the wrong time—adding more money to the economy once it is already improving or pulling money out of the economy as it is declining.

Total U.S. Debt 1968 to 2008	
Date	Amount
09/30/2008	$10,024,724,896,912.49
09/30/2007	$9,007,653,372,262.48
09/30/2006	$8,506,973,899,215.23
09/30/2005	$7,932,709,661,723.50
09/30/2004	$7,379,052,696,330.32
09/30/2003	$6,783,231,062,743.62
09/30/2002	$6,228,235,965,597.16
09/30/2001	$5,807,463,412,200.06
09/30/2000	$5,674,178,209,886.86
09/30/1999	$5,656,270,901,615.43
09/30/1998	$5,526,193,008,897.62
09/30/1997	$5,413,146,011,397.34
09/30/1996	$5,224,810,939,135.73
09/29/1995	$4,973,982,900,709.39
09/30/1994	$4,692,749,910,013.32
09/30/1993	$4,411,488,883,139.38
09/30/1992	$4,064,620,655,521.66
09/30/1991	$3,665,303,351,697.03
09/28/1990	$3,233,313,451,777.25
09/29/1989	$2,857,430,960,187.32
09/30/1988	$2,602,337,712,041.16
09/30/1987	$2,350,276,890,953.00
09/30/1986	$2,125,302,616,658.42
12/31/1985	$1,945,941,616,459.88
12/31/1984	$1,662,966,000,000.00
12/31/1983	$1,410,702,000,000.00
12/31/1982	$1,197,073,000,000.00
12/31/1981	$1,028,729,000,000.00
12/31/1980	$930,210,000,000.00
12/31/1979	$845,116,000,000.00
12/29/1978	$789,207,000,000.00
12/30/1977	$718,943,000,000.00
12/31/1976	$653,544,000,000.00
12/31/1975	$576,649,000,000.00
12/31/1974	$492,665,000,000.00
12/31/1973	$469,898,039,554.70
12/29/1972	$449,298,066,119.00
12/31/1971	$424,130,961,959.95
12/31/1970	$389,158,403,690.26
12/31/1969	$368,225,581,254.41
12/31/1968	$358,028,625,002.91

Note: Total U.S. debt includes both privately held debt and intergovernmental holdings. Figures for 1974 to 1984 rounded to nearest million.
Source: U.S. Treasury Department

Federal Budget Outlays: Defense, Human and Physical Resources, and Net Interest Payments 1980 to 2002
(in billions of dollars)

	1980	1990	1995	1998	1999	2000	2001	2002
National defense	134.0	299.3	272.1	268.5	274.9	294.5	308.5	348.0
Human resources								
Education, training, employment, and social services	31.8	37.2	51.0	50.5	50.6	53.8	57.3	71.7
Health	23.2	57.7	115.4	131.4	141.1	154.5	172.6	195.2
Medicare	32.1	98.1	159.9	192.8	190.4	197.1	217.5	226.4
Income security	86.6	148.7	223.7	237.7	242.4	253.5	269.8	310.7
Social security	118.5	248.6	335.8	379.2	390.0	409.4	433.1	459.7
Veterans benefits and services	21.2	29.1	37.9	41.8	43.2	47.1	45.8	51.5
Human resources, total	313.4	619.3	923.8	1,033.4	1,057.7	1,115.4	1,196.1	1,315.3
Physical resources								
Energy	10.2	3.3	4.9	1.3	0.9	−1.1	0.1	0.6
Natural resources and environment	13.9	17.1	21.9	22.3	24.0	25.0	26.3	30.2
Commerce and housing credit	9.4	67.6	−17.8	1.0	2.6	3.2	6.0	3.8
Transportation	21.3	29.5	39.4	40.3	42.5	46.9	55.2	62.1
Community and regional development	11.3	8.5	10.7	9.8	11.9	10.6	12.0	15.4
Physical resources, total	66.0	126.0	59.1	74.7	81.9	84.7	99.7	112.1
Other functions								
International affairs	12.7	13.8	16.4	13.1	15.2	17.2	16.6	23.5
Agriculture	8.8	12.0	9.8	12.2	23.0	36.6	26.6	28.8
Administration of justice	4.6	10.0	16.2	22.9	26.1	28.0	30.4	34.4
General government	13.0	10.6	14.0	15.6	15.6	13.3	15.2	18.3
Other functions, total[1]	45.0	60.7	73.2	82.1	98.1	113.8	108.6	153.8
Net interest payments	52.5	184.4	232.2	241.2	229.8	223.0	206.2	178.4
Undistributed offsetting receipts	−19.9	−36.6	−44.5	−47.2	−40.4	−42.6	−55.2	−55.2
Federal outlays, total	590.9	1,253.2	1,515.8	1,652.6	1,701.9	1,788.8	1,863.9	2,052.3

[1] Totals include outlays not listed separately.

Source: U.S. Office of Management and Budget, *Budget of the United States Government, Historical Tables,* 2002.

Fiscal policy is largely determined by federal budget outlays.

In many cases, governments have little choice about fiscal policies. For example, during periods of war, governments are forced to spend large sums on defense regardless of the state of the economy. For example, in 1945, during World War II, government spending accounted for 44 percent of all economic activity in the United States.

Further Research
U.S. Budget Watch
www.usbudgetwatch.org
U.S. Budget Watch is a project designed to increase awareness of fiscal issues facing the country. The project seeks to inform the public about government tax and spending policies.

—*Carl Haacke*

Futures Markets

The futures markets are the most volatile portion of the stock market. A futures contract is an obligation to buy or sell a specific commodity, for example, wheat, silver, or Treasury bonds, on a specific day for a preset price. Purchasing such a contract is called taking a long position. Futures can be extremely profitable—and also extremely risky—because investors are required to put up only a fraction of the contract's value. This is called margin and is usually between 5 and 10 percent of the price of the contract.

The most basic concept of investing money is that the return, or profits, will be proportional to the risks taken. The safest investments produce little reward but offer investors the security that their money is safe. Conversely, investors can make tremendous profits, but only by taking a chance on enormous losses. Both kinds of investors—those interested in high risk and those in low—can benefit from futures markets.

High-risk futures investors can risk an enormous amount with only a small investment. For example, if gold cost $500 per ounce, an investor could purchase a contract for 100 ounces of gold for future delivery for $5,000 ($500 × 100 ounces × 10 percent = $5,000). That money is a good-faith deposit and provides leverage over the 100 ounces of gold. Gold is a volatile commodity and the price could easily gain $100 per ounce over the life of the contract. If the price rose to $600 per ounce, the value of the investment would rise by (100 ounces × $100/ounce = $10,000). Conversely, if the price dropped by $100 per ounce, the investor would lose $10,000. This example shows why futures trading can be so dangerous. Investors can lose far more than they initially invested and run the risk of bankruptcy. Investors can also use the

Commodity Futures Markets

Exchange	Year Established	Major Commodities
Chicago Board of Trade (CBOT)	1848	Grains, U.S. Treasury notes and bonds, other interest rates, stock indexes
Kansas City Board of Trade (KCBT)	1856	Wheat, natural gas, and stock indexes
MidAmerica Exchange (MIDAM)	1868	Soybeans, wheat, and corn
New York Board of Trade (NYBOT)		
• New York Cotton Exchange (NYCE)	1870	Cotton
• Coffee, Sugar, and Cocoa Exchange (CSCE)	1882	Sugar, coffee, and cocoa
• New York Futures Exchange (NYFE)	1979	Currencies and stock exchanges
Chicago Mercantile Exchange (CME)	1919	Livestock, dairy products, stock indexes, Eurodollars and other interest rates, currencies
The COMEX Division (COMEX)	1933	Metals
Minneapolis Grain Exchange (MGE)	1947	Spring wheat
New York Mercantile Exchange (NYMEX)	1956	Energy products
Philadelphia Board of Trade	1986	Currencies
Cantor Financial Futures Exchange (CX)	1998	U.S. Treasury and Agency notes
Island Futures Exchange	2000	Security futures products
Merchants' Exchange (ME)	2000	Barge freight rates and energy products
OnExchange Board of Trade (ONXBOT)	2000	Treasury securities
BrokerTec Futures Exchange (BTEX)	2001	Government securities
Nasdaq LIFFE Markets (NQLX)[1]	2001	Security futures products
OneChicago (OCX)	2002	Security futures products

[1] Joint venture between Nasdaq and the London International Financial Futures and Options Exchange.

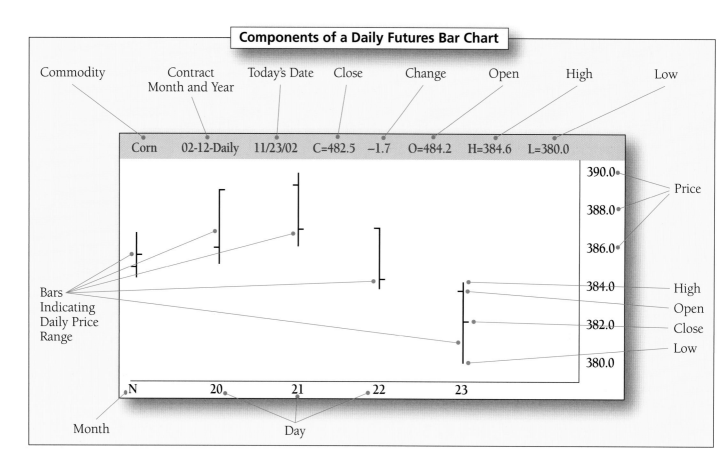

Components of a Daily Futures Bar Chart

Commodity — Corn

Contract Month and Year — 02-12-Daily

Today's Date — 11/23/02

Close — C=482.5

Change — −1.7

Open — O=484.2

High — H=384.6

Low — L=380.0

Price — 390.0, 388.0, 386.0

High — 384.0

Open

Close — 382.0

Low

380.0

Bars Indicating Daily Price Range

Month — N

Day — 20, 21, 22, 23

Futures traders review bar charts like this one to track the price fluctuations of commodities.

futures market to go short, or bet that the price of a commodity will decrease. In this case, the above math works in reverse and investors gain profits as the price of the commodity decreases.

Futures markets allow investors to take large risks. The futures markets also allow investors to control their risks by hedging. This technique is defined as limiting gains and losses as a protection against large swings in the markets.

A practical example is when a farmer is concerned that the price of his wheat may drop. He may then short-sell wheat in the futures market, purchasing contracts where he will profit if the price drops. If the farmer's fears are realized and the price of wheat falls, he still loses some money on the sale of his wheat. However, these losses are offset by the gains from short-selling wheat; the farmer has thereby reduced his risk.

If the price of wheat remains strong, the farmer will make a profit on the sale of his wheat. However, he must also buy an offsetting contract to cancel his short-selling and pay the additional cost. In

either case, his profits or losses are limited and he has controlled the risk to his business. Businesses from construction companies to mutual funds find futures useful to control risk, thus futures contracts are sold on a wide variety of commodities, ranging from meat and livestock to precious metals and orange juice.

These uses also explain why so few futures contracts—roughly 2 percent—actually result in the exchange of goods. The vast majority of trades are offset, or canceled out, with a contract that carries the opposite promise as the original. For example, if an investor purchases a September corn contract at $2 per bushel with a $1,000 margin payment, she expects the price of corn to rise. If the price of corn climbs to $3 per bushel, her account is credited with $5,000 and she is ahead. To collect her profits, she must sell the September wheat contract, which cancels her obligation to buy. She is left with the difference between the two contracts, less the commissions paid to the broker for making the trades.

The usefulness of futures has made them an accepted part of doing business.

They are sold and traded on markets in the United States and across the world, in person or by computer. In either case, they are exchanged by a specialist, called a trader, who charges a fee to purchase or sell the future.

Several dramatic news stories have been published about rogue futures traders and the impact they can have on their employers. The most famous is the case of Nicholas Leeson, who was employed by the reputable and conservative Barings Bank of England during the late 1990s. Leeson was assigned to the Singapore trading office with responsibilities that included trading futures and hedging risk for the bank. Over time he incurred trading losses and concealed them from his superiors at the bank, using false paperwork and other methods to create the appearance of success.

By the time his activities were fully understood, Leeson had exceeded all previous standards of using futures as a means of speculation, investing more than $27 billion on the Japanese stock exchange. Through a complicated series of financial maneuvers, he essentially bet that the Nikkei would trade in a narrow range. Unfortunately, he was wrong; the result was a loss of about $950 million. This loss was greater than the total value of the bank and resulted in its collapse. This was especially shocking because Barings was more than 300 years old and had a strong reputation as a stable institution.

The inherent risk of futures markets has created the need for regulation. In the United States, the Commodity Futures Trading Commission (CFTC) is the federal agency responsible for monitoring the various futures markets. Like the Security and Exchange Commission in the stock market, it works to ensure the stability and fairness of the market by investigating questionable trades and acting as a deterrent to misbehavior.

The futures exchanges also use price limits to protect investors in volatile periods. These are preset limits on the range a futures contract may trade in. This system limits price swings from unexpected news and thus creates some limitations on gains and losses.

Nonetheless, the futures markets hold both promise and peril for investors. They are valuable business tools because they allow the exchange and control of risk. They also illustrate the fundamental principle of investing: profits and losses are proportional to the risks taken.

Further Reading

How Leeson Broke Barings
riskinstitute.ch/137560.htm
The full account of the Barings debacle by the
     International Financial Risk Institute.

U.S. Commodities Futures Trading Commission
www.cftc.gov
The home page of the independent government
     agency that has the mandate to regulate com-
     modity futures and option markets in the
     United States. The "Education Center" pages
     offer a clear description of the futures trading
     process and its regulation.

—David Long

A commodities trader relays trade information to the Standard and Poor's 500 stock index futures pit at the Chicago Mercantile Exchange.

Globalization

From the last quarter of the twentieth century, there has been an unprecedented boom in international trade and commerce and growing financial links between nations around the world. This phenomenon is generally referred to as economic globalization, and it involves more than the importing and exporting of goods between companies in different countries. Economic globalization also involves increased integration between investors, manufacturers, workers, and customers around the globe, as well as the ability to quickly exchange research, information, and ideas. This increase in the pace of international activity was made possible by the advances in computer technology and communications.

Globalization is often described as a force that is shrinking the world, as many transactions now take place across international borders at speeds that were not before possible. In this new era, globalization is creating major shifts in the worldwide distribution of money and jobs. In much the same way that the invention of the steam engine engendered the Industrial Revolution and resulted in large numbers of people leaving their villages to work in urban factories, so are computers, satellites, robots, and the World Wide Web changing the world economy and the lives of workers in fundamental ways.

Positive and Negative Effects

Globalization has brought increased prosperity to people in many countries by opening new trade opportunities and creating worldwide networks of markets for goods and services. It has led to increased competition, which has resulted in lower prices and improvements in the quality of goods and services as companies increasingly strive to outdo each other to win customers.

Socioeconomic inequality between the rich and the poor appears to have increased from the late twentieth century and beyond, however. Studies by worldwide economic

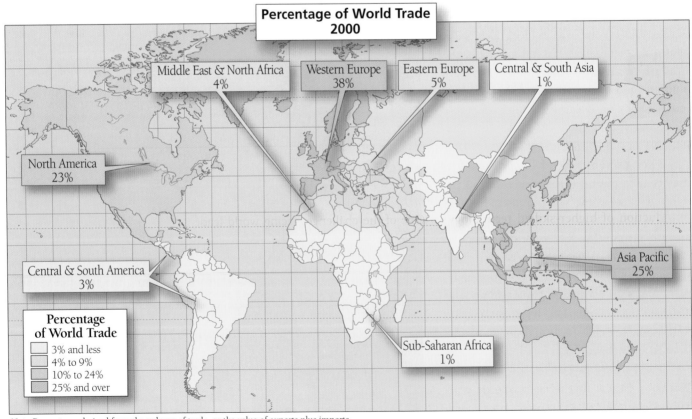

Percentage of World Trade 2000

Middle East & North Africa 4%

Western Europe 38%

Eastern Europe 5%

Central & South Asia 1%

North America 23%

Central & South America 3%

Asia Pacific 25%

Sub-Saharan Africa 1%

Percentage of World Trade
- 3% and less
- 4% to 9%
- 10% to 24%
- 25% and over

Note: Percentages derived from the volume of trade, or the value of exports plus imports.
Source: Computed from the figures in International Monetary Fund, *Directions of Trade Statistics, May 2001.*

Employees of a 24/7 customer service center in Bengaluru (Bangalore), India, provide phone support for British and American clients.

organizations show that income gaps are generally widening between the wealthiest and most impoverished countries. Such research makes clear that the economic benefits of globalization have not been evenly distributed. Indeed, they have not been realized at all in some of the world's least developed nations, which remain wracked by poverty and are largely cut off from economic progress.

Income gaps have also widened within individual countries, even in nations with advanced economies. One reason is the introduction of higher-skilled technology jobs into economies that once relied heavily on lower-skilled manufacturing jobs. As technology creates more demand for better educated workers, opportunities become fewer and fewer for less-educated people, who are then left on the lower rungs of the economic ladder.

These income disparities have prompted growing criticisms that globalization is a system that is helping the rich get richer at the expense of the poor. Thousands of protest-ers have gathered in cities where major international financial summits are held. The protesters argue that the world is becoming increasingly dominated by the interests of wealthy investors and huge multinational corporations to the detriment of average working people.

Most economists see globalization as neither good nor bad in itself, but rather as a force that includes both positive and negative aspects, just as fire can be thought of as good or bad depending on whether it is used to cook a meal or burn down a house. One of the challenges facing world leaders is to promote the positive attributes of globalization while also finding ways to counteract its negative effects.

Historical Perspective

Michael Mussa, an economic counselor and director of research for the International Monetary Fund, describes globalization as a process that has been occurring in fits and starts for hundreds of years, driven forward or back by consumer preferences,

Change in Trade as Share of GDP 1980 to 1999
(in percent)

Country	%	Country	%	Country	%
Negative growth		Norway	14.8	Sweden	67.0
Iran	-63.3	Myanmar	17.0	New Zealand	67.5
Niger	-46.9	Senegal	21.0	Italy	68.5
Zambia	-45.1	South Africa	23.2	Costa Rica	69.0
Benin	-44.3	Israel	25.1	Brazil	72.1
Egypt	-40.9	Burundi	26.8	Austria	72.5
Nigeria	-39.9	Morocco	30.4	Australia	72.9
Gambia	-34.7	Mauritius	32.6	Colombia	80.7
Malawi	-32.4	Swaziland	38.1	Hungary	81.8
Sudan	-32.2	Congo, Dem. Rep.	38.2	Uruguay	90.9
Syria	-31.7	Cote d'Ivoire	38.8	Rwanda	97.7
Chad	-29.4	Japan	39.3	United States	99.1
Guinea-Bissau	-27.9	Sri Lanka	40.1	Thailand	99.5
Burkina Faso	-25.6	Germany	40.6	*100 to 200 percent increase*	
Mauritania	-25.5	Jamaica	42.2	Greece	103.1
Madagascar	-25.1	Sierra Leone	42.6	Canada	113.3
Algeria	-24.6	Tunisia	43.7	Portugal	118.5
Togo	-22.3	Netherlands	44.4	Korea, South	121.6
Honduras	-21.8	Belgium	44.5	Malaysia	124.8
Indonesia	-16.5	Peru	45.9	Mali	125.5
Guatemala	-13.4	Bolivia	46.3	Nepal	127.1
Pakistan	-13.3	El Salvador	48.7	Ireland	129.1
Kenya	-9.1	*50 to 99 percent increase*		Bangladesh	130.7
Papua New Guinea	-7.5	Switzerland	50.6	Zimbabwe	139.6
Jordan	-7.3	Dominican Republic	51.5	Paraguay	142.3
Ghana	-1.3	Denmark	55.3	Philippines	142.3
0 to 49 percent increase		United Kingdom	55.6	Spain	154.6
Lesotho	0.9	Cameroon	56.4	Argentina	154.9
Gabon	2.8	Finland	57.6	Haiti	168.1
Ecuador	3.1	India	61.6	*More than 200 percent increase*	
Trinidad and Tobago	9.3	France	63.1	Hong Kong	209.7
Congo, Rep.	10.9	Nicaragua	65.2	Mexico	223.4
Venezuela	12.1	Chile	65.5		

Source: World Bank, *World Development Indicators*, 2002.

The liberalization of trade under globalization has had varied impacts, as evidenced by the table showing the change in trade, measured as a share of gross domestic product (GDP), for selected countries.

political influences, or advances in human knowledge. For centuries, the difficulties of moving goods from one country to another limited the scope of global commerce. Over time, international trade became more feasible through the development of steam-powered ships, railroads, and, later, airlines. By the late nineteenth century, goods like French wines, German watches, and Oriental silks had worldwide reputations for quality and conse-quently were in demand by consumers from different countries. However, many countries levied surcharges, or tariffs, on foreign imports as a method of raising money and as a way of encouraging their citizens to buy domestic goods. For these reasons, high-quality foreign imports tended to be expensive compared with products made in one's homeland.

Early in the 1900s globalization came to a virtual standstill during a period of international political instability that culminated in two world wars. Growing economic rivalries led many governments to become more protective of their own national economies. They put regulations in place that banned imports from enemy countries and encouraged economic self-sufficiency at home. This climate of economic protectionism accelerated after a major economic collapse in the United States, resulting in the Great Depression, which helped fuel a worldwide downturn in economic activity in the 1930s. The United States reacted by imposing substantial tariffs on foreign imports, which caused other countries to retaliate by erecting similar trade barriers to protect their economies.

These domestically oriented economic policies continued for several decades to greater or lesser degrees throughout the period known as the cold war. This period, roughly from 1945 to the late 1980s, was characterized by suspicion and mistrust between the two global superpowers, the democratic, capitalist United States and the communist Soviet Union. The two superpowers competed for political, military, and economic dominance, and their rivalry had the effect of restricting international trade.

During this period, global commerce was largely, though not totally, limited to democracies trading with other democracies and communist nations trading with other communist nations. However, this period also saw the birth of many international organizations, programs, and policies that wanted to facilitate world trade and lay down rules by which it might be governed. These include the International Monetary Fund, the World Bank, and the General Agreement on Tariffs and Trade (GATT), forerunner to the current World Trade Organization.

By the 1980s the economic failures of communism were becoming increasingly apparent both inside and outside the Soviet Union. Communism's hallmark—the planned economy where all economic activity was directed by the government rather than by the free market laws of supply and demand—had led to economic stagnation characterized by widespread

shortages of food and consumer goods in communist nations. In the 1980s some Eastern European countries under communist control began to rebel and break away. In 1991 the Soviet Union itself collapsed and split into numerous separate countries.

As the cold war was thawing, the United States and some other countries started shifting from economic protectionism and lifted some old restrictions on foreign trade and investment. Increasingly, they began to open their economies to the outside world. This new freer-trade philosophy was one of two major factors that helped pave the way for rapid globalization in the late twentieth century.

Technology and Globalization

The other major factor that made globalization possible to the degree it exists today was the technology boom. For the first time, rapid advances in microchip processing, robotics, and satellite communications made it practical for corporations to establish over-

Wealthy versus Poor Nations

Economists note that many factors help to explain why the results of globalization have been uneven so far. One major reason for the current disparities is that countries were not in an equal position to participate when the global boom began. For example:

- Wealthy nations like the United States, Japan, and those of Western Europe had huge advantages because communications and information technology were much more advanced and computer use much more widespread than in poorer countries. This technological inequality between nations is often referred to as the "digital divide." The World Bank noted that in 2000, about 90 percent of Internet host computers were located in the world's wealthiest countries, while half of the world's population had never made a phone call.
- Education, banking, and government systems are also more advanced and more stable in wealthier countries and thus benefit business.
- Government corruption, chronic hunger and disease, illiteracy, and political instability are preventing many of the poorest countries from getting a toehold in the global economy. When millions of people are starving and dying from AIDS, tuberculosis, and malaria, as is the case in many parts of Africa, they are generally not concerned with global commerce.
- In a vicious circle, international investors generally shun unstable countries when deciding where to locate new operations; thus fewer opportunities for reversing economic stagnation are provided, leading to more instability.
- The vast majority of foreign investment has occurred in a limited number of emerging markets: Brazil, Mexico, Russia, Indonesia, and China. Smaller, frontier markets, such as Vietnam, receive less investment.

Burmese refugees sewing in a Thai sweatshop.

seas affiliates and branch operations almost anywhere in the world.

Far-flung business operations can be linked by e-mail, video conferencing, fax machines, and cell phones. Research can be conducted anywhere and the results transmitted instantaneously to head offices worldwide. News and information can be quickly shared around the globe over the Internet, allowing corporate decision makers to keep abreast of events that might affect their business interests. As computerization streamlines the airline and shipping industries, travel has become faster and more economical for both goods and for people.

The technology boom also sparked a revolution in the investment world. For the first time, investment capital could be moved around electronically over the World Wide Web without anyone physically crossing a border. Companies and individuals can put money into markets around the globe in the hope of earning higher returns on their investments.

The ease of moving money and the lifting of old trade and investment barriers prompted many corporations, particularly those engaged in manufacturing, to transfer portions of their operations to other countries. Such relocation allowed them to take advantage of lower wage costs in those countries or to build factories closer to where large pools of their customers live.

For example, from 1980 automaker General Motors and its former parts division Delphi have built dozens of automobile assembly and parts plants in Mexico and elsewhere in Latin America, where parts can be produced more cheaply because wages are so much lower than in the United States. Japanese automakers like Toyota and Honda have built numerous auto plants in the United States and Canada, eliminating the need to ship finished vehicles across the ocean before they can be sold to North American consumers.

Changes in Manufacturing

The displacement of manufacturing jobs to lower-wage countries benefited consumers because finished goods usually could be priced lower. The huge American chain store Wal-Mart, for example, is able to offer discount merchandise to shoppers because it buys products from lower-wage factories throughout the world, then uses advanced technology, for example, computerized just-in-time inventory systems, to keep costs down. Toasters made in Mexico, stereos assembled in China, and clothing manufactured in Sri Lanka can all be found on the shelves of any Wal-Mart. The bargain prices Wal-Mart offers also put pressure on other retailers to find ways to keep their prices down to be able to compete for customers.

This transfer of money and jobs to other nations has brought much-needed opportunities for economic growth to some underdeveloped countries. However, critics have expressed concerns that many of these new jobs are menial, high-turnover, low-paid positions, and that the working conditions of these new employees are substandard compared with the conditions found in more developed economies. In addition, the global economic downturn of 2008–2009 showed that the economies of these underdeveloped countries risk becoming dependent on the ebbs and flows of the U.S. economy, and U.S. rates of consumer spending in particular.

The global redistribution of manufacturing jobs has also had a harsh impact on blue-collar workers in economically advanced countries like the United States, where tens of thousands of employees have seen their factory jobs relocated overseas or their wages reduced. High school–educated males in the United States—the segment of the workforce that traditionally held factory jobs—earned $5,000 less in annual wages in 2005 than in 1969.

Critics say that by transferring less-skilled jobs to poorer countries, companies in rich nations are effectively putting downward pressure on wages worldwide. Critics also charge that multinationals are exploiting foreign workers by paying them lower wages, essentially trapping them in standards of living lower than those of workers in wealthier nations. This phenomenon has been described by critics as a "race to the bottom."

U.S. sportswear maker Nike, for example, came under extreme criticism for entering into manufacturing contracts with foreign factories known as sweatshops.

Global Locations of General Motors

Americas	Africa/Middle East	Asia	Eastern Europe	Western Europe
Argentina	Bahrain	Australia	Croatia	Austria
Brazil	Egypt	China	Czech Republic	Belgium
Canada	Israel	Hong Kong	Hungary	Denmark
Chile	Jordan	India	Poland	Finland
Colombia	Kenya	Indonesia	Russian Federation	France
Ecuador	Kuwait	Japan	Slovakia	Germany
Mexico	Lebanon	Korea	Slovenia	Greece
Paraguay	Nigeria	Malaysia		Ireland
United States	Oman	New Zealand		Italy
Uruguay	Qatar	Singapore		Netherlands
Venezuela	Saudi Arabia	Taiwan		Norway
	South Africa	Thailand		Portugal
	Syria			Spain
	United Arab Emirates			Sweden
	Yemen			Switzerland
				Turkey

Source: General Motors, "Global Locations," http://www.gm.com/company/corp_info/global_locations/ (January 28, 2003).

The global reach of the multinational corporation General Motors.

Jose Bové: Antiglobalization Activist

Jose Bové, a French farmer, activist, and trade unionist, is probably best known for dismantling a half-built McDonald's in southern France in August 1999. Following the McDonald's incident, Bové cultivated a media image as a simple, sheep-farming David to the Goliath of one of America's most recognizable multinationals.

In 1987 Bové, by then an established sheep farmer and maker of Roquefort cheese, helped found Confédération Paysanne, now France's second-largest farmer's union. As a union representative, Bové staged witty, symbolic media events. In 1988, as a protest against the farm policies of the European Economic Community, Bové called the lawn of the Champs de Mars around the Eiffel Tower "the only real field in Paris," and proceeded to plow it. In the same spirit, Bové grazed his sheep at the Paris stock exchange and brought a cow to the Louvre.

On August 12, 1999, Bové led a rally at the building site of the McDonald's in the small town of Millau near the river Tarn. Bové decried McDonald's as a symbol of "economic imperialism," and coined two of his most famous phrases: *malbouffe* (lousy food) and "McDomination." Plainclothes police officers watched as the farmer–activists took their tools to the half-constructed building and loaded the pieces onto tractors, which were then driven to the city council office.

Bové and five other members of Confederation Paysanne were arrested, and the press dubbed the ensuing trial "Seattle on the Tarn," a French extension of the antiglobalization movement that began with the World Trade Organization protests in Seattle. Bové arranged to arrive at the courthouse in an open cart made to resemble the ones used to bring prisoners of the French Revolution to the guillotine. After two years of failed appeals, Bové returned to jail to serve his three-month sentence.

While Bové remains most infamous for taking on McDonald's, his actions, from protesting against French nuclear testing to destroying genetically modified crops in France and Brazil, have addressed a range of issues. Some of Bové's fellow French farm unionists disparage him as a media opportunist, noting that he spends more time protesting than farming. Such criticisms have diminished Bové's reputation as a folk hero, but he remains a key voice in the antiglobalization struggle. Indeed, Naomi Klein, antiglobalization notable and author of *No Logo* (2000), credits Bové with bringing the complicated issues surrounding the industrialization of food and farming to the table.

—*Laura Lambert*

Jose Bové is taken away by security forces during a WTO protest in Paris.

Foreign workers sometimes worked in conditions that would be illegal under U.S. labor laws. Nike responded to the criticisms by ordering investigations and pledging to eliminate undesirable practices. Some other large multinational corporations have taken similar steps, adopting mission statements that include commitments to be socially responsible in their business practices.

Technology and Globalization

The success of the international protests against Nike's contract factories was largely made possible by some of the same technological advances that have fueled globalization. The Internet, for example, allows labor advocates and human rights activists around the world to keep in touch, compare notes, and plan multi-country publicity campaigns aimed at improving the business practices of multinationals.

Some economic sectors, most notably technology industries, have prospered enormously from globalization. Bill Gates, the head of the Microsoft empire, became the richest man in America, amassing a fortune of nearly $30 billion during the 1980s and 1990s. The world's growing interconnectedness and its increasing reliance on technology has created a groundswell of demand for high-tech workers and products.

A good example can be found in Silicon Valley in California, a community with a worldwide reputation for having made numerous advances in information technology. Its population is global: in 2008, 36 percent of Silicon Valley residents were foreign-born; of those, 57 percent were from Asia, according to Joint Venture, Silicon Valley Network's index of economic activity. The median household income was 65 percent higher than the national average: in Silicon Valley, the average annual income was more than $79,000 per person.

Even this success story has a downside, however. At the same time that salaries were soaring at the top of Silicon Valley's economic ladder, income disparity also increased. The percentage of households earning more than $100,000 per year grew to 42 percent of all Silicon Valley households; but at the same time, the percent of the population earning less than $35,000 also reached 20 percent. The cost of living in Silicon Valley has risen so fast that lower-wage earners find it challenging to afford to live in the area.

Income Gaps

Worldwide, income gaps between the rich and poorest countries appear to have worsened. A briefing paper by the World Bank attempted to measure this gap by comparing the average incomes per person for the 20 wealthiest countries with those of the 20 most impoverished nations. In 1960 per capita Gross Domestic Product (GDP)—the value of a nation's economic output measured on a per person basis—was 15 times higher in the 20 richest nations than in the 20 poorest. By 2000 that income gap had doubled, with per capita GDP in the wealthiest countries 30 times higher than that of the poorest.

Globalization also appears to have lifted millions of people out of poverty. Another World Bank report compared the economic performance of dozens of poorer countries by dividing them into two groups: those that had become more globalized and those that remained less globalized. The more globalized nations—those that had substantially increased their export of manufactured goods—grew at an average rate of 5 percent during the 1990s. This group, which included India, China, Mexico, and 19 other countries, saw increases in life expectancy and education levels during that period.

In the less-globalized nations, including those in much of sub-Saharan Africa, incomes declined during the same period. "For many of the poorest least-developed countries, the problem is not that they are being impoverished by globalization, but that they are in danger of being largely excluded from it," the World Bank concluded. Critics point to such disparities as proof that globalization is not working. Supporters say the inequalities show that the international community must do much more to help less-developed countries catch up.

In the early twenty-first century, many economists and commentators on globalization are calling for the international community to do more to alleviate the economic disparities between rich and poor nations. Failure to do so may result in worsening income gaps over time, with less-developed nations becoming even more impoverished and disease-ridden. This increased instability could fuel problems that affect all nations. In a global society, sickness and turmoil can easily spread beyond international borders, and desperation in poor nations can lead to violent conflicts and increased illegal immigration.

International financial crises, like those experienced by both Latin American and Asian countries in the 1990s and early 2000s, and the genuinely global economic and financial crisis that began in 2008, are another subject of debate. The prevention of such crises and how to better manage them when they do occur are significant concerns. Until 2008, the concept of "decoupling," or economic independence, was gaining ground, and economists saw signs that national economies were becoming less interlinked. However, the speed at which the economic crisis spread beyond the United States in 2008 stymied this line of thinking. Many observers feel that future debates will revolve around setting and reforming the rules of global capitalism. The globalization debates of the future may not be about whether "to globalize or not to globalize." Instead, they will address the questions of how, when, and on what terms global trade takes place.

Further Research
Globalization 101
www.globalization101.org
A student's guide to globalization, this Web site, run by the Levin Institute of the State University of New York, offers news analyses, issue briefs, and interviews.
World Bank
www.worldbank.org
The World Bank's Web site offers a research database as well as a library of more than 65,000 downloadable documents.
—*Carol Alaimo*

Gross Domestic Product

The gross domestic product (GDP) is a measurement of economic activity within a certain area—most commonly the borders of a nation, but sometimes another kind of region, like the American Northeast or the European Union. The GDP provides an estimate of the value of goods and services purchased during a specific period.

The GDP is often consulted by economists and policy makers as an indication of how well a country or region is performing financially and whether specific policies are working. The GDP is widely reported, as are fluctuations in its value—an increasing GDP, for example, is usually what is meant when observers talk of "a growing economy" or "economic growth," while a shrinking GDP indicates an economic recession or depression.

Calculating the GDP

Determining the value of goods and services produced in a year in a country as large as the United States is an arduous task; the GDP is always an estimate and is often revised. To begin, economists must agree on the value of various goods and services. As the United States is a market economy, a relatively simple way to do this is to accept the market's judgment of value and say that goods and services are worth whatever price people choose to pay for them. In that case, the GDP is based on the total sales of goods and services in a given region over a given time.

Obviously, inconsistencies can arise. A retail store could sell a swimsuit for $60 in May, then sell the same swimsuit for $20 at an end-of-season clearance sale in late August. Most economists would argue that accepting the judgment of the market is ultimately more useful than attempting to create an abstract master value for swimsuits.

Services provided by the government are more problematic, however, as they are usually provided free of charge. Nonetheless, services like police and fire protection have value and should be counted somehow. So economists use the amount of money the government spends to provide the services. Obviously this method does not give a perfect measure of value either—the government could overpay or underpay for the services it provides—but the GDP is an estimate, not a precise measurement, so it is good enough.

If the GDP is calculated using sales of goods and services, economists have to guard against "double-dipping," or the counting of multiple sales of the same good. Take the swimsuit: supplies are sold to the fabric manufacturer, the fabric is sold to the swimsuit manufacturer, and the resulting swimsuit is sold to the wholesaler, the retailer, and finally to the customer. Add up all those sales and the swimsuit by itself could account for hundreds of dollars of economic activity. However, the swimsuit is not worth hundreds of dollars, it is worth $60 in May and $20 in August. When calculating the GDP, economists count only final sales, not what are known as intermediate sales. In addition, economists omit sales of goods that have already been sold once—used cars, for example. Otherwise, a $20,000 car that is bought new and promptly sold could be counted as $40,000 worth of goods.

Another way to calculate the GDP is to determine all the value added to goods and services in a given region. The value added to something is the price it is sold for, minus the cost of raw materials. If a baker takes 50 cents of supplies and makes a muffin he sells for $1, then 50 cents of value has been added to the muffin by the baker. If the baker sells the muffin for $1 to

---

Components of the GDP

- Personal consumption expenditures
- Gross private domestic investment
- Net export of goods and services
- Government consumption expenditure and gross investment

a convenience store, which sells it for $3 to someone who eats it, $2 of value has been added by the convenience store. Notice that the cost of raw materials, 50 cents, plus the amount of value added, $2.50, equals the muffin's final sale price, $3. Whether economists calculate the GDP by looking at total final sales or calculate it by looking at the value added to goods and services, they will come to the same number.

The amount of value added to goods and services can be determined another way—by looking at income. When a convenience store sells a muffin for $2 more than it paid for it, the store uses that $2 to pay salaries—which yield personal income—and records whatever is left over as profit—which is business income. As the total income in a region is the same as the total value added to goods and services in a region, the total income of a region is just as good a measure of the GDP as the total value added to goods or the total final sales in a region. Such figures make life much easier for economists, because personal and business incomes are routinely reported to the government for tax purposes.

Limitations of the GDP

Although the GDP is an important measure of how well the economy of a region is doing, it is by no means the only or the perfect measure. For one, the GDP measures only the economic activity of a specific place. That place can be very large, like Europe or the Western Hemisphere, but if people in that place have substantial investments or own businesses located someplace else, the GDP will not capture that economic activity. That kind of activity can be measured using something called the gross national product (GNP). The GNP essentially measures the economic activity of a people—Swiss citizens, for example, rather than Switzerland itself.

The GDP is also restricted to a specific time, often a year or a quarter, so it does not directly indicate the base from which a country is starting. Two countries with a similar GDP might be in very different

Gross Domestic Product 1929 to 2002 (in billions)			
Year	Gross domestic product	Year	Gross domestic product
1929	103.7	1966	789.3
1930	91.3	1967	834.1
1931	76.6	1968	911.5
1932	58.8	1969	985.3
1933	56.4	1970	1,039.7
1934	66.0	1971	1,128.6
1935	73.3	1972	1,240.4
1936	83.7	1973	1,385.5
1937	91.9	1974	1,501.0
1938	86.1	1975	1,635.2
1939	92.0	1976	1,823.9
1940	101.3	1977	2,031.4
1941	126.7	1978	2,295.9
1942	161.8	1979	2,566.4
1943	198.4	1980	2,795.6
1944	219.7	1981	3,131.3
1945	223.0	1982	3,259.2
1946	222.3	1983	3,534.9
1947	244.4	1984	3,932.7
1948	269.6	1985	4,213.0
1949	267.7	1986	4,452.9
1950	294.3	1987	4,742.5
1951	339.5	1988	5,108.3
1952	358.6	1989	5,489.1
1953	379.9	1990	5,803.2
1954	381.1	1991	5,986.2
1955	415.2	1992	6,318.9
1956	438.0	1993	6,642.3
1957	461.5	1994	7,054.3
1958	467.9	1995	7,400.5
1959	507.4	1996	7,813.2
1960	527.4	1997	8,318.4
1961	545.7	1998	8,781.5
1962	586.5	1999	9,268.6
1963	618.7	2000	9,872.9
1964	664.4	2001	10,208.1
1965	720.1	2002	10,445.6

Source: Bureau of Economic Analysis, "National Accounts Data," http://www.bea.gov/bea/dn1.htm (March 24, 2003).

situations because one has a well-developed infrastructure due to years of careful investment and the other has a terrible infrastructure due to years of corruption

Average GDP Per Capita: 20 High-Income and 20 Low-Income Countries 1970 to 2000		
Year	Average GDP per capita in high-income countries	Average GDP per capita in low-income countries
1970	10,066	524
1971	10,755	543
1972	12,283	553
1973	14,828	613
1974	15,683	652
1975	16,309	700
1976	16,750	662
1977	17,686	705
1978	19,670	777
1979	20,978	829
1980	21,536	692
1981	18,812	713
1982	17,008	667
1983	16,085	533
1984	15,584	395
1985	15,441	384
1986	19,346	393
1987	22,749	364
1988	24,554	373
1989	24,129	358
1990	27,262	334
1991	27,199	296
1992	28,178	283
1993	26,392	250
1994	27,960	209
1995	31,313	240
1996	30,952	253
1997	29,145	247
1998	28,786	242
1999	28,987	233
2000	27,591	211

Note: Adjusted for inflation.
Source: World Economic Outlook.

Note:
Average based on 20 countries with the highest GDP per capita and 20 countries with the lowest.

High-income countries:
Australia, Austria, Belgium, Canada, Denmark, Finland, France, Germany, Hong Kong, Iceland, Ireland, Japan, Luxembourg, Netherlands, Norway, Singapore, Sweden, Switzerland, United Kingdom, and United States.

Low-income countries:
Burkina Faso, Burundi, Central African Republic, Chad, Ethiopia, Ghana, Guinea-Bissau, Kenya, Madagascar, Malawi, Mali, Mozambique, Myanmar, Nepal, Niger, Nigeria, Rwanda, Sierra Leone, Tanzania, and Uganda.

period. As a result, money invested in the stock market or used to pay off a debt does not show up in the GDP because no good or service has been purchased. Both actions may result in a better future, but the GDP is not focused on the future—it only shows how the economy of a place moves during a narrow time span.

Estimating the GDP with any accuracy in countries where records are poorly kept and practices like smuggling, the cultivation of drugs, and prostitution are common is extremely difficult. People who engage in illegal activities usually do not report their income to the government, nor do they usually keep records of their purchases and sales, so their actions are effectively invisible. Even in the United States, which has a largely legitimate economy, the GDP is believed to be undervalued by roughly 10 percent because of unrecorded criminal activity.

The GDPs of various countries are often compared to establish which countries are doing well and which are doing poorly. However, comparisons between countries can be complicated because of limits to what the GDP indicates. For example, a country may have a very low GDP, but to observers, the population looks prosperous and well. It may turn out that the country's government has onerous tax policies, so everyone engages in tax evasion, and incomes are vastly underreported.

Poorer countries tend to have extremely low GDPs, so low that almost no economic activity appears to be occurring. If a poor country gets a little richer, the GDP will shoot up, as though everyone suddenly decided to buy goods and services. Although increased incomes do lead to more spending, the way the GDP is measured tends to exaggerate this effect because it measures only things that are sold on a market for money. A family of subsistence farmers may work very hard to grow crops, tend animals, and make clothing and other goods. Family members may even barter with neighbors, swapping their eggs for fruit they do not grow themselves. However, none of this activity will be

and warfare. Obviously the quality of the infrastructure may have an indirect effect on the GDP, but the GDP alone will not tell observers which country is actually better off.

Just as the GDP does not tell much about the past, it also tells little about the future. The GDP records only the goods and services bought and sold in a specific

indicated by the GDP, because no money changes hands. If a factory opens nearby and one of the family members goes there to work, receiving a salary and buying the goods she used to make herself, then that activity is recorded, and her contribution to the GDP is suddenly much larger, even though she may be only a little better off.

A high GDP likewise does not always indicate that all is well in a nation. If people spend lots of money on security or cleaning up toxic wastes, that spending will increase the GDP just like any other spending, but it will not help the economy grow long-term and may indicate deeper social problems. A country with a high GDP may be relying entirely on nonrenewable mineral wealth and not developing the rest of its economy at all. Indeed, many oil-rich nations have very high GDPs but also high rates of unemployment and dissatisfaction.

For all its limitations, however, the GDP remains a useful snapshot of economic activity. Monitoring the GDP, especially to see if it is growing or shrinking, can give economists and policy makers a much better idea of how the economy is doing overall. Being able to measure economic growth gives policy makers a much better idea of

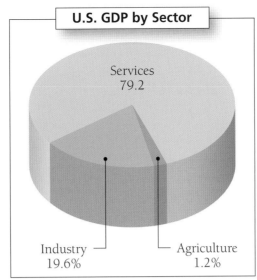

U.S. GDP by Sector

Services
79.2

Industry
19.6%

Agriculture
1.2%

Source: CIA World Factbook.

what kinds of economic and fiscal policies actually promote economic health.

Further Research
Bureau of Economic Analysis
www.bea.gov
This division of the U.S. Commerce Department calculates U.S. GDP and other metrics.
International Monetary Fund
www.img.org
The United Nations' International Monetary Fund is a source of international GDP data, as well as other news and resources.

—*Mary Sisson*

A child sleeping in a homeless shelter in Atlanta, Georgia. A healthy gross domestic product for a nation is no guarantee against severe poverty for individuals.

Human Capital

Human capital equals people. In the business world, the term has a more specific meaning: the combination of a person's experience, knowledge, values, social and communication skills, and the capacity to learn and grow.

When a company talks about its human capital, it is referring to the unique set of individuals working in that company, particularly those with the ability to produce results. For example, Microsoft is known not only for its software products, but also as a place where brilliant software engineers work. The software products are what generate the company's revenue. However, the company's real value springs from its software engineers' ability to create software. The talent phenomenon explains why Microsoft's stock sells so high above its book value—the book value refers to the value of its hard assets. The trading value is partly a reflection of the confidence buyers have in the people who work there.

The term *human capital* comes from the world of economics. It was first used by Theodore Schultz to describe the potential of developing countries. His concept, for which he won the Nobel Prize in 1979, was that the potential of countries did not lie in things but in knowledge. He argued that investing in the people to teach skills and provide knowledge would help eliminate poverty.

Human capital is sometimes referred to as intellectual capital, and people who provide intellectual capital are called knowledge workers. Knowledge workers are those who use their knowledge, rather than manual labor, to generate an income. Even factory workers who used to stand in a production line doing manual labor now sit behind computer terminals to monitor machines that do the work. Statistics show that approximately 60 percent of the workforce in the United States consisted of knowledge workers—a number that seems sure to grow.

The Shift from Industrial Age to Information Age

By the mid-1980s the Information Age was in full swing, firmly leaving the Industrial Age behind. The key difference between the Industrial Age and the Information Age lies in how a company generates wealth. In the Industrial Age, wealth came from machines. Whoever had the most, best, or fastest machines was typically ahead of the competition. In the Information Age, companies generate wealth from knowledge. Whoever employs the brightest, most creative, most productive employees gets ahead. This shift in the locus of wealth creation has had a profound effect on organizations at all levels: financial, structural, and in their human resources processes.

Most of our current financial practices are rooted in the Industrial Age. Machines generated wealth and machines are a finite entity that can be owned, upgraded, depreciated, or sold. Anything done to a machine has a measurable financial consequence. Companies could look at their financial reports and see exactly how much their company was worth by checking their assets against their liabilities. In the Industrial Age, machines were assets, and people's salaries and benefits were considered liabilities.

In the Information Age, machines and hard assets are only part of the financial picture. Knowledge workers are an asset, not a liability, because wealth is generated from their productivity rather than a machine's productivity. Talented knowledge workers, those with exceptional skills, creativity, and managerial ability, are particularly valuable to a company.

Two problems are encountered by companies that rely on knowledge workers to generate wealth. First, knowledge cannot be owned like a machine. The knowledge of a worker is specific to that worker. If the worker leaves the company, then the company loses an asset. Second, no way yet exists to financially measure a person's value as an asset. Therefore, most of a company's assets do not show up on its balance sheets. In the Microsoft example, this accounts in part for the difference in the book value of its stock versus the trading value.

To fully enter the Information Age, companies must change through reinvention and restructuring or through acquisitions and mergers. The traditional hierarchical structure of companies has proven to be a hindrance in the Information Age. As the needs for technology and information increase and change rapidly, companies must adopt a flat, flexible management structure to respond quickly. The hierarchical structure typically required changes to be reviewed and approved up and down a chain of command before they were implemented. A flat organization of multiple business units within a company allows the various units to move ahead, even leapfrogging each other, when needed.

However, a flat organization also requires open communication and support among business units. One of the biggest expenditures in human capital in the future will be the investment in savvy managers who can motivate their own people as well as other business units to accomplish their unit's goals and realize the organization's vision.

Human Resources

Another structural change is the rise of the Human Resources (HR) department. In the past, HR was responsible for employees and for seeing that their needs were met. With a company focused on investing in human capital, HR becomes a partner with managers in assembling a successful knowledge-worker base. HR also becomes a much more powerful area within the corporate culture.

The increased power does not come without change for the human resources process. Recruiting practices take a 180-degree turn. Traditionally, recruiting would be informed of a need, run an ad, collect resumes, interview candidates, and hire an employee. By the 1990s the demand for knowledge workers outpaced the supply. This forced a switch from a passive recruiting

To take full advantage of human capital, Information Age firms usually need to loosen the normal hierarchical structure. Traditionally, information traveled up the chain of command and back down. An Information Age structure involves communication between all levels.

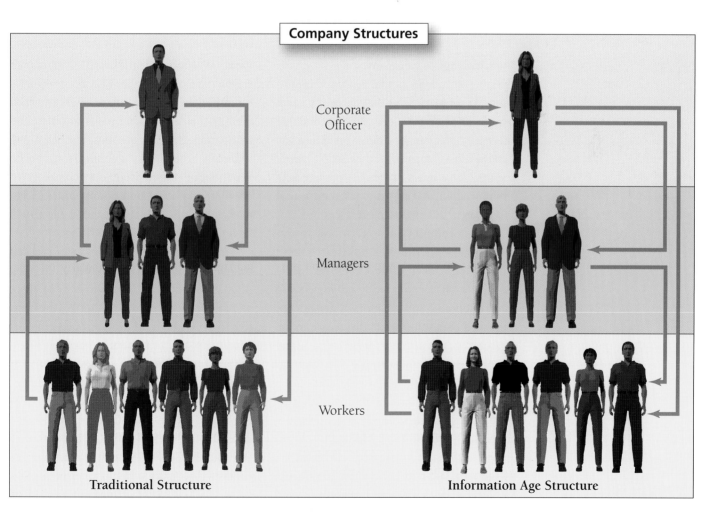

Company Structures

Corporate Officer

Managers

Workers

Traditional Structure

Information Age Structure

process to a more proactive plan for producing a continual supply of talent to meet the organization's business needs. Recruiters have to search for talent through a variety of sources. Internet resume postings and employee referrals offer the advantage of finding passive job seekers—those who might change companies for a better opportunity but are not actively searching for a job. Recruiting is a constant search rather than one executed on an as-needed basis.

Another change for HR comes in the hiring stage. In the past, the hiring packages were as structured as the companies. Now HR must be flexible in creating hiring packages for desirable individuals. HR has to know what people are looking for and work to meet those needs. For example, a job hopper with 30 years of experience may want to start with three weeks of vacation time. The option to telecommute for most or all of the time is another possibility. Signing bonuses or paying moving expenses may be offered. HR must be flexible and adapt the package to the potential of the candidate.

The Challenge to Companies

Investing in human capital creates a conundrum for companies. Should an organization invest in an asset that it does not own and that can depart at any time? Employees rarely stay with the same company for their whole career. The traditional business formula of increasing profits while managing risks takes on a new dimension in this environment.

First, a company must learn how to create internal opportunities to attract talent. This includes everything from the hiring package to challenging work assignments to recognition and appreciation. Management must set a high value on all the people in the organization, not just the star performers, and be consistent in implementing the organization's vision across the whole organization.

Developing people as human capital is more than providing skills training. Mentoring or coaching provide the backbone for developing individuals to their next level of expertise and productivity. The ideal: employees are matched with a coach or mentor to help them become more productive for the company while helping them move along their individual career paths. Both employee and employer win: employees progress along their career paths and the employer, because of the high level of investment, tends to keep people from job hopping.

Another important management issue is retaining high-caliber talent while unloading unproductive workers. No one enjoys working below their potential for extended periods, but that can happen to star performers if they are put to work under an unproductive manager. Avoiding this situation requires organizations to institute a review process for all workers that includes a formal, in-depth review similar to a traditional performance review, plus frequent informal reviews in the form of suggestions and encouragement on how to reach the next level of growth.

The Challenge to Individuals

For the individual, becoming "human capital" creates its own set of uncertainties. No longer can employees expect to enter a company and find a career path laid out to retirement. Workers are in charge of their own career development. Because no guarantees of employment are in place, workers must identify their own career paths and then find companies that are stepping stones along that path. Sometimes a stepping stone will be a deliberate move from one company to another for a better opportunity or to get out of a career rut. Other times, that move will be forced through a layoff or firing.

Individuals need a career plan to keep on track. A career plan should include a list of goals: short-term (the next two or three steps along the path), midterm (the next five to 10 years), and long-term (last half of career up to retirement). Thus, when a wished-for opportunity comes or a worker is asked to leave a company unexpectedly, the next step can be evaluated in terms of the larger career plan. Career plans should be evaluated periodically: (1) in relation to the marketplace, (2) when the season of life changes (becoming a homeowner or parent), and (3) when major changes in technology occur. These are all major shifts that can affect career goals.

Every career path requires the acquisition of new knowledge and skills. Education opportunities come in a variety of forms. The more traditional forms include degrees from colleges and universities or attending technical schools. However, some technical staff are actually self-taught; they grew up with the computer industry and learned on their own. Self-teaching is almost a requirement along many career paths because technology changes so quickly and training can be expensive. Still others attend classes to learn a specific skill like network administration or network security.

One big leap along a career path is from hands-on staff person to manager. Management requires a whole new area of expertise: "people skills." Career paths that include management aspirations should have intermediate steps of supervisory or team leader roles to gain skill in dealing with people. Solid people skills, coupled with several years of hands-on experience, create a very attractive human capital package. Typically, these are the people who command high salaries and receive outstanding career opportunities.

Reaping the Rewards

The rewards for companies that understand human capital and work to develop it are tremendous. Investors are beginning to review human-capital management before investing in an otherwise financially sound company. Good human-capital management can significantly increase the return on an investment.

Businesses, too, have recognized that increased profits can be achieved by managing their human capital. Working through the human-capital management process requires removing unproductive employees, investing in existing employees at all levels, and rewarding those who produce great results.

Knowledge workers have the opportunity to prosper, too. Instead of the company providing an income (and an associated career path) for the individual, the individual provides income for the company. This

gives workers more responsibility but also greater opportunities, not only to follow their career plans but also to contribute to the growth and development of the companies they work for.

Further Research
Managing Knowledge Workers: Developing Capabilities
www.babsoninsight.com/contentmgr/showdetails.php/id/852
This article, by Professor Thomas Davenport of Babson College, is excerpted from his book on knowledge management, published by Harvard Business School.

Society for Human Resource Management
www.shrm.org
The home page of the world's largest professional association devoted to human resource management offers news summaries, research, and information about human resources as a profession.

—*Stephanie Buckwalter*

In the Information Age, knowledge workers with the right education and training can become more valuable than the rapidly changing tools they use.

Income Distribution

Income can be defined as earnings from employment. The distribution of income is a fundamental issue for every political system; if income were equally distributed, everyone in a country would earn the same amount. Historically, income has been concentrated among the richest in society. Income distribution is a subset of wealth distribution; it answers the question of who earns how much through work. Wealth distribution addresses who has how much, adding the element of productive assets that are accumulated over time.

Income Distribution in the United States

The illustration below shows the income distribution in the United States from 1949 to 1999. It divides society into quintiles, or groups of 20 percent. The far left quintile represents the group with the lowest incomes, and the far right quintile is the group with the highest incomes. This chart demonstrates: first, income is skewed, or unevenly distributed—the poorest 20 percent earned only 3.6 percent of all income in 1999, compared with the richest quintile earning 49.4 percent. Thus, the richest 20 percent earned nearly half of all income in 1999.

Second, income distribution has been getting more unequal since 1969. In 1969 the poorest quintile earned 45.6 percent of all income; by 1999, that figure had shrunk to 3.6 percent. The top quintile saw its share of income grow from 40.6 percent in 1969 to 48 percent in 2001.

Family income in America rose very rapidly from 1949 to 1969 and very slowly since. What may have caused this pattern? The earlier period was typified by economic growth and low unemployment. Manufacturing jobs, which tended to pay well, were plentiful and helped raise the incomes of less-educated Americans. This period ended with a number of economic shifts in the 1970s and 1980s. The oil price shocks of 1973 ushered in a period of inflation and recession that hurt household income. This was accompanied by a general decrease in government assistance to the poor and changes in the tax structure.

A second trend since 1969 has been the shift of the American economy from manufacturing to service jobs. The latter tend to pay significantly less, thus holding down household incomes. This effect was partly

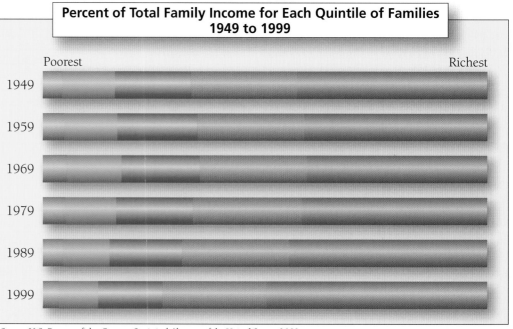

Percent of Total Family Income for Each Quintile of Families 1949 to 1999

Poorest   Richest

1949
1959
1969
1979
1989
1999

Source: U.S. Bureau of the Census, *Statistical Abstract of the United States,* 2001.

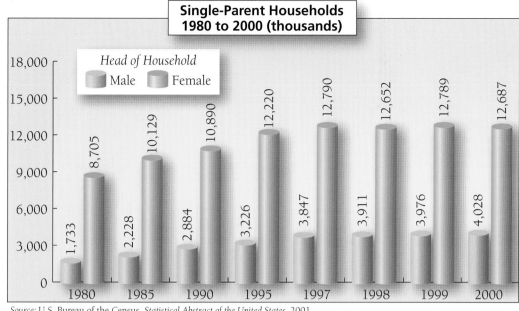

**Single-Parent Households
1980 to 2000 (thousands)**

Head of Household
■ Male   ■ Female

18,000
15,000
12,000
9,000
6,000
3,000
0

1980: 1,733 / 8,705
1985: 2,228 / 10,129
1990: 2,884 / 10,890
1995: 3,226 / 12,220
1997: 3,847 / 12,790
1998: 3,911 / 12,652
1999: 3,976 / 12,789
2000: 4,028 / 12,687

Source: U.S. Bureau of the Census, *Statistical Abstract of the United States*, 2001.

By 2007, there were more than 14 million single-parent households headed by women and over 5 million headed by men.

offset by the increasing frequency of dual earner couples, with more and more women leaving the home to work.

The trend away from manufacturing and toward service jobs also explains the continued income growth in the top quintile. These workers tend to be professionals in the service sector—doctors, computer programmers, and lawyers. Their high levels of education and job specialization increase their job security and income potential, thus increasing their share of income.

A third related trend is the growth of single-parent households, a product of higher divorce rates and increased out-of-wedlock births. Raising children while working almost eliminates the time needed to get the education and gain the job skills to improve income, and it has an especially negative effect on the economic status of women.

Overall, the news presented by these figures is mixed. The best-educated Americans have generally seen their incomes rise steadily and are typically in the top income quintile. Other Americans have experienced improved living standards, though at a much slower rate. Minorities generally fare less well, with higher poverty rates and lower incomes.

People are income mobile, however, and can change their income quintile. Generally, workers gain income with education and job

experience into their fifties; income tends to decline after retirement. Statistics indicate that 60 percent of Americans change quintile each decade, meaning the poor can get richer and the rich poorer.

Global Income Distribution

Comparing income distribution in the United States with other countries yields several findings. First, incomes in Europe tend to be spread more evenly. The more progressive tax systems of European nations impose higher

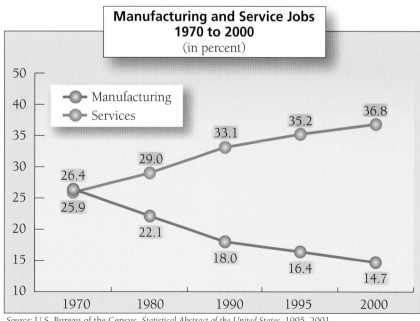

**Manufacturing and Service Jobs
1970 to 2000**
(in percent)

● Manufacturing
● Services

50
40
35
30
25
20
15
10

Manufacturing: 1970: 26.4, 1980: 22.1, 1990: 18.0, 1995: 16.4, 2000: 14.7
Services: 1970: 25.9, 1980: 29.0, 1990: 33.1, 1995: 35.2, 2000: 36.8

1970   1980   1990   1995   2000

Source: U.S. Bureau of the Census, *Statistical Abstract of the United States*, 1995, 2001.

A pedestrian passes a mother and children in downtown Durban, South Africa, where the gap between the haves and the have-nots is wide.

income tax rates on the rich, and countries' higher levels of spending on social programs aid the poor.

Second, incomes in the poorer countries of South America, Africa, and Asia tend to be far less equally divided. The share of income controlled by the top quintile of developing nations tends to be much larger than in the United States, while the remaining four quintiles generally enjoy a much smaller proportion of total income. Several factors contribute to this disparity. Access to education and job training is extremely limited in these regions. Also, societal disruptions—war, famine, and epidemic disease—are more frequent and all harm economic activity.

Although poverty rates are still high, incomes for the poor in Asia and Latin America have generally improved. The spread of free market economies, higher rates of economic growth, and a decrease in internal conflicts have been given the credit for rising incomes in these regions.

Africa, however, has more than 65 percent of the world's poor. Economic progress on the continent has been much slower than in other regions because of internal conflicts, poor economic management, and environ-

mental degradation. The AIDS epidemic is having and will continue to have a devastating impact on many African nations.

Debates about income distribution frequently take on the character of an argument about whether a glass is half full or half empty. Pessimists argue that the poor are getting poorer and the rich richer because of the disruptive effects of globalization. Optimists state that overall living standards have consistently improved over time for most people and that economic mobility for the poor remains a possibility.

Further Research
Economic Policy Institute
www.epi.org
The nonprofit Economic Policy Institute researches the living standards of working people.
The UC Atlas of Global Inequality
ucatlas.ucsc.edu
Created by the University of California Santa Cruz, this atlas examines global income inequalities using downloadable and interactive maps and graphics.
U.S. Census Bureau
www.census.gov/hhes/www/income/income.html
The Census Bureau provides income distribution data for the United States.

—David Long

Inflation

In economics, inflation is defined as a steady and persistent rise in the cost of goods and services. In an inflationary situation, a rise in prices causes a fall in the value of money. Distinction must be made between inflation and a rise in relative prices; a rise in prices of certain limited items (a weather-related rise in coffee prices, for example) is not necessarily inflationary, while a rise in the price of a vital product (oil, for example) can be.

In the United States, inflation is generally measured by the Consumer Price Index (CPI), which is calculated monthly by the U.S. Bureau of Labor Statistics. The CPI is a measure of the average change over time in the prices paid by urban consumers for a market basket of consumer goods and services, and the inflation rate is the percentage of change in the CPI. Economists recognize that the CPI is not a perfect indicator of inflation: The items included in the index do not necessarily reflect what all consumers buy; different families have different needs; a national CPI does not account for regional differences; and new products may be slow to be included.

Throughout history, inflation has often accompanied wars, but inflation was rare until the twentieth century. In the United States, for example, the price level of a good in 1900 was about the same as it was in 1770. One often cited historical example of inflation was the "price revolution" that occurred in Europe between 1500 and 1650, which economists usually attribute to a combination of an influx of gold from the New World, increased silver production in Europe, and a rapidly rising population. At a rate of 1 percent a year, however, the episode rates as only mildly inflationary by contemporary standards.

The twentieth century witnessed some spectacular examples of runaway inflation, or hyperinflation. In Hungary from 1945 to 1946, for example, inflation reached almost 20,000 percent a month. A more famous example is the hyperinflation in Germany in 1923; at one point the conversion rate for deutsche marks was four trillion to the dollar. In the United States prices began to rise steadily after World War II. Although the inflation rate reached 14.5 percent in 1947, inflation remained low in the 1950s and did not become worrisome again until the late 1960s. Overall inflation for the decade of the 1970s was 103 percent, with the annual inflation rate peaking at 13.5 percent in 1980. Recessions in the early 1980s and the early 1990s served to slow inflation, and the inflation rate remained low in the late 1990s despite heady economic growth. In 2008, the inflation rate rose from 5.0 percent to 5.6 percent, the sharpest year-on-year increase

In the 1920s in Germany, inflation was so bad that deutsche marks were essentially useless except for lighting stoves.

Inflation can hit people on fixed incomes very hard, if prices go up but their income does not.

since 1991, a response to the high oil prices experienced that year.

In modern economies an inflation rate of less than 2 or 3 percent is considered normal and acceptable. Inflation is harmful, however, when it increases economic uncertainty, thus discouraging investment and saving. If one nation experiences excessive inflation while most others do not, its exports become more expensive and its imports cheaper, thus leading to a trade deficit. Although inflation can cause wages to rise, prices normally rise faster than compensation, resulting in a lowering of real wages. Inflation also hurts people on fixed incomes, for example, people receiving pensions. Their incomes decline as inflation rises (an inflation rate of 6 percent a year causes prices to double every 12 years). Inflation is beneficial to borrowers, however, as they may be able to pay their debts in

money that has less value than when they borrowed it.

Causes of Inflation

Economists disagree on inflation's causes. Broadly speaking, inflation analysts are often divided into two camps—advocates of the "demand pull" view (also known as monetarists) and advocates of the "cost push" theory (also known as institutionalists).

Monetarists consider the money supply to be the most significant factor in determining the level of spending. Demand pull inflation is seen as a matter of supply and demand—it occurs when there is a constant demand for a particular good or service but the supply of that good or service decreases or, alternatively, occurs when the demand rises and the supply does not keep pace. Demand pull inflation can also be explained as a relationship between the economy's output (supply) at full capacity and the level of overall spending (demand). Monetarists generally argue that hikes in the cost of goods and services will not normally cause inflation unless the government increases the money supply.

The key is whether the economy is operating at full capacity. If it is not, demand pull theory states that increasing the money supply will raise real income and will not cause inflation. If, however, productive capacity is at maximum, an increase in the money supply will serve only to raise prices—the classic inflationary scenario.

The demand pull theory includes what is known as the Phillips Curve. Developed by the American economist A. W. Phillips in the late 1950s, the Phillips Curve establishes a relationship between unemployment and inflation—low unemployment is associated with rising prices—an uncomfortable thought, as it leads to the conclusion that inflation can be held in check only if unemployment is relatively high (or, conversely, a certain level of inflation must be accepted to minimize unemployment). Thus, price stability depends on the level of unemployment; the point at which this is possible is known as the Non-Acceleration Interest Rate of Unemployment (NAIRU). The legitimacy of the Phillips Curve seemed certain in the 1960s but was called into question in the 1970s, when many industrialized countries entered a period of "stagflation," which combined high unemployment with high inflation. In response, the monetarists, led by Milton Friedman, adopted the theory of "the natural rate of unemployment," which, they argued, is consistent with a stable rate of inflation. The economy, in this view, should find its own natural rate of employment.

Economists who support the cost push view of inflation argue that economic and social conditions in developed countries are not sufficiently appreciated by the demand pull theorists. In the institutionalists' view, inflation is caused by strong economic forces—increased taxes, for example, or the actions of corporations and the labor market (in the form of trade unions). Corporations can cause a rise in prices by eliminating competition and establishing near-monopoly conditions. Collusion and price fixing are possibilities, but price stability or price rises are more likely if a particular area of production is dominated by a small number of firms: none will attempt to undercut the others' prices because the interests of all are served by keeping prices high.

On the other hand, the upward pressure on prices may be the result of wage gains by workers. When workers win increased wages, their employers seek to cover those costs through price increases, resulting in inflation. Some institutionalists, however, see this model as somewhat old-fashioned, harking back to an era when the economic landscape was more commonly viewed as a struggle between capitalism and organized labor. Given the decline in the importance of labor unions in developed economies, this view has credibility. However, certain groups of workers are still able to win inflationary wage increases.

Coping with Inflation

Just as theories about the causes of inflation differ, so do theories about its cure. Speaking for the monetarists, Friedman dramatically demonstrated their viewpoint in his 1970s television series on economics, *Free to Choose*. Standing in front of a Treasury Department printing press spewing out $20 bills, he announced, "This is how you stop inflation," and turned off the machine. Inflation is caused by too rapid growth in the money supply, thus slowing that growth will slow inflation. One way to reduce the money supply is to raise interest rates—a step often taken by the Federal Reserve Board, the nation's central bank (which also tends to lower interest rates in periods of slow growth). As reducing the money supply will also slow the economy, the monetarist cure is painful because it leads to a period, which might last several years, of lower economic output and higher unemployment.

Institutionalists are more willing to turn to direct government control as a cure

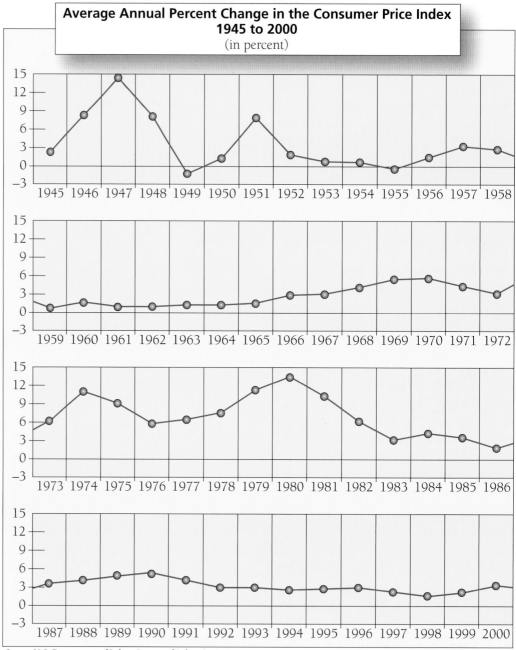

Average Annual Percent Change in the Consumer Price Index 1945 to 2000
(in percent)

Source: U.S. Department of Labor, Bureau of Labor Statistics.

for inflation. One side of this equation would be government-imposed wage–price controls, which were attempted in the United States in the early 1970s and proved difficult to implement, politically unpopular, and distorted the normal operation of the economy. The equation's other side would be encouraging lower prices by promoting greater competition among corporations, which can be done by enforcing antitrust legislation (restraining monopolies) and by dismantling government regulations that depress competition (a move that monetarists would also applaud). A third approach has been called the "living with inflation" theory, which advocates protecting those most hurt by inflation by linking Social Security payments to a cost-of-living index. Although such a policy can indeed mitigate inflation's harsher effects, it does not address the real causes of inflation.

Further Research
Inflation Calculator
data.bls.gov/cgi-bin/cpicalc.pl

—*Joseph Gustaitis*

International Monetary Fund

The International Monetary Fund (IMF) is an organization of the United Nations that exists primarily to improve cooperation between its 185 member states in matters of foreign exchange. Other key parts of its work include lending money and providing technical assistance to nations to solve short-term economic problems.

The IMF has its origins in the financial instability of the early twentieth century. Before World War I, foreign exchange had been underpinned by the gold standard: Nations could always balance their payments (compensate for differences between their imports and exports) by exchanging their reserves of gold, which acted like a common international currency, instead of their own currencies, whose values fluctuated in relation to one another. However, the war and the Great Depression of the 1930s brought considerable instability to the international economy. With gold providing the only certain means of foreign exchange, demand soon exceeded reserves. Some countries abandoned the gold standard; others continued with it. Without the stability of a universal gold standard, nations became more wary of trading with other nations and international trade suffered dramatically.

The solution to the problem was the creation of the International Monetary Fund—effectively an agreement between members to keep the system of foreign exchange running smoothly for the benefit of their own economies and of international trade. Originally signed at a conference at Bretton Woods, New Hampshire, in 1944 (and modified in 1969, 1978, and 1990), the agreement delineates the IMF's six objectives: to promote international financial cooperation; to encourage the growth of international trade and thereby high levels of employment and real income; to promote the stability of foreign exchange; to help establish a system of current international payments and to eliminate exchange controls; to promote confidence between members by

In 2002 Argentine president Eduardo Duhalde (far end of table) and his Economy Minister, Roberto Lavagna (lower right), meet with representatives of the IMF to seek a new loan to stave off an economic crisis.

Demonstrators outside a meeting of the IMF in Washington, D.C.

The IMF is perhaps best known for providing emergency assistance to nations that find themselves in economic difficulties. When a nation joins the IMF, it pays a membership fee known as a quota subscription, which varies in size according to the strength of its economy and is reviewed every five years. Quotas range from around $35 billion for the United States (the largest economy) to about $3.8 million for Palau (the smallest). The quotas are measured in a unique IMF currency known as special drawing rights (SDRs). Collectively, the quota subscriptions of the IMF's members form a huge fund from which individual member nations can borrow when they cannot maintain their balance of payments; the fund can be enlarged when necessary with loans from commercial banks and governments around the world. Quotas also determine a member's say in how the IMF is run.

Another important aspect of the IMF's work is providing technical expertise. IMF staff members often work inside member countries—especially newly created ones—to help establish central banks or devise new currencies, for example. Based at the IMF's headquarters in Washington, D.C., the IMF Institute provides training courses and seminars for thousands of economists and other staff from member nations.

The IMF has played a key role in the development and regulation of the international economy for more than half a century. Since the 1980s it has devoted much of its attention to the international debt crisis in the developing world. Much of this work has involved joint programs with the World Bank. (Although the two organizations often work together and are sometimes mistaken for each other, the Bank's work focuses on making loans to relieve poverty in developing countries, while the IMF's job is to ensure the smooth running of the international financial system through cooperation between its members.) During the 1990s the IMF worked extensively with nations in Eastern Europe and the former Soviet Union to help them transform from centralized to market economies. Also during the 1990s the IMF

offering temporary loans to correct balance-of-payments problems; and to make payments in foreign currency smoothly and quickly.

The IMF carries out three broad kinds of work: monitoring and consultation (or "surveillance"), financial assistance, and technical assistance. Surveillance involves studying the economic policies of IMF members in an attempt to anticipate future financial problems that could imperil the international economy. In practice, this involves not just passively monitoring each member nation but also consulting it, at least annually, to discuss its exchange rates, general economic policies, balance of payments, and international debt obligations, and the effects these are likely to have on the international economy.

Afghan money dealers display banknotes at the open air "Shahzada" money market in Kabul, while a team of World Bank and IMF experts met to begin talks on ways to help revive Afghanistan's economy.

made a series of huge loans to avert financial crises in Mexico ($17.8 billion in 1995), Indonesia ($11.2 billion in 1997), Thailand ($4 billion in 1997), and Russia ($9.2 billion in 1996 and $11.2 billion in 1998). While in 2004, many countries, benefiting from positive economic fundamentals, began repaying their loans, the global recession that began in 2008 gave the IMF a new focus: lending to countries hit by the economic crisis.

Like the World Bank, the IMF has frequently been criticized for its role in the politics of the international economy. Some economists charge that by lending very large amounts to unstable economies the IMF causes some of the global financial instability that it seeks to prevent. Others argue that the IMF encourages financial imprudence, corruption, and inefficiency by providing a safety net for its members, who might follow more responsible economic policies if countries had to operate by the rules of the market as do commercial concerns. Some economists question why the IMF is apparently transferring huge wealth from rich Western nations to, for example, East Asian governments and banks; others link the IMF and the World Bank in what they claim is a conspiracy to transfer wealth from the devel-

oping world to the industrialized nations through the perpetuation of the international debt crisis. Environmental and social justice campaigners question why the IMF lends money to nations—Indonesia, for example—that have questionable records on issues like human rights.

While critics call for the IMF's abolition or reform, the IMF, for its part, replies that it is not an economic subsidy for developing nations, nor a centralized world bank, nor an international financial police force coercing its members into austere economic reform. Although IMF policies constantly evolve according to the changing world economy, the IMF is simply a cooperative agreement between nations that exists purely to smooth the system of international finance and trade.

Further Research
Bretton Woods Project
www.brettonwoodsproject.org
An independent watchdog that scrutinizes the IMF and the World Bank.
International Monetary Fund
www.imf.org/external/index.htm
The home page of the IMF has member information, evaluations, news, and resources.

—*Chris Woodford*

International Trade

Individuals trade to acquire goods or services that are difficult or expensive to make or perform for themselves. International trade extends this idea to trading with people and firms in foreign countries. International trade is a central feature of the world economy. Currently, almost one-third of all production is for consumers in other countries. Trade is the central engine of globalization and directly affects politics, consumers, and culture worldwide.

Trade is beneficial because it allows people to specialize, or produce, what they do best. Economists call this concept comparative advantage, which is defined as the ability to produce an item at a lower cost than another party. For example, an individual may be an excellent doctor, but inefficient at producing automobiles. The doctor should spend her time doing what she does best—working with patients—rather than building her own car. This concept explains why most people pursue one profession and trade for almost all of the goods they consume.

International trade works on the same principle. Nations export goods that they are particularly good at producing and import items that other nations make better. Both nations benefit by maximizing efficiency.

A Short History of Trade

The history of international trade dates to the earliest civilizations. Ancient rulers understood that trade and commerce were powerful tools for uniting the empires they built through conquest. In general, the economies of ancient empires, for example, the Roman Empire, were based on the premise of taxation in exchange for protection and increased trading opportunities for the subjects. The duration of such empires largely depended on their capacity to guarantee these conditions.

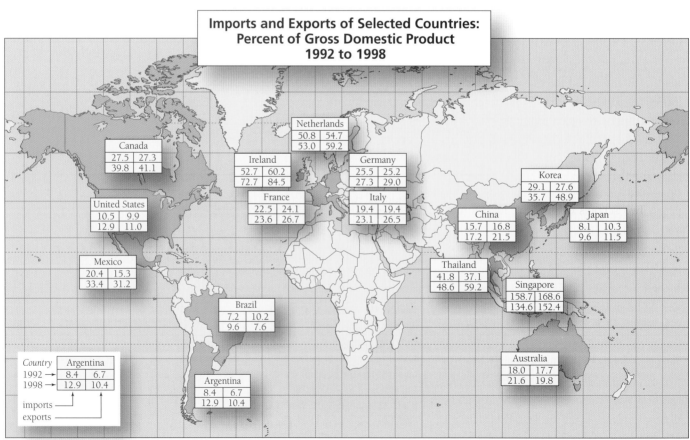

Note: Includes goods and services.
Source: International Monetary Fund.

Trade played a critical role in the development of the modern world. Europe was relatively backward in comparison to the Muslim and Chinese cultures after the fall of Rome in the fifth century C.E. After the Crusades, however, trading routes to the Middle and Far East were reestablished and foreign inventions, including the compass and gunpowder, began to reach Europe.

European nations eagerly embraced trade, the profit motive, and technological change, whereas the Muslim and Chinese cultures did not. Over time, the latter two declined economically. In contrast, Europe began to develop rapidly. Europeans' quest for profits, combined with the competition between European nations for power, resulted in the age of discovery: Columbus sailed west in search of a quicker trading route for spices from the Far East. His success inspired other explorers who first sought to trade with, then to conquer, the peoples they encountered. Thus, the modern world is dominated by European ideas largely because Europeans embraced trade and the changes it brought.

Governments and Trade

One misperception about international trade is that nations trade with one another. This suggests that governments plan what will be traded, the prices, and so on. In reality, international trade is simply exchanges made by firms and individuals for goods and services produced in foreign countries.

The role of governments in international trade has been controversial for hundreds of years. Two schools of thought, mercantilism and liberalism, have argued over whether governments should interfere with trade or allow it to operate without restrictions. Mercantilists believed that wealth formed the foundation of a powerful nation. Therefore, they asserted that nations should attempt to increase their wealth by promoting exports and limiting imports through subsidies to businesses, permitting monopolies, and other means.

Adam Smith, the founder of economics and champion of liberalism, made the case for free trade in his landmark work *The Wealth of Nations* (1776). He argued that

U.S. Shares of World Trade by Type: 1990 to 2003 (in percent)			
	1990	*2000*	*2003*
Exports			
Merchandise	11.4	12.3	9.7
Manufactures	12.2	14.0	10.8
Chemicals	13.3	14.3	11.5
Clothing	2.4	4.3	2.5
Iron and steel products	3.3	4.4	3.7
Machinery and transport equipment	15.1	16.1	NA
Automotive products	10.2	11.9	9.6
Office machines and telecom equipment	17.3	16.3	12.1
Textiles	4.6	7.0	6.4
Agricultural products	154.3	12.7	11.3
Commercial services	17.0	19.1	16.0
Transportation services	16.7	15.5	11.7
Travel services	19.0	21.6	16.0
Other commercial services	15.3	19.2	18.1
Imports			
Merchandise	14.6	18.8	16.8
Manufactures	5.4	20.0	17.8
Chemicals	7.7	12.7	12.7
Clothing	24.1	31.6	29.1
Iron and steel products	9.5	11.7	7.2
Machinery and transport equipment	17.5	21.6	NA
Automotive products	24.7	29.4	24.0
Office machines and telecom equipment	21.1	22.5	17.9
Textiles	6.2	9.4	10.3
Agricultural products	9.0	11.0	10.7
Commercial services	12.0	13.8	12.8
Transportation services	13.6	15.8	13.6
Travel services	14.6	15.5	12.0
Other commercial services	8.2	11.3	12.9
Balance			
Merchandise	−3.2	−6.5	−7.1
Manufactures	−3.2	−6.0	−7.0
Chemicals	5.6	1.6	−1.2
Clothing	−21.7	−27.3	−26.7
Iron and steel products	−6.2	−7.3	−3.5
Machinery and transport equipment	−2.4	−5.5	NA
Automotive products	−14.5	−17.5	−15.4
Office machines and telecom equipment	−3.8	−6.2	−5.8
Textiles	−1.4	−2.4	−3.9
Agricultural products	5.3	1.7	0.6
Commercial services	5.0	5.3	3.2
Transportation services	3.1	−0.3	−1.9
Travel services	4.4	6.1	4.0
Other commercial services	7.1	7.9	5.2

Note: NA = Not available. Balance equals exports minus imports.
Source: World Trade Organization, *International Trade Statistics.*

Countries with the Greatest and Least Growth in Trade 1989 to 1999

Lithuania 12.0
Poland 11.2
Czech Republic 9.9
Bulgaria -4.1
Albania 10.5
Iran -9.0

Estonia 13.0
Belarus -5.1
Slovak Republic 11.1
Moldova 14.6
Armenia -11.7
Azerbaijan 25.2

Mexico 10.3

The Gambia -3.0
Togo -3.5
Botswana -3.6

Congo, Dem. Rep. -4.9

China -6.5
Vietnam 22.3
Singapore -4.6

Greatest Growth
Least Growth

Source: World Bank, *2001 World Development Indicators.*

mercantilism was inefficient because it would increase the money supply and cause harmful inflation. Instead, Smith argued that the best way to improve wealth and living standards was through reducing trade restrictions. He proposed a policy called laissez-faire, or hands off, dictating minimal government interference with trade.

Modern economists generally agree that Smith is right: free trade does result in higher living standards and increases national wealth. One clear example is the United States, which has practiced relatively unrestricted trade within its borders and is now the wealthiest nation in the world.

Kinds of Trade Restrictions

Most nations practice mercantilist policies to some extent. Governments use several strategies to limit trade. The most common is tariffs, which are taxes on imports. Tariffs take one of two forms. The first is a revenue tariff, which is levied as a way for the government to make money. Revenue tariffs are similar to sales taxes and are usually only a small percentage of the

price of the item. The second is a protective tariff. A protective tariff is set to protect domestic industry from foreign competition and is much larger than revenue tariffs. Protective tariffs increase the price of foreign goods dramatically and make domestic goods more appealing.

Quotas are a set limit on imports of a foreign good. For example, in response to economic problems in the American auto industry during the 1980s, the U.S. government set a limit on the number of cars that could be imported from Japan. The result of a quota is to reduce the supply of the targeted good. This results in its price rising and a reduction in competition for domestic producers. The quotas on Japanese cars in the 1980s increased their prices and made it easier for American automobile producers to be profitable.

A third common trade restriction is an export subsidy, which occurs when a government makes payments to domestic producers of a good. The subsidy allows them to sell their products at lower prices and therefore be more competitive.

Several arguments have been made for nations imposing trade restrictions. One is the national defense argument. This posits that certain specific industries are crucial to the nation's security. Allowing them to go bankrupt would leave the nation vulnerable because foreign production might not be available during war or other hostilities. Another argument asserts that certain industries must be protected from cheap foreign labor. Wages in poor countries are much lower than those in developed nations. This allows low-wage producers to sell at lower prices. Producers in high-wage nations are threatened by the cheaper imports and often ask for trade restrictions.

A third justification is referred to as the infant industry argument. It asserts that nations that are beginning to industrialize cannot compete against more developed economies. Therefore, such countries must impose trade restrictions until their industries have had a chance to mature and can compete with foreign rivals.

Most economists reject these arguments for trade restrictions. Studies consistently show that quotas and tariffs are economically harmful because they allow domestic producers to increase prices. Businesses may benefit, but consumers lose.

Regardless of the justifications, trade restrictions often lead to international tensions. Reducing imports reduces the profits of foreign producers, often resulting in their firing workers or going out of business. These companies often appeal to their governments to act, asking for retaliation and sometimes leading to trade wars in which each side increases restrictions against the other.

Overseeing International Trade

Governments attempt to avoid such problems through negotiating international trading agreements. Such agreements come in several forms, including the creation of common markets and international institutions to govern trade. Common markets are agreements to remove trade barriers between member nations while imposing common tariffs on nonmember countries. This idea is

based on the success of the United States, which became the wealthiest nation in the world in part because it is a free-trade zone between all 50 states.

The two most important common markets are the European Union and the North American Free Trade Agreement. Member nations of the European Union have agreed to drop trade restrictions against each other, and many have adopted a common currency, the euro, as a means to promote economic growth. The North

Not everyone greets increased trade as a positive development. At a protest in Seoul, Korea, protesters burned a miniature model of a foreign car and packs of foreign cigarettes; the banner at the back reads, "Expel foreign luxury goods."

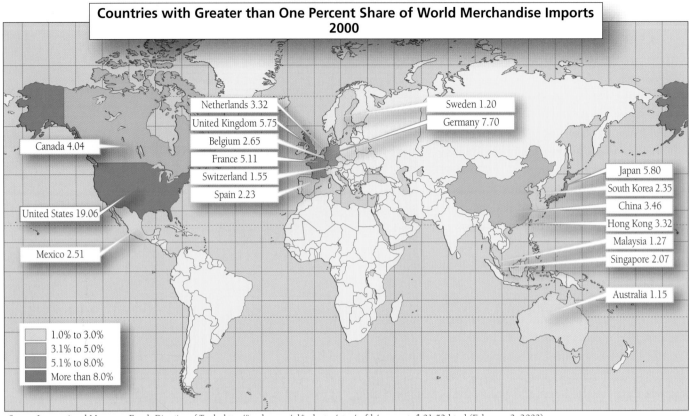

Countries with Greater than One Percent Share of World Merchandise Imports 2000

Netherlands 3.32
United Kingdom 5.75
Belgium 2.65
France 5.11
Switzerland 1.55
Spain 2.23

Sweden 1.20
Germany 7.70

Canada 4.04

United States 19.06

Mexico 2.51

Japan 5.80
South Korea 2.35
China 3.46
Hong Kong 3.32
Malaysia 1.27
Singapore 2.07

Australia 1.15

1.0% to 3.0%
3.1% to 5.0%
5.1% to 8.0%
More than 8.0%

Source: International Monetary Fund, *Direction of Trade,* http://ita.doc.gov/td/industry/otea/usfth/aggregate/h01t52.html (February 3, 2003).

American Free Trade Agreement (NAFTA) created a common market among Mexico, the United States, and Canada. It features the gradual elimination of trade barriers and contains other policies to make trade easier and more profitable, but it has not been without its controversies.

A second method for promoting international trade is the creation of international institutions. The most important of these are General Agreement on Tariffs and Trade (GATT) and the World Trade Organization (WTO). GATT was created after World War II as an attempt to promote peace through encouraging international trade. Member nations agreed to three conditions: treating all member nations equally on trade issues; reducing tariffs through continuing negotiations; and reducing quotas. One of the most important results of GATT was the creation of the WTO. Unlike GATT, which was an agreement, the WTO is a permanent institution located in Geneva, Switzerland. Its main functions are to analyze trading policies and resolve disputes among member nations.

Trade and Development

One of the most important benefits of international trade is the improvement in living standards that results as additional goods and services are made available at lower prices. Accordingly, nations with less-developed economies have focused on trade as a method to modernize their economies.

In general, nations that have successfully developed after World War II emphasized exporting as a means to create capital. Their basic strategy was to deliberately create a trade surplus by exporting more than they imported, then investing the extra capital in modernizing their industries. This approach was successful for Japan, Korea, and the nations of Europe as they recovered from the war. However, relatively few other nations have since modernized successfully. Economists agree that many developing nations generally lack political stability and access to education and often suffer from government corruption.

The World Bank and International Monetary Fund advise poor nations and

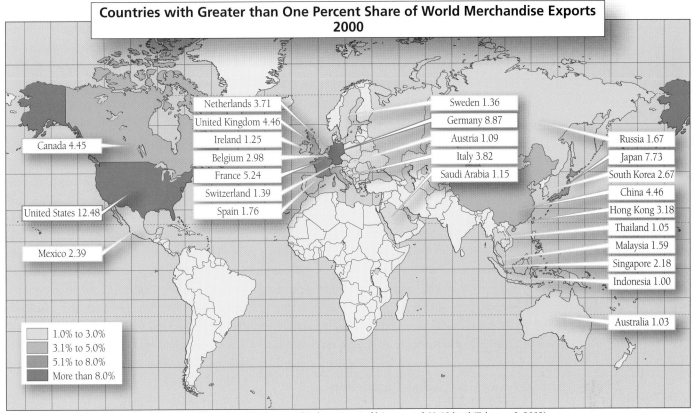

Countries with Greater than One Percent Share of World Merchandise Exports 2000

Netherlands 3.71
United Kingdom 4.46
Ireland 1.25
Belgium 2.98
France 5.24
Switzerland 1.39
Spain 1.76

Sweden 1.36
Germany 8.87
Austria 1.09
Italy 3.82
Saudi Arabia 1.15

Canada 4.45

United States 12.48

Mexico 2.39

Russia 1.67
Japan 7.73
South Korea 2.67
China 4.46
Hong Kong 3.18
Thailand 1.05
Malaysia 1.59
Singapore 2.18
Indonesia 1.00

Australia 1.03

1.0% to 3.0%
3.1% to 5.0%
5.1% to 8.0%
More than 8.0%

Source: International Monetary Fund, *Direction of Trade,* http://ita.doc.gov/td/industry/otea/usfth/aggregate/h01t53.html (February 3, 2003).

provide funding in the forms of loans and grants. These efforts have created much controversy. Some critics have argued that the reforms required by these institutions to qualify for funds are unrealistic for most clients. Others state that much of the money has been wasted by corrupt politicians. Although international trade has been increasing, its benefits have not.

The most critical current issue related to international trade is economic globalization—the process of the world becoming a single market for goods and services. Critics charge that the result is the dominance of large, mostly Western, international corporations that pursue profits at the cost of environmental and cultural degradation. However, these arguments lie outside the scope of economic theory.

Increased trade brings concrete benefits in lower prices and access to new goods and services. Moreover, with the failure of socialism and the collapse of the Soviet Union, no other economic models offer a viable alternative. The cost is that capitalism emphasizes the pursuit of profits without regard to the cultural identity or traditional values of societies. Therefore, conflicts will continue as nations attempt to balance the benefits of economic efficiency with the continual process of change that capitalism demands.

Further Reading
The Adam Smith Page
www.utdallas.edu/~harpham/adam.htm
Maintained by the University of Texas–Dallas, the Web site includes biographic and bibliographic information.
Global Trade Negotiations
www.cid.harvard.edu/cidtrade/index.html
A centralized resource on international trade.
International Monetary Fund
www.imf.org
Home page of the United Nations' International Monetary Fund has member information, evaluations, news, and resources.
World Bank
www.worldbank.org
Home page of the World Bank.
World Trade Organization
www.wto.org
Home page of the World Trade Organization.

—*David Long*

Labor Market

The labor market refers to buying and selling the services of workers. The market for labor is just as much a market as, say, the market for tomatoes or televisions. Of course, workers are not literally being bought and sold in a labor market, rather the services of the workers are being bought and sold. The labor market also differs from most other markets in other respects.

In 2007 approximately 146 million people were working in the United States, with another six million not holding a job but looking for work, adding up to a labor force equal to one-half of the U.S. population. Approximately two-thirds of all income in the United States goes to employees, with the rest going to the owners of capital (the other main factor of production) via dividends paid to shareholders, interest payments, or profits kept within a firm to be used for future projects.

This ratio has remained remarkably constant. The people who are not working or looking for work are a varied lot. They include students, retirees, homemakers, those who are institutionalized, hospitalized, or otherwise unable to work, and those who choose for whatever reason not to participate in the labor market.

Those who participate in the labor market are equally varied. In reality, markets for workers number in the millions. For instance, because of state certification requirements, those who want to buy and sell the services of a math teacher in Rutland, Vermont, have nothing to do with the market for math teachers in San Francisco, California. In addition, the market for math teachers in San Francisco is unrelated to the market for chefs in San Francisco, because buyers or sellers who participate in the market for teachers do not participate in the market for chefs.

Each market has many different buyers and sellers, each with different characteristics. For instance, the ability of computer consultants varies widely from consultant to consultant. Some who sell their services as a computer consultant can diagnose problems quickly and repair a computer in a short time, while others are better at long-term technology strategy and might struggle to find and solve problems on a specific machine or network. Likewise, some employers are very easy to work for, and offer their workers flexibility, freedom, and annual pay increases, while others seem to go out of their way to antagonize employees. Such differences do not exist in the market for televisions—Sanyo and Sony make TVs that are remarkably similar. The labor market exhibits a great amount of heterogeneity: no two workers, and no two jobs, are alike.

Economists spend a lot of time studying how firms and individuals behave in the labor market, and how government policies affect it. For instance, some economists have

Employment Status of U.S. Civilian Population 1960 to 2007

	Civilian labor force (in thousands)	Percent of population	Not in labor force (in thousands)	Percent of population
1960	69,628	59.4	47,617	40.6
1970	82,771	60.4	54,315	39.6
1980	106,940	63.8	60,806	36.2
1985	115,461	64.8	62,744	35.2
1989	123,869	66.5	62,523	33.5
1990	125,840	66.5	63,324	33.5
1991	126,346	66.2	64,578	33.8
1992	128,105	66.4	64,700	33.6
1993	129,200	66.3	65,638	33.7
1994	131,056	66.6	66,758	33.4
1995	132,304	66.6	66,280	33.4
1996	133,943	63.2	66,647	33.2
1997	136,297	67.1	66,837	32.9
1998	137,673	67.1	67,547	32.9
1999	139,368	67.1	68,385	32.9
2000	140,863	67.2	68,836	32.8
2001	143,734	66.8	71,351	33.2
2002	144,863	66.6	72,707	33.4
2003	146,510	66.2	74,685	33.8
2004	147,401	66.0	75,956	34.0
2005	149,320	66.0	76,762	34.0
2006	151,428	66.2	77,387	33.8
2007	153,124	66.0	78,743	34.0

Source: U.S. Bureau of the Census, *Statistical Abstract of the United States,* Bureau of the Census, Washington, D.C.

At a "pink-slip party" in Austin, Texas, unemployed high-tech workers meet with recruiters.

come to the conclusion that making poor people pay social security taxes on their income removes their incentive to leave welfare and find work. In response, the federal government created the earned income tax credit, which gave low-income employees a subsidy to cover their taxes.

Another example of government's role in the labor market can be found in the creation of the Occupational Safety and Health Administration (OSHA). OSHA's assigned role is to regulate the working conditions in the country and improve on-the-job safety. However, some economists have argued that well-informed employees already perform this service, by requiring higher wages to do more dangerous or more difficult work. Rather than pay higher wages, many firms instead attempt to reduce the risk or unpleasantness of the work environment, achieving the very result that OSHA was designed to bring about. Economists thus debate whether an entity like OSHA is necessary.

The United States has no single labor market. When someone speaks of the labor market, he is really considering an aggregation of many smaller markets that share common characteristics and are affected by the same outside forces, but in the end function independently of one another. For example,

during the economic recession that began in 2008, unemployment increased nationally, and the the financial services labor market experienced a particularly severe downturn, as many companies closed or cut back and others stopped hiring new workers. Were the math teacher and food-service markets mentioned above affected? Not necessarily, but possibly—a powerful force like an overall downturn of the economy affects every job market in one way or another. The labor market deserves our attention not only because nearly all of us will participate in the market at some time, but also because of its central role in the overall economy and its unique traits that distinguish it from all other markets.

Further Reading
International Labour Organisation
www.ilo.org
A UN agency promoting labor rights.
Labor and Worklife Program
www.law.harvard.edu/programs/lwp/index.html
This program from Harvard Law School includes research about labor markets worldwide.
Occupational Health and Safety Administration
www.ohsa.gov
The home page of this arm of the U.S. Department of Labor provides statistics, news, and publications.

—*J. Isaac Brannon*

Macroeconomics

Traditionally economics has been divided into two areas: microeconomics and macroeconomics. The two terms are derived from Greek: *micro,* meaning small, and *macro,* meaning large. Microeconomics is the study of individual consumers, workers, and producers functioning in specific markets. It explores how those individuals and markets function and generate (or do not generate) efficient outcomes for a society. Macroeconomics uses many of the same tools, but focuses on somewhat different problems. While microeconomics focuses on individuals, firms, and specific markets, macroeconomics considers the behavior of the economy as a whole—all individuals, firms, and markets together.

For example, the determination of stock and bond prices and the functioning of individual banks fall under the purview of microeconomics, while the effects of

Macroeconomics founder John Maynard Keynes in his study in 1940.

Goals of Federal Macroeconomic Policy

- Full employment
- Price stability
- Healthy rate of economic growth

changes in stock prices on investors' overall spending plans and the effects of changes in interest rates on total spending are macroeconomic issues. The trend in economic research and understanding has been increasingly to apply the principles of microeconomics to many of the issues studied in macroeconomics.

In 1936 John Maynard Keynes published his *General Theory of Employment, Interest, and Money*, which began the study of macroeconomics. At the time, the United States and much of the rest of the developed world were in the midst of the Great Depression, with unemployment rates above 25 percent and economic activity shrinking significantly. Keynes analyzed how consumption and investment spending are determined and how fluctuations in spending can cause unemployment and falling output.

Macroeconomics begins with the generation of data that describe conditions in the economy. For example, levels of employment and unemployment and the percentage of the labor force that is unemployed make up one set of indicators of conditions in a country's economy. Index numbers are used to measure average price levels; changes in those index numbers give us rates of inflation—the rise in the average or overall level of prices. A number of different indexes are used, depending upon the goods and services included in the index. The most well known is the Consumer Price Index, which calculates average price levels for a collection of goods and services (called a market basket) that a typical consumer might buy. Another measure of economic well-being is an estimate of total production in the entire economy during a year, the real gross domestic product (GDP). These measures indicate the status of unemployment, inflation, and growth, and help us understand how well the economy is doing in relation to its potential.

Perhaps the most important area of study within macroeconomics is economic growth. Growth in real GDP per person raises standards of living and explains differences in incomes among individuals in different countries. Considerable effort has been and continues to be devoted to identifying the importance of technological advances, the amount and skills of labor, and the quantity and kind of investment spending in determining the rate of growth in an economy over time.

Macroeconomics includes analysis of the determinants of spending in relation to an economy's capacity. GDP consists of a number of different kinds of spending: consumption, investment, government, and net export spending. Fluctuations in any of these kinds of spending cause total spending to change and can cause temporary periods of inflation or unemployment. Research has helped economists and politicians understand that a trade-off between

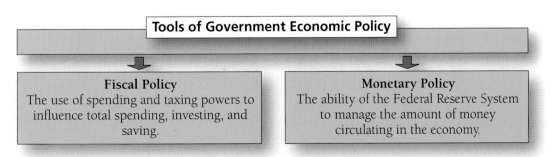

Tools of Government Economic Policy

Fiscal Policy
The use of spending and taxing powers to influence total spending, investing, and saving.

Monetary Policy
The ability of the Federal Reserve System to manage the amount of money circulating in the economy.

Three Primary Macroeconomic Indicators		
Indicator	**Function**	**Key Index**
• Unemployment rate	• Measures underutilization of labor in nation	• Unemployment rate
• Inflation rate	• Measures rate of change in average level of prices	• Consumer Price Index
• Growth rate in real national output	• Measures pace of what economy is producing in goods and services	• Gross domestic product

unemployment and inflation is sometimes necessary. At other times, they both can move in the same direction.

Macroeconomics and Politics

Government policies about how and whether to respond to periods of rising unemployment, rising inflation, or falling real GDP are important, often controversial, parts of macroeconomics, which affects both fiscal and monetary policy. Fiscal policy is the federal government's use of its spending and taxing powers to influence total spending, investing, and saving in the economy and thereby encourage economic growth, reduce inflationary pressures, or decrease unemployment. The effectiveness of those policies and how best to manage fiscal policy are important matters of research and debate. The roles of government deficits and surpluses, as well as changes in government debt, are also important macroeconomic issues.

Monetary policy is the ability of the Federal Reserve System to manage the amount of money that circulates in the economy. Changes in the money supply and in interest rates influence businesses in making decisions about spending on new plants and machinery, and individuals in purchasing automobiles, appliances, and homes. Changes in the money supply help determine total spending. Because of the importance of the availability of money and the level of interest rates, a field known as money and banking is included in macroeconomics. The study of the banking system, how loans are made, and even how money is created are key components of the field.

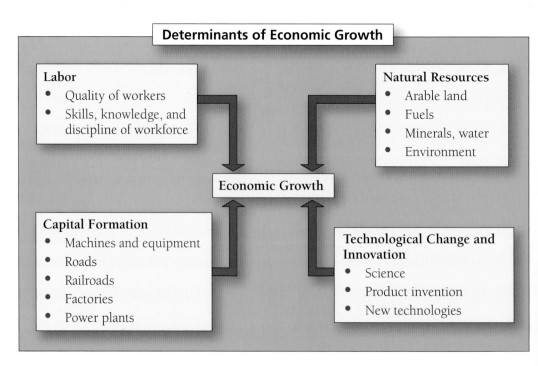

Determinants of Economic Growth

Labor
- Quality of workers
- Skills, knowledge, and discipline of workforce

Natural Resources
- Arable land
- Fuels
- Minerals, water
- Environment

Economic Growth

Capital Formation
- Machines and equipment
- Roads
- Railroads
- Factories
- Power plants

Technological Change and Innovation
- Science
- Product invention
- New technologies

Schools of Macroeconomics

School	Themes
• Classical	• Advocates laissez-faire. Government should allow the economy to function without interference.
• Keynesian	• Stresses primacy of fiscal policy in influencing output and employment. In times of depression the government should run deficits; in times of inflation it should have surpluses.
• Monetarist	• Emphasizes the importance of monetary policy to influence macroeconomic activity over the short term. Advocates fixed rate of growth of money supply through all economic conditions.
• New classical economist	• Predictable macroeconomic policies have no real effect on output or employment because people anticipate government actions and act to protect their interests, thereby negating government policy.

Macroeconomics is not without its controversies, particularly on the frontier of research and new understanding of how our overall economy works and how best to use policy. Although Keynes proposed using fiscal policy to bring the world out of the Depression, he also argued that monetary policy is ineffective in stimulating spending. Later, other researchers, led by Milton Friedman, provided evidence that not only is monetary policy effective, it is so effective that mistakes are often made. They found that mistakes in monetary policy are the cause of most periods of inflation, and they argued that fiscal policy is difficult to use and often ineffective.

Controversy exists over the implementation of macroeconomic policy. Because policies take time to influence output, employment, and inflation, effective use of policy requires the forecasting of future conditions and acting in the present to influence the future. However, forecasts tend to be imprecise, which leads to mistakes that may actually worsen conditions.

Macroeconomic issues and concerns are on the front pages of newspapers almost daily. The unemployment, inflation, and economic growth announcements receive significant attention as indicators of how well the economy is working. Political parties often debate spending and taxing policies that may improve conditions. The Federal Reserve policy committee meets approximately every six weeks to discuss economic conditions and whether monetary policy should be changed. Understanding how the overall economy works and how policy functions are important tools in developing an understanding of modern societies.

Further Research

Bank of Canada

www.bankofcanada.ca/en/monetary/monetary_main.html

The Bank of Canada sets monetary policy in Canada, published in the Monetary Policy Report.

Classic Works in Economics and Economic Thought

www.oswego.edu/~economic/oldbooks.htm

Web site of the State University of New York–Oswego's Economics Department lists and provides links to various transcribed and excerpted texts.

The Economists' Papers Projects

library.duke.edu/specialcollections/collections/economists

Duke University library's Web site featuring special collections and archival texts of 30 modern economists.

Federal Reserve Board

www.federalreserve.gov/monetarypolicy/default.htm

The Federal Reserve Board sets monetary policy in the United States; its committee reports are issued to the public.

History of Economic Thought Web Site

www.cepa.newschool.edu/het/index.htm

Home page of the New School University's repository of links and information on economic history and theory.

—Stephen Buckles

Management

Management is work done by supervisory individuals (managers) responsible for guiding formal organizations toward accomplishing their intended purposes. Management includes providing vision and leadership, establishing environments for effective work, analyzing and solving problems, making decisions, fostering communication, and ensuring accountability.

Modern concepts of management have evolved together with the large organizations that arose during and after the Industrial Revolution. Management is now a popular field of study in colleges and universities at both the undergraduate and graduate levels, and many people use the study of management to prepare themselves for eventual assignment to managerial responsibilities. Formal study is not an absolute requirement for becoming a manager—many managers have learned management on the job.

Managerial Functions
Just as there is no one way to manage, there is no comprehensive, precisely defined theory of management. Over the years, however, managers and people who study management have developed a substantial body of knowledge. Most management textbooks published since about 1950 have emphasized a functional approach based on the writings of management theory pioneers like Henri Fayol (1841–1925). Of the managerial functions Fayol identified, the ones most commonly referred to are planning, organizing, directing, and controlling.

Henri Fayol's basic management principles.

Planning is a decision-making process in which managers set goals and objectives (consistent with their organizational purpose), select courses of action, make action assignments, determine means of assessment, allocate resources (typically through budgets), and authorize actions to be taken. Plans can specify unique, one-time sets of actions to be undertaken for special purposes, for example, designing a new model of a car, or routine, recurring sets of actions directed to recurring requirements, for example, managing university students' registration for courses. Decisions made within the plan may rely on conceptual analysis and judgment as well as a variety of quantitative analytic methods. Computers and database systems are vital aids to today's managers in planning and making decisions.

Organizing is the process managers use to structure organizations, design jobs, and select and assign people to individual jobs and work groups. Two critical aspects of organizing are authority (the legal right to direct certain actions) and responsibility (a moral requirement to do certain things and behave in certain ways). Authority, responsibility, and channels of communication are necessary for empowering and coordinating the actions of an organization's members. Managers delegate authority (empower others to act) and determine the means of communication to be used in the activity in question.

Managers, however, never surrender responsibility. A manager who empowers a subordinate to take certain actions or perform specific tasks is considered to be responsible for the outcome even if the subordinate fails to perform. Delegation is important because, especially in large organizations, managers must rely on others to shoulder part of the workload. As organizations grow, the need for increased delegation fosters the creation of additional levels of managerial responsibility, often clustered according to organizational functions like production, marketing, and finance. The model for complex, formal

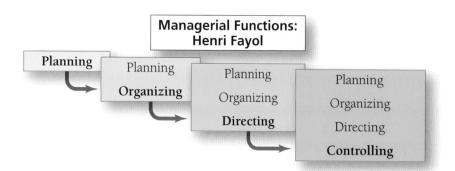

Managerial Functions:
Henri Fayol

Planning

Planning
Organizing

Planning
Organizing
Directing

Planning
Organizing
Directing
Controlling

Good management often involves leading and inspiring workers rather than simply asserting authority over them.

organizations was described by the German sociologist Max Weber (1864–1920).

Directing is the process managers use to mobilize, engage, and guide the actions of members of the organization. Directing depends upon four essential components: power (the ability to compel compliance), leadership (inspiring and guiding), motiva-

tion (arousing the ability and desire to be productive), and communication (effectively exchanging meaning). Many modern textbooks speak of leading rather than directing in describing this managerial function.

Managers possess several kinds of power. Depending upon the circumstances, they can give orders, reward performance, punish failure or improper behavior, and employ expertise and social skills to guide and encourage their subordinates. Power alone is usually not sufficient for managers to be successful in supervising others.

Communication is the process of exchanging meaning between two or more individuals. Managers must become skilled at receiving and interpreting messages, at creating and transmitting messages, and at providing or seeking feedback. Managers must therefore write well and speak effectively to a wide variety of audiences, but that is not sufficient. Managers must also learn to solicit information, invite the input of others, share information effectively, be able to shape information from raw data, and master modern communication technologies. The directing function is rendered impotent without effective communication.

Controlling is how managers evaluate the effectiveness of plans and decisions made. It requires setting standards for performance, measuring performance against standards,

determining whether significant deviations exist, and, if they do, making corrections as necessary to revise the plan of action, adjust performance standards, or correct performance failures. Controlling is the partner of planning. Just as planning is useless without a means to evaluate effectiveness, controlling in the absence of planning is equally inappropriate.

Managerial Functions Applied

The managerial functions described above provide a general, abstract picture of management. Managers do not work in the abstract, however; they manage real people and projects, and they are responsible for the effectiveness and efficiency of actual organizations. In planning, organizing, directing, and controlling, they apply themselves to a range of business activities including:

- *Marketing*—defining the customer and the customer's needs, selecting products and services, designing advertising and promotional material, determining

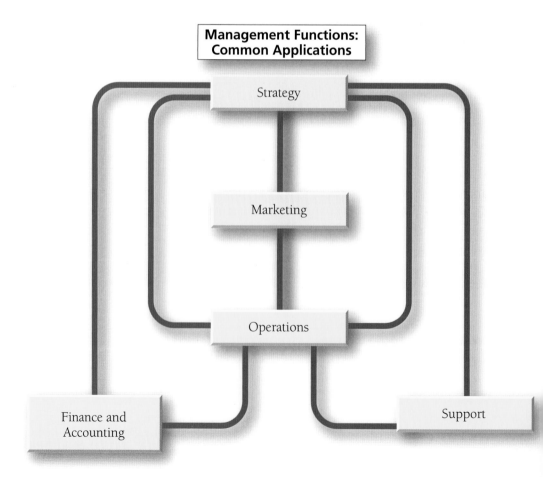

Finance and accounting, and support functions like office and facilities management, form a foundation for the more product- and sales-oriented management functions including operations, marketing, and strategy.

prices, and providing products and services to customers in convenient ways or places.

- *Operations*—designing and operating the processes and systems by which firms create and make products and services available to marketers.
- *Finance and Accounting*—acquiring and managing financial resources including invested, borrowed, and operating cash.
- *Support*—managing necessary auxiliary actions, including human resources, physical plant, insurance, legal, security, and information processing.
- *Strategy*—supervising all organizational functions and functional managers simultaneously to ensure that all the pieces fit together.

In small, entrepreneurial businesses, the owners perform all of these actions. Because of the risks and challenges involved in juggling so many activities, the world of the entrepreneurial owner–manager looks especially exciting and attractive to some people and daunting to others.

Every generation of managers must contend with important social, political, legal, economic, and ecological realities specific to their era. Managers in the twenty-first century must pay attention to issues of equal opportunity and diversity, frequent litigation, a network of laws and regulations, differing perspectives rooted in the age and experience levels of employees and customers, electronic commerce and the Internet, global competition, economic cycles, rapid technological change, pollution control, worker safety and quality of work life, and recurring challenges to ethical and socially responsive behavior.

Individuals can learn about management by reviewing relevant scholarship and by observing managers in action. They should assess themselves, too, determining whether they want to be accountable for the behavior and performance of others in organizational settings. They should want to influence others for work-related better-

Leadership and Motivation

Leadership is a much used but much misunderstood term. Leadership and management are not synonymous, although many people use the term *leadership* when referring to organizational managers as organizational leaders. Leadership is the ability to gain the willing compliance of others in doing what the leader wants done. Leadership ability is closely related to the personality of the leader, but being an effective leader is not the result of following a set of given procedures. Obviously, developing leadership skills is very useful to a manager. Power can force others to comply, but leadership can inspire others to go beyond mere compliance.

Motivation is the force that drives individuals to act and sustains them in their action. In general, job performance depends upon a worker's ability (mental and physical capacity), skill (ability refined and improved through practice, learning, and experience), and motivation (the desire to perform to a certain level). Although ability and skill are obviously important, low levels of motivation can adversely affect able, skilled workers, decreasing their productivity. Managers, therefore, must strive to increase workers' motivation.

Unfortunately, as is the case with leadership, no simple, fail-safe procedure is available to address motivational shortfalls. Some theories emphasize human needs (what motivates people?), some focus on the process of motivation (how does motivation occur and how do individuals choose to be motivated?), and some emphasize behavior reinforcement. Probably most important for managers to understand is that a worker's motivation is "owned by" the worker, not by the manager, and must be addressed by leadership skills, not merely authority.

ment. They should develop skills in mastering the functions of management and managerial roles through actual managerial experience. Potential managers must be able to deal with complexity, handle multiple and often divergent demands, and not be dismayed by unpredictable human behavior. In a competitive business climate, managers must also grasp the relationship between product or service quality and business success.

Further Reading

Communications, Principles of Management, and Organizational Behavior

www.csupomona.edu/~wcweber

Course materials from a California professor.

The Economist

www.economist.com/business/management

Writings on management and business education from the respected magazine.

MIT Open Courseware

ocw.mit.edu/OcwWeb/web/courses/courses/index. htm#SloanSchoolofManagement

MIT OpenCourseWare is a free publication of MIT course materials, including courses from the Sloan School of Management.

—*John Washbush*

Microeconomics

Economics is the study of how societies use scarce resources to produce goods and services and how societies distribute those goods and services. Resources—land, natural resources, and labor, as well as machines, tools, and buildings—are scarce because people want more goods and services than there are resources and abilities to produce them. Given this fundamental condition of scarcity, economic efficiency becomes an important concept. A society is economically efficient if resources are being used to make itself as well off as possible. These two concepts, scarcity and economic efficiency, underlie all of economics.

Economics has been traditionally divided into two areas: microeconomics and macroeconomics, with *micro* meaning "small" and *macro* meaning "large." Macroeconomics considers the behavior of the economy as a whole; microeconomics is the study of individual consumers, workers, and producers functioning in specific markets. Microeconomics topics include: the behavior and decision making of individuals and businesses; how their decisions affect themselves and society; how the kind of market that is formed affects prices, profits, and production within the market; how the incomes are determined; and the appropriate economic role of government in influencing the use and distribution of resources. Microeconomics explores how those markets function and generate or do not generate efficient outcomes for society. It also considers where markets can fail and suggests solutions to improve market efficiency and fairness.

For example, the number of personal computers a company and an industry produce is a microeconomic issue, but the total amount of output of all goods and services in the economy is a macroeconomic issue. Pricing of personal computers is a microeconomic topic, while the rate of change in prices of all goods and services produced in an economy is a macroeconomic topic. Changes in unemployment rates of high school dropouts fall within the confines of microeconomics, but the causes of changes in unemployment rates for all individuals are analyzed by macroeconomics. Although microeconomists may study large markets and large companies, they are still individual markets and companies.

Adam Smith, whose *The Wealth of Nations* was published in 1776, is the founder of microeconomics. He examined how the prices of goods, services, and resources are determined, and the strengths and weaknesses of different markets. In particular, he discussed the effectiveness of markets where individuals pursue their own self-interests. He also explored how markets can fail to be efficient.

The Basics of Microeconomics

Microeconomics begins with an examination of the fundamental economic problem—scarcity. Given scarcity, choices must be made about how resources are used. Microeconomics focuses on the consequences of the choices made by individuals, firms, and governments, and evaluates those decisions for their effectiveness in making consumers, workers, businesses, and all of society as well off as possible.

The microeconomic concept of comparative advantage explains why individuals and businesses benefit when they specialize and trade. If individuals specialize instead of trying to produce everything they need or want, two consequences result. Total production in a society increases, but each individual becomes dependent upon others. To consume goods and services other

Microeconomic Methodology

- Recognizing cost of decisions
- Thinking on the margin
- Comparing costs and benefits
- Examining effects of incentives
- Evaluating efficiency of markets and governments

than the ones they produce, the specializing individuals must trade for the other goods and services they want. That trade takes place in markets. How those markets work is at the heart of microeconomics. Microeconomic principles are the same for local, national, and international markets and in markets for goods and services, labor, land, financial instruments, currencies, and other resources.

The analysis of markets begins with an exploration of supply and demand. Economists study how firms make decisions about how to set prices and quantities to produce. The supply side of any market depends upon costs and availability of productive resources and the technology that is available to firms. Once these are determined, firms can decide whether and how much to produce based on their costs compared with the prices they can receive in the market. Consumers, in efforts to maximize their own well-being, decide whether to purchase goods and services. The decision of how much to buy depends upon the price of the goods and services as well as the consumers' tastes, incomes, and available alternatives. The market outcome—price and quantity of the good or service—results from the interaction of both sides of the market.

Whether a market is economically efficienct is highly dependent upon market structure. Much of microeconomics concentrates on development of one model that describes a perfectly competitive market, a market with many buyers and sellers, much knowledge about prices and qualities, a homogeneous product, and relatively easy entry and exit by firms into the market. The opposite extreme is a market with only a single producer—a monopoly. The outcomes, in terms of economic efficiency, of those two markets are quite different. The perfectly competitive market most often provides an economically efficient use of resources, while the monopolist will charge a higher price, produce less, and not have the incentives to hold costs to the lowest possible levels.

Between these two extremes is oligopoly, market models with only a few producers,

and monopolistic competition, markets with many producers, each one producing its own unique product. A useful tool, game theory, is often used to analyze firm behavior in these markets. Game theory is used to explore how individuals and firms act when their actions affect other individuals and firms, which, in turn, can cause a reaction by the other individuals and firms, which affects the outcome of the initial decision. Tools like game theory, along with cost-benefit comparisons, are important practical parts of research and decision making.

Another aspect of microeconomics is the study of factors of production (labor, land, natural resources, and capital) and resulting income distribution. Through application of the appropriate supply and demand tools, the process of determining prices, and therefore incomes, can be understood.

Microeconomics and Politics

Out of the analysis of markets comes an economic role for government. Although portions of the economic role of government fall within macroeconomics, a substantial economic role for government exists that is directly connected with individual, firm, and market behavior. If mar-

Determinants of Supply and Demand

Supply	Demand
• Technology changes • Cost factors of production • Prices of other goods • Taxes • Expectations about prices • Number of sellers	• Price of the good • Desire for the good • Income of consumer • Availability and price of other goods • Expectations for income and prices

Example of Gains from Specialization

	Unspecialized production capability (units)		Specialized production capability (units)	
	Product 1	Product 2	Product 1	Product 2
Company A	50	40	76	30
Company B	19	34	13	58
Total production	69	74	89	88

kets are not competitive, for example, they are not efficient. Thus, one economic role for government is antitrust regulation aimed at encouraging competition, holding prices down, promoting innovation, and providing economically efficient results. In other cases, competition may not work perfectly because consumers do not have the ability to understand the product fully—prescription drugs, for example—or where a monopoly can actually produce goods or services at lower costs than competitive firms, as with many public utilities. Here, the role of the government is regulatory.

Governments also produce some goods and services that a market cannot produce in economically efficient amounts. Often businesses in such markets would earn a profit only with great difficulty. Therefore, the amount produced would be less than economically efficient. National defense is one example. A private firm may not be able to set a price because, if national defense already exists, everyone is protected whether they choose to be or not. Many individuals would not buy the services, and businesses would have to contract, and perhaps disappear.

In other cases, governments produce or subsidize goods that offer external benefits.

External benefits are those received by individuals other than those directly involved in producing or consuming the good. Public education and research and development in basic science are good examples. In these cases, buyers will tend to not purchase an amount sufficient for economic efficiency because they do not pay attention to the extra benefits received by others (or are unaware of those benefits). Only through government subsidies or production can an economy come closer to an efficient level of production in these areas.

Governments may find it necessary to tax or regulate how other goods are produced when external costs exist. The best example is when significant pollution is created in a production process. External costs (the pollution itself) are borne by individuals other than those directly involved in producing or consuming the good or service. As a result, too much of the good or service is produced, as businesses and consumers do not pay all of the costs. Only if government adopts regulations or taxes business will businesses adjust their production levels or methods.

All of these government activities must be paid for, and market economies normally use taxes to do so. The effect of the taxation

The Free Electron Laser, developed at the Los Alamos National Laboratory in New Mexico; relying on the private sector to provide national defense and pure scientific research can be economically inefficient, so governments frequently provide subsidies.

on incentives to work, produce, and save—and therefore on economic efficiency—is another part of microeconomics.

Incentives are a fundamental part of economics not only for firms and individuals, but for governments also. Government decision making often involves incentives different from those of consumers and producers. As a result, governments can make decisions that are not economically efficient, a situation characterized by microeconomics as a government failure. Microeconomics includes analysis of the effects of government policy decisions that influence markets by setting minimum prices (for wages, as an example) and maximum prices (rent controls in some

areas) in markets for labor and tariffs and quotas on imported goods and services.

Microeconomics is a method of thinking about issues. Microeconomics, with its methodology of recognizing the costs of decisions, thinking on the margin, comparing costs and benefits, examining the effects of incentives, and evaluating economic efficiency of markets and governments, is the core of all of economic analysis. Microeconomics focuses those tools and methods on how societies organize their resources to produce and then distribute goods and services.

The waste produced by this petrochemical plant is an external cost that is borne by the society as a whole, rather than the chemical producers themselves. Governments regulate waste-producers in order to force them to keep these external costs under control.

Themes in Microeconomics

- Behavior and decision making of individuals and businesses
- How decisions of businesses and individuals affect themselves and society
- How the kinds of markets formed affect prices, profits, and production within the market
- How incomes are determined
- The appropriate economic role of government in influencing the distribution of resources

Further Research
The Adam Smith Page
www.utdallas.edu/~harpham/adam.htm
Maintained by faculty at the University of Texas–Dallas, the Web site includes biographic and bibliographic information.
American Economics Association—Resources for Economists on the Internet
www.aeaweb.org/RFE
Site sponsored by the American Economics Association and compiled by faculty at SUNY–Oswego has links to Web-based resources on economics.
A Glossary of Political Economy Terms
www.auburn.edu/~johnspm/gloss
A useful glossary, compiled by a professor at Auburn University.

—*Stephen Buckles*

Monetary Policy

Monetary policy controls a country's money supply, which in turn determines how much an economy can expand or contract. By manipulating the total amount of money available, a country's central bank (in the United States, the Federal Reserve) can influence monetary and credit conditions to promote employment, economic growth, and low inflation. The Federal Reserve (also known as the Fed) typically seeks to control the supply of money and the level of key short-term interest rates as means of implementing its policy.

The Objectives of Monetary Policy

The U.S. government is required by the Employment Act of 1946 (which was later reaffirmed in the Full Employment and Balanced Growth Act of 1978) to aim for high employment and stable prices. As a government agency, the Fed must pursue a policy course consistent with achieving these objectives. As evidence suggests that monetary and credit conditions are statistically linked to employment, output, and inflation, the Fed must control money growth or the level of short-term interest rates to meet these objectives.

Observers sometimes disagree about the extent to which monetary policy objectives are consistent with one another. For example, some researchers argue that efforts to lower unemployment and stimulate growth of output can be inflationary, thereby interfering with Fed attempts to deliver price stability. Still others argue that monetary policies that prove inflationary can lead to inefficiencies in the use of economic resources and can cause output to grow less rapidly in the long run. Uncertainties about the economic effects of monetary policy can markedly complicate the decisions of the Fed.

Evidence suggests that in the short run (probably as long as 18 months), monetary policy can and does influence employment and output growth. To see how this might happen, imagine that the Fed has decided to make credit more plentiful by expanding the supply of money. Increased availability of credit tends to make the cost of obtaining credit (the interest rate) decline. These lower rates make financing the construction of new homes less costly; businesses can also invest in new equipment, machinery, and structures at a lower cost. Consumers also find purchasing new motor vehicles, furniture, and appliances less expensive. These greater expenditures lead to more output. With more spending on new output, firms must hire more people to achieve production goals. Thus, employment increases and unemployment falls when the Fed increases credit availability. The opposite can be expected to occur when the Fed tightens monetary policy.

The Tools of Monetary Policy

The Fed uses three tools to influence the money supply and short-term interest rates: open market operations, discount policy, and reserve requirements. Before these tools can be explained, understanding the role of bank reserves in the implementation of monetary policy is crucial. Banks hold reserves as cash in vaults or as deposits that they maintain at a regional Federal Reserve bank. When reserves in the banking system become more plentiful, the federal funds rate decreases; the federal funds rate is the rate that banks charge one another for the overnight use of reserves (this interest rate is unfortunately named as there is really nothing "federal" about this market-determined rate). The federal funds rate has played a key role in Federal Reserve monetary policy operations in recent years. When newspapers report that the Fed has lowered interest rates, what they are actually reporting is that the central bank's target for the federal funds rate has

Tools of Monetary Policy	
Required reserves	Portion of funds a depository institution is required to maintain as vault cash or on deposit with a Federal Reserve Bank
Discount rate	Rate of interest the Fed charges on loans to member banks
Open market operations	The Fed's purchase and sale of previously issued U.S. government securities

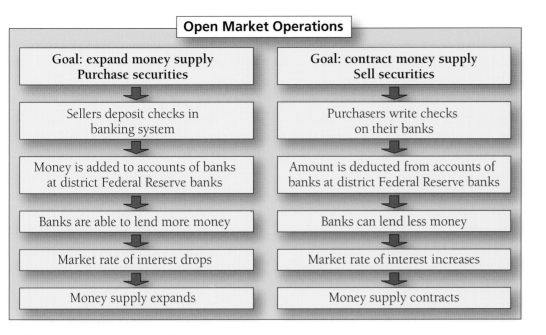

Open Market Operations

Goal: expand money supply — Purchase securities	Goal: contract money supply — Sell securities
Sellers deposit checks in banking system	Purchasers write checks on their banks
Money is added to accounts of banks at district Federal Reserve banks	Amount is deducted from accounts of banks at district Federal Reserve banks
Banks are able to lend more money	Banks can lend less money
Market rate of interest drops	Market rate of interest increases
Money supply expands	Money supply contracts

been lowered. When the Fed wishes to ease monetary policy, it uses its tools to increase the supply of reserves in the banking system and reduce the cost of obtaining these reserves (which is the federal funds rate). A reduction in bank reserves has the opposite effect, causing the federal funds rate to rise.

Open market operations are the buying and selling of existing government securities by the Federal Reserve. When the Fed arranges to purchase existing Treasury bonds, notes, or bills, the supply of reserves in the banking system increases and the federal funds rate falls. Open market operations are easily the most frequently used tool of monetary policy. For example, if the Fed wishes to pursue a more expansionary monetary policy, it will lower the federal funds rate target and take a more aggressive approach to the buying of existing government securities. This will naturally cause the supply of reserves in the banking system to rise and will likely stimulate short-term economic activity. Again, this also works in the reverse: determination to tighten the availability of credit will typically involve the selling of existing government securities (otherwise known as open market sales), leading to a reduction in the supply of bank reserves and an increase in the federal funds rate.

The second most frequently used monetary policy tool is discount policy. The discount rate is the rate the Fed charges banks that borrow reserves (in the form of discount loans) from Federal Reserve banks. This rate is set by Fed policy makers and is not market determined. Banks are typically discouraged from using discount loans because the Fed expects banks to use market sources of funds to meet their short-term need for reserves. Banks that "overuse" the discount facility are likely to attract Fed scrutiny. Perhaps the most important function of discount policy is that it allows the Fed to provide liquidity to financial markets during times of heightened

Aggregate Reserves of Depository Institutions 2008
(in million dollars)

Date	Total	Required
January	42,150	40,509
February	42,826	41,100
March	44,299	42,321
April	43,561	41,716
May	44,128	42,115
June	43,364	41,089
July	43,330	41,353
August	44,559	42,568
September	102,784	42,733
October	315,516	47,612
November	609,937	50,883
December	820,942	53,530

Source: Federal Reserve Board, "Aggregate Reserves of Depository Institutions and the Monetary Base," http://www.federalreserve.gov/release/h3/

uncertainty. For example, in the days following the September 11, 2001, terrorist attacks, the Fed supplied $45 billion of discount loans to the banking system. This represented an almost unimaginable 76,000 percent increase in the level of discount loans from the ordinary level of $59 million in the weeks before the terrorist attacks. When the banking system has no other immediate source of funds, the Federal Reserve can use its discount facilities to make funds available to banks. This allows the Fed to promote economic stability by serving as lender of last resort.

The Fed is usually very reluctant to change reserve requirements, the third tool of monetary policy. Banks do not keep all the money deposited with them immediately on hand; much of the money saved in banks is, in fact, invested or lent out to others.

However, all U.S. depository institutions are required to maintain a fraction of depositors' checking accounts in the form of reserves. This fraction was one-tenth, or 10 percent, at the beginning of 2009. This fraction, known as the required reserve ratio, had not been raised since April 1992. To illustrate how reserve requirements are tabulated, imagine a bank in which customers hold $100 million in checking accounts. This bank is required to hold 10 percent of this, or $10 million, in the form of vault cash or as deposits at its regional Federal Reserve bank.

A decision by the Fed to raise the required reserve ratio would require banks to hold more of their assets in the form of reserves. As banks cannot make loans out of their required reserves, such requirement would effectively cause the money supply to decline. Conversely, a reduction in the required reserve ratio would lead to an increase in the money supply. Because a change in reserve requirements can have a very powerful effect on monetary and credit conditions, the Fed rarely uses this tool for ordinary day-to-day monetary policy operations.

Further Research
Bank of Canada
www.bankofcanada.ca/en/monetary/monetary_
    main.html
Federal Reserve Board
www.federalreserve.gov/monetarypolicy/default.
    htm.
These agencies set monetary policy.

—*Rich MacDonald*

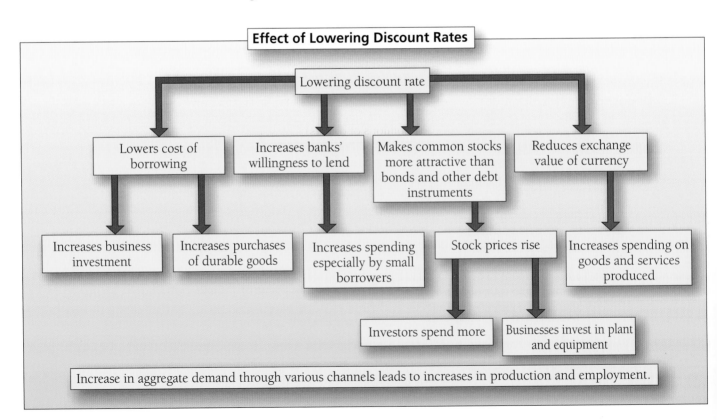

Multinational Corporation

Although some companies sell their products in a strictly local or national market, many companies have tried to increase sales by selling in foreign markets. Companies may simply export the same goods they sell at home to other countries, or they might license their brand names to foreign manufacturers who build and sell goods in their home country. True multinational corporations take matters a step further, establishing some combination of actual manufacturing, distribution, and sales, or other operations in more than one country.

By the start of the twenty-first century, most large companies were multinationals—a development that has not been viewed with equanimity in all quarters. Becoming a multinational can open new markets to firms, and the increased sales and flexibility that come with having operations abroad can help them cut costs and improve efficiency. Multinational companies, also called transnational companies, are also to a certain degree outside the control of any one national government. The large numbers of multinationals complicate efforts to shape the economy of any one country.

The Evolution of Multinationals

Multinational companies have a long history in the United States. Pioneering U.S. firms like Singer Sewing Machine Company established manufacturing plants abroad as early as the 1860s. During the 1920s, more and more U.S. companies established operations in foreign countries, especially in Europe.

The severe economic recession of the 1930s and the war that followed forced U.S. companies into retreat. When World War II ended in the mid-1940s, U.S.–backed agreements were put into place that encouraged international commerce, which was seen as vital to the rebuilding of Europe. Once again, U.S. companies led the charge abroad; by the late 1960s most multinationals were based in the United States.

The 1970s and 1980s saw a substantial increase in the presence of European and Japanese multinationals, which made serious inroads into the U.S. market and posed a significant competitive threat to U.S. firms. This sparked something of a nationalist backlash in the United States, with U.S. companies emphasizing their American roots. Most contemporary multinationals describe themselves as "global"

U.S. Multinational Companies 2006
(in billions of dollars)

Industry	U.S. parents				Foreign affiliates			
	Total assets	Sales	Employment (1,000)	Total employee compensation	Total assets	Sales	Employment (1,000)	Total employee compensation
All industries	18,520	8,273	21,748	1,365	11,540	4,731	10,935	426
Mining	326	108	179	17	518	243	191	9
Manufacturing	4,868	3,847	7,546	572	1,851	2,168	1,132	5
Wholesale trade	722	873	1,061	66	642	1,072	793	46
Finance, insurance, and real estate	8,754	959	1,148	145	4,334	328	338	32
Services	243	344	1,158	98	232	141	604	41
Other industries	1,451	1,440	8,564	295	3,532	NA	3,302	4

Note: A U.S. parent is a U.S. person or business enterprise that owns or controls 10 percent or more of the voting securities of an incorporated foreign business enterprise, or an equivalent interest in an unincorporated foreign business enterprise. A foreign affiliate is a foreign business enterprise owned or controlled by the U.S. parent company.
Source: U.S. Bureau of Economic Analysis.

companies, suggesting that their home country is the world at large.

Managing a Multinational

Building and running a multinational corporation are complicated. Language barriers must be surmounted and cultural differences must be negotiated. In some cases, countries have laws limiting foreign ownership of or foreign investment in businesses, although these can usually be circumvented by establishing independently owned subsidiaries. Having operations in many different countries exposes a company to different political or currency crises that can pose a threat to business. During times of nationalist feeling, for example, multinational corporations are sometimes singled out as symbols of foreign domination.

Even without crises, multinational corporations face certain challenges, largely because of the difficulty of controlling operations that occur half a world away. A company based in San Diego, for example, must make a greater effort to monitor a factory located in Munich, Germany, than one located down the street.

One approach is to have a very centralized chain of command—the San Diego company can send executives from San Diego to run the Munich plant, using the same techniques and strategies used in San Diego. Most successful multinationals have learned to fragment control, recruiting people in Munich to run the factory there, for example. In many cases a company tries to ensure that operations abroad fit into a worldwide business plan, but some multinationals exercise very little control over their foreign operations, demanding only that profits be kept high.

Decentralizing control is sometimes referred to as being a "global" strategy (rather than an "international" one) and is considered preferable for a number of reasons. Local management of a multinational's operations usually helps defuse potential cultural tensions—local managers know the language and customs, they know how the

Revenues: Nations vs. Multinationals		
	Revenue *(in billion U.S. dollars)*	Year
United States	1,722.0	1998
Germany	977.0	1998
Italy	559.0	1998
United Kingdom	487.7	1998
Japan	407.0	1998
France	222.0	1998
Netherlands	163.0	1998
General Motors	161.3	1999
DaimlerChrysler	154.6	1999
Brazil	151.0	1998
Ford Motor	144.4	1999
Wal-Mart	139.2	1999
Canada	121.3	1998
Spain	113.0	1998
Sweden	109.4	1998
Mitsui	109.4	1999
Itochu	108.7	1999
Mitsubishi	107.1	1999
Exxon	100.7	1999
General Electric	100.5	1999
South Korea	100.4	1998
Toyota Motor	99.7	1999
Royal Dutch/Shell Group	93.7	1999
Marubeni	93.6	1999
Australia	90.70	1998
Sumitomo	89.0	1999
AXA	78.7	1999

Source: 1999 Fortune Global 500 *Fortune;* and *CIA World Factbook,* 1999, http://www.globalpolicy.org/socecon/tncs/tncstat2.htm (February 21, 2003).

labor market is structured, and they have a better idea of what regulators care about.

In addition, a multinational will more easily recruit talented people abroad if they know that their nationality will not pose a barrier to promotion. In contrast, if all the high-ranking executives at the Munich plant are from San Diego, any ambitious and enterprising German at the plant will go work somewhere else where the prospects for promotion are better.

An even more decentralized business model is common among industries like apparel—for example, the Oregon-based shoemaker Nike. With apparel like athletic

The production line at a Nike factory in Chi Chu, Vietnam. Nike was Vietnam's largest private employer.

shoes, what makes a particular brand desirable tends to be the design of the shoes, not how they are manufactured. So Nike relies on independent contractors in other countries to make its shoes. This way of doing business requires Nike to work closely with its contractors to make sure quality remains high. In recent years, however, the company has attracted substantial criticism from labor activists who charge that Nike and other multinationals do not adequately monitor their contract manufacturers to ensure that they do not abuse workers.

Multinational corporations can also choose to take an international outlook regarding the products they sell, adjusting the presentation depending on the particular market.

Local tastes vary, and a company generally will sell more products if they are tailored to fit local preferences. Such customizing is a common practice among makers of foods, as food traditions vary widely from place to place and most people feel very strongly about what they are willing to eat. India has a large Hindu population that does not eat beef, so McDonald's restaurants there offer sandwiches made with lamb. The Domino's Pizza restaurant chain has had great success in Japan by offering pizza topped with mayonnaise. Customization does not work as well with, for example, heavy industrial machinery, but for restaurant companies, it costs roughly the same to top a pizza with mayonnaise as it does to top it with tomato sauce, so whatever sells pizza is used.

Pros and Cons of Multinationals

Multinationals also tend to locate different kinds of business operations in different countries because each country may offer a different advantage. Many European pharmaceutical companies, for example, have research and development facilities in the United States to take advantage of the well-educated workforce.

This practice gets far more controversial, however, when it involves manufacturing jobs that, unlike the production of pharmaceuticals, do not require highly specialized skills. No special education is required to perform tasks like putting together parts on an assembly line, thus multinational corporations tend to seek the cheapest workers. Multinationals, accordingly, locate factories in poorer countries where wages tend to be very low and environmental and labor regulations lax. The United States has lost much of its manufacturing base since the 1950s because many companies have discovered that they can save a great deal of money by

locating factories in countries with lower prevailing wages.

The mobility of multinationals is a source of great concern to many labor and environmental activists, who worry that multinationals will trigger a "race to the bottom" among countries. As multinationals often seek out cheap labor, labor activists worry that countries that want to attract and keep multinationals will try to keep labor costs down by banning labor unions and allowing unsafe work conditions. Environmental activists worry that multinationals will force countries to weaken environmental regulations because such regulations add to the cost of doing business.

Multinationals have benefited from government behavior that protected business interests. Some notorious incidents occurred in Nigeria throughout the 1990s, when numerous protests against pollution caused by the oil operations of Royal Dutch Shell were viciously put down by the Nigerian government, which in 1995 executed several

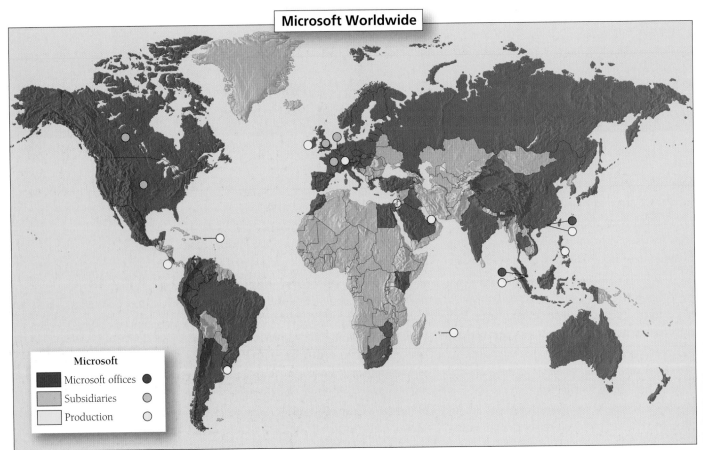

Microsoft Worldwide

Microsoft
- Microsoft offices ●
- Subsidiaries ◐
- Production ○

Source: http://www.microsoft.com/worldwide/ (February 21, 2003); and Transnational Corporations Observatory, http://www.transnationale.org/anglais/fiches/45.htm (February 21, 2003).

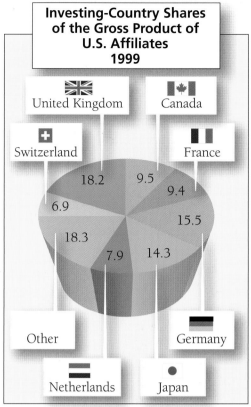

Investing-Country Shares of the Gross Product of U.S. Affiliates 1999

United Kingdom

Canada

Switzerland

France

18.2

9.5

9.4

6.9

15.5

18.3

7.9

14.3

Other

Germany

Netherlands

Japan

Note: Does not include banks.

Source: William J. Zeile, "U.S. Affiliates of Foreign Companies: Operations in 1999," *Survey of Current Business,* August 2001, http://www.bea.gov/bea/ARTICLES/2001/08august/0801FDIUS.pdf (February 24, 2003).

Ogoni activists including Ken Saro-Wiwa. Saro-Wiwa's family sued Shell in 2001, charging that the company was responsible for the executions, an allegation the company denies. One weapon activists have is publicity; indeed, the publicity surrounding Saro-Wiwa's death was enough to force Shell to pull out of Ogoni territory.

National economic policies are complicated by the fact that multinationals may build something in one country, sell it in a second country, and be based in a third country. For example, a country might want to lower unemployment, so its trade ministers might negotiate favorable trade pacts with other countries, hoping that boosting exports will lead to more hiring at home. The multinationals headquartered in the country do sell more abroad—but unemployment in the country remains the same because the multinationals' manufacturing operations are also located abroad. In addition, a multinational corporation that strongly objects to a country's economic policies can just move elsewhere—a

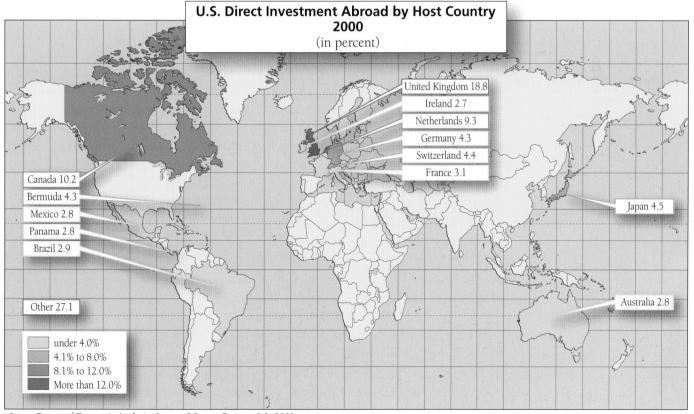

U.S. Direct Investment Abroad by Host Country 2000
(in percent)

United Kingdom 18.8

Ireland 2.7

Netherlands 9.3

Germany 4.3

Switzerland 4.4

France 3.1

Japan 4.5

Canada 10.2

Bermuda 4.3

Mexico 2.8

Panama 2.8

Brazil 2.9

Australia 2.8

Other 27.1

under 4.0%
4.1% to 8.0%
8.1% to 12.0%
More than 12.0%

Source: Bureau of Economic Analysis, *Survey of Current Business,* July 2001, http://www.bea/gov/bea/ARTICLES/2002/07july/0701dip.pdf (February 21, 2003).

Multinational Corporation 145

Hundreds of women of the Ijaw tribe occupied a ChevronTexaco oil export terminal at Escravos, Nigeria, for more than a week. The women demanded jobs for their relatives as well as electricity, water, and other amenities. Here, the women escort a Chevron worker who had been held hostage, as they allow him to leave.

significant problem for countries like Sweden with high corporate taxes.

However, the rise of multinational corporations has also created many benefits. For all the debate about conditions in factories in poorer countries, for the people who live there, factory work generally represents a major step up from subsistence farming, for example. Countries like Mexico and South Korea that once attracted the lowest-paying factory work can leverage the experience and education their workers get in industry to move up the ladder and attract skilled and better-paying manufacturing jobs.

In addition, the breaking down of national barriers has led to the spread of new and innovative ways of doing business. In the 1980s, for example, Japanese multinationals made serious inroads into U.S. markets. Although the competitive pressure was hardly welcomed, U.S. companies began to study their Japanese counterparts and discovered many clearly superior management and manufacturing practices. These practices were eventually adopted by many U.S. companies, making them stronger in the long run. For many supporters of multinationals the flow of ideas across cultural barriers is a major appeal of multinational corporations—they seem to embody the benefits of global cooperation, as opposed to nationalist hostility and competition. Especially in Europe, trade across borders has explicitly been promoted as a way to promote peace and stability. The rise of multinational corporations has hardly led to the end of war, but multinationals have, for good or ill, made the world a smaller, more interconnected place.

Further Reading

Global Issues—Corporations

www.globalissues.org/issue/50/corporations

A Web site looking at globalization has a section on multinational corporations.

Multinational Corporations

www.econ.iastate.edu/classes/econ355/choi/mnc.htm

A comprehensive treatment of the subject from the Iowa State University economics department.

Transnational Corporations

www.globalpolicy.org/socecon/tncs/indxmain.htm

Data on multinationals from the Global Policy Forum, an independent watchdog.

—*Mary Sisson*

Nonprofit Entities

In the United States, a large number of different kinds of organizations are identified as worthy of tax exemption, ranging from business associations to charitable organizations and social clubs. The Salvation Army, the Republican Party, the American Heart Association, the Guggenheim Museum, and the United Automobile Workers of America are all nonprofit entities or nonprofits. Although nonprofit entities vary widely in their goals and functions, they share five critical features. To be considered part of the nonprofit sector, an entity must be an institution with some meaningful structure and permanence; not part of the apparatus of government; self-governing; non-profit-distributing (not permitted to distribute profits to its owners or directors, but rather required to reinvest them in the objectives of the organization); and supportive of some public purpose.

All organizations that meet these five criteria are formally part of the nonprofit sector in the United States; however, an important distinction exists between two broad categories of these organizations. The first category is primarily member-serving organizations. Although serving some public purpose, these organizations address the interests, needs, and desires of the members of the organization, for example, social clubs, business associations, labor unions, mutual benefit organizations of various kinds, and political parties.

The second group of nonprofit organizations is primarily devoted to public service. These organizations exist exclusively to serve the needs of a broader public audience, for example, a variety of charitable, grant-making foundations; religious congregations; and a wide range of educational, scientific, charitable, and related service organizations providing everything from nursing home care to environmental advocacy.

That nonprofit organizations play such an important role in American life is, in part, a historical accident. In most areas, American society came into existence before the government did. Frontier settlers had to find ways to provide needed public services for themselves. They did so by joining voluntarily with their neighbors to create schools and build public facilities.

America's first nonprofit corporation was Harvard College; it was founded with public subsidies in 1636. As urbanization and industrialization accelerated in the nineteenth-century United States, the limited capability of purely voluntary responses to human needs became increasingly apparent. Demand grew for government assistance and authority to address serious poverty, ill-health, inadequate housing, recurrent unemployment, and related problems. Indeed, nonprofit organizations were often in the forefront of pressing for increased government involvement.

Perhaps because of this long history, under U.S. law the formation of nonprofit organizations is considered a basic right that

Number of National Nonprofit Associations by Type 1980 to 2000			
	1980	1990	2000
Trade, business, commercial	3,118	3,918	3,880
Agriculture	677	940	1,102
Legal, governmental, public admin., military	529	792	789
Scientific, engineering, technology	1,039	1,417	1,301
Educational	12,376	1,291	1,296
Cultural	(^{1})	1,886	1,785
Social welfare	994	1,705	1,828
Health, medical	1,413	2,227	2,494
Public affairs	1,068	2,249	1,775
Fraternal, foreign interest, nationality, ethnic	435	573	524
Religious	797	1,172	1,122
Veteran, hereditary, patriotic	208	462	834
Hobby, avocational	910	1,475	1,329
Athletic sports	504	840	716
Labor unions	235	253	231
Chambers of Commerce[2]	105	168	142
Greek and non-Greek letter societies	318	340	295
Fan clubs	NA	581	380
Total	14,726	22,289	21,840

NA = Not available. [1]Data for cultural associations included with educational associations.
[2]National and binational.
Source: Gale Group, Farmington Hills, Mich., compiled from *Encyclopedia of Associations*, annual.

Every night St. John's Hospice in Philadelphia serves hundreds of meals to the homeless. Religious and charitable institutions are key parts of the nonprofit sector.

does not depend on government approval. This is particularly true of religious congregations, which are specifically exempted from obligation to register and to file the annual reporting form that registered organizations are required to submit.

Nonprofits and the Economy

The distinction between member-serving and public-serving organizations is far from perfect. Nevertheless, it is sufficiently important to find formal reflection in U.S. law. Public-serving organizations fall into a special legal category—Section 501(c)(3) of the U.S. tax code—that makes them eligible not only for exemption from federal income taxation and most state and local taxation, but also for receipt of tax-deductible gifts from individuals and corporations. Individuals and corporations can deduct the value of gifts given to these organizations from their own income in computing their tax liabilities. For its tax implications alone, this public-benefit portion of the American nonprofit sector is a major economic force.

The approximately 850,000 organizations that comprise this core, public-benefit service portion of the American nonprofit sector had total expenses in 2004 of approximately $1 trillion. If this set of organizations were a nation, its economy would thus be larger than all but 10 national economies—larger than the economies of Australia, India, Mexico, and the Netherlands. What is more, if the volunteer labor that these organizations utilize is added in, the total economic activity these organizations represent would rise by another $80 to $100 billion.

Not all portions of this nonprofit sector contribute equally to the sector's economic scale, of course. By far the largest component is the health subsector. Health organizations alone account for more than 60 percent of all nonprofit expenditures. Higher education is second with about 20 percent. The remaining 20 percent of nonprofit expenditures are split among all the other kinds of organizations—social services, arts and culture, international assistance, advocacy, community development, and many more.

Further Research
National Center for Charitable Statistics
nccs.urban.org
The NCCS is is the national repository of data on the nonprofit sector in the United States. Its Web site provides broad information on the sector.

—John Riddle

Opportunity Cost

In thinking about cost, we ordinarily think about money: How much will a pair of new shoes or some new tires for the car cost? The concept of opportunity cost, however, refers to the cost of choices, not things, and the cost of choices is not always measured in money.

What does it mean to talk about the cost of choices? The answer is implicit in a favorite adage among economists, "There is no such thing as a free lunch." If you were to object to the adage, mentioning a time when you enjoyed a lunch that someone else paid for, an economist would reply that you could have spent your lunchtime doing something else—washing your car, perhaps, or caring for a younger sibling. In choosing to go to lunch instead, you gave up that alternative use of your time, and the value of that alternative was the real cost—the opportunity cost—of the decision to enjoy the lunch. It was not free, even though someone else paid for it.

Economists maintain that all choices entail an opportunity cost. Consider the broader context in which decisions must be made—a context marked by scarcity. We experience scarcity when we want more than we can have. Material things, including housing, food, and clothing are only the first items on our wish list. People also want education, health care, protection from criminals, clean air, good roads, mass transit systems, opportunities to travel, time to pursue hobbies, confidence in a secure retirement, and so forth. The list is endless. Society is limited, however, in what it can produce. Productive resources (labor resources, capital resources, and natural resources) are finite. As a result, choices must be made among alternative possibilities. Scarcity and choice are a universal condition applying to all societies.

For example, a teenager wakes up on Saturday morning and considers three choices:

1. Roll over and go back to sleep.

All decisions bring with them some cost: for example, choosing to go to lunch means sacrificing time that might have been spent doing something else.

Sometimes people choose risky activities—football, for example—because they accept the risk of injury as a cost of the activity.

might have been earned in the job market, for example, or the value of leisure time—young people give up when they choose to stay in school. A high school education is never free, even when the dollar costs are distributed among taxpayers, rather than being paid directly by students or their parents.

The analysis of opportunity cost can yield surprising insights. How much is a human life worth? It is priceless, some might say. Does this mean all people would sacrifice anything to preserve their lives? Maybe not. In many instances people risk their lives because safe, healthful living seems to come at too high a price. Many people smoke, despite the advice of the surgeon general. Some play football or climb mountains or drive too fast, despite the risk of accident and injury. Some work at jobs that put them at risk of death. They choose the satisfaction they derive from risky behavior over safer or healthier options (choosing to be a nonsmoker, for example, or choosing to be an accountant rather than a firefighter). Sometimes these choices seem foolish, sometimes they seem heroic; either way, the concept of opportunity cost enables us to describe and explain these choices.

Opportunity cost is fundamental to business decisions. Business leaders constantly seek to measure opportunity costs and keep them as low as possible. Consider a grocery store with 25 rows of shelving for displaying groceries. What is the opportunity cost of offering one brand of potato chips or coffee over another? What is the opportunity cost of removing a shelf to make space for a new advertising display? If the owner borrows money to expand her parking lot, will she have to drop plans for adding a floral department? In each instance of choice, which opportunity cost can the business best afford to pay? Such decisions, taken together, are critical to business success.

2. Get up and help his parents with the grocery shopping.
3. Get up and jog two miles before breakfast.

He is looking at scarcity; he has more alternatives than time, and he will have to choose. If he decides to jog, he gives up the opportunity to sleep late. If he decides to sleep, he gives up jogging, at least for now. The opportunity cost for either choice is the value of what he did not choose.

Consider the cost of a high school education. Most young people attend public high schools; it may seem that a high school education is free because no tuition is charged. An economist would say that the real cost, the opportunity cost, of going to high school is the next-best alternative—income that

Further Research
NetMBA
www.netmba.com/econ/micro/cost/opportunity
A clear and concise discussion of the concept of opportunity cost in economics as well as its applications.

—*Mark C. Schug*

Organisation for Economic Co-operation and Development

The Organisation for Economic Co-operation and Development (OECD) is an international organization of nations formed in 1961 to pursue global economic growth and stability. The organization is a forum for members to discuss, develop, and refine social and economic policies. The OECD is one of the most important international organizations in the world, with an annual budget greater than $480 million. The 30 member countries of this Paris-based organization produce about 60 percent of the world's goods and services. Some critics charge that the OECD is primarily designed to benefit wealthy nations, and that its decisions reflect the agendas chiefly of the European Union, Japan, and the United States.

The origins of the OECD date to 1947. In that year, European and North American nations formed the Organisation for European Economic Co-operation to administer American and Canadian aid for the reconstruction of postwar Europe under the Marshall Plan.

The OECD is one of the world's largest and most reliable sources of comparable statistical, economic, and social data. Exchanges between member states flow from information and analysis provided by the Secretariat. Various departments of the Secretariat collect data, monitor trends, analyze, and forecast developments, while others research social changes or evolving patterns in trade, environment, agriculture, technology, and taxation.

Member countries compare experiences, seek answers to common problems, and work to coordinate domestic and international policies to help members and nonmembers function and prosper in an increasingly globalized world. Their exchanges may lead to agreements to act in a formal way—for example, by establishing legally

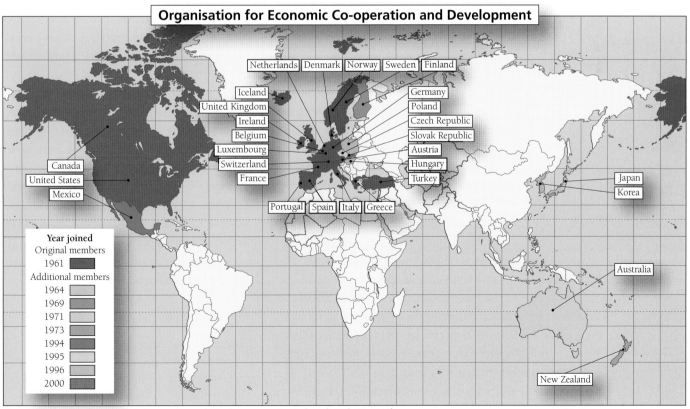

Source: Organization for Economic Cooperation and Development, www.oecd.org (March 12, 2003).

Police and protesters clash during an anti-OECD demonstration in Bologna, Italy.

ideas and review progress in defined areas of policy, including, trade, money laundering by international terrorists, food safety, poverty, electronic commerce, science and technology, development assistance, and financial markets. Approximately 40,000 senior officials from national administrations attend OECD committee meetings each year to inquire, review, and contribute to work undertaken by the Secretariat.

The OECD has two official languages: English and French. Staff members are citizens of OECD countries but serve as international civil servants with no national affiliation during their posting. The OECD is funded by member nations. Contributions to the OECD annual budget are based on a formula tied to the size of a nation's economy. The United States provides 25 percent of the OECD budget; Japan is the second largest contributor.

The emergence of globalization has seen the scope of the OECD's work move from examination of each policy area within member states to analysis of how various policy areas interact between OECD countries and beyond OECD areas. The OECD has a cooperative relationship with about 70 nations. In May 2007, the OECD countries invited Chile, Estonia, Israel, Russia, and Slovenia to discussions regarding membership and offered enhanced engagement with the possibility of membership to Brazil, China, India, Indonesia, and South Africa. In such areas as eliminating harmful tax practices and combating terrorist and other illicit use of global financial systems, the OECD is working with nonmember economies to find solutions acceptable to all. The Centre for Co-operation with Non-Members (CCNM), established in 1998, is the focal point for these relationships. It manages multicountry programs of OECD work, as well as individual country programs with major nonmember economies.

binding agreements to prohibit bribery or codes to assure the free flow of capital across borders. The OECD is also known for "soft law"—nonbinding instruments on difficult issues like guidelines for multinational enterprises. Beyond agreements, the discussions at the OECD make for better-informed work within member countries' own governments in public policy and help clarify the effect of national policies on the international community.

Member countries meet and exchange information in committees. They assemble representatives from member countries, either from national administrations or permanent delegations to the OECD in Paris. The most powerful decision-making body is the Council, which is composed of one representative from each member nation and a representative from the European Union. The Council meets regularly at the OECD ambassador level and once per year at the ministerial level. Due to the perception that the OECD is a tool of wealthy nations, these meetings sometimes inspire anti-globalization protests similar to those sometimes seen at meetings of the World Trade Organization.

Specialized committees (of which there are approximately 200) meet to advance

Further Research
Organisation for Economic Co-operation and Development
www.oecd.org
The Web site of the OECD.

—Carl Pacini

Organization of Petroleum Exporting Countries

The Organization of Petroleum Exporting Countries (OPEC) is an association of 12 developing nations with revenues heavily dependent on the production and export of oil. OPEC, commonly referred to as a cartel, coordinates its members' crude oil production policies in an attempt to maintain stable world oil prices and a steady supply of oil to consuming countries. Since the 1960s OPEC has been a major influence on the world market for oil.

Representatives from five nations—Iran, Iraq, Kuwait, Saudi Arabia, and Venezuela—founded OPEC on September 14, 1960, at a meeting in Baghdad, Iraq. In the late 1950s the petroleum industries of these countries were controlled by U.S. and Western European oil companies, who extracted crude oil and sold it on the world market at posted prices—prices kept artificially low by the oil companies. The host governments then received payments, known as royalties, based on the revenues of these companies. Production quantities varied widely from one year to the next, as the oil firms operated independently of one another.

In 1959 and 1960 oil production outpaced demand, prompting several of the oil companies to reduce their posted prices, thus reducing their profits and the royalties paid to the host governments. OPEC was formed in response to this unexpected drop in national income. In addition to forming the cartel, some of the countries also nationalized the oil producing and refining equipment of the petroleum companies through buying out the Western firms or negotiating better terms,

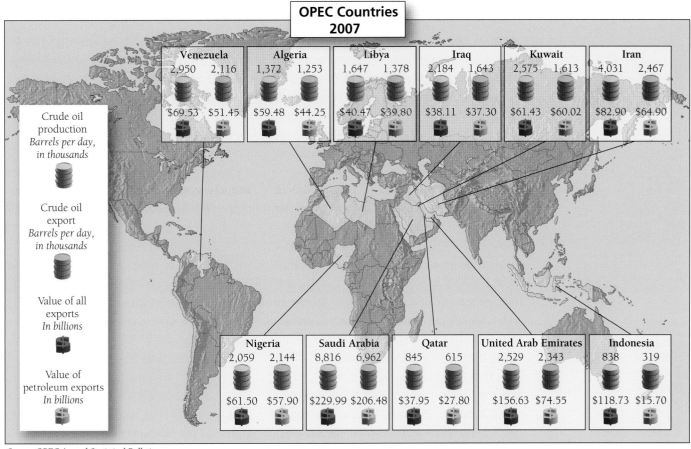

Source: OPEC Annual Statistical Bulletin.

OPEC leaders during a summit in 2000: (left to right) the emir of Qatar, Sheik Hamad ben Khalifa ben Hamed Al Thani; Iraqi vice president Taha Yassin Ramadan; Iranian president Seyyed Mohammad Khatami; Libyan colonel Mustafa Al-Kharroubi; and Algerian president Abdelaziz Bouteflika.

which gave greater pricing control to the local governments.

Membership in OPEC, according to the organization's charter, is open to any country with substantial exports of crude oil and interests similar to those of the member countries. Any application for membership must be approved by at least three-quarters of the current members, including all five of the founding members. Current members of OPEC are: Algeria, Angola, Ecuador, Iran, Iraq, Kuwait, Libya, Nigeria, Qatar, Saudi Arabia, the United Arab Emirates, and Venezuela. Indonesia joined in 1964 but suspended its membership in January 2009.

OPEC members collectively produce about 41 percent of the world's crude oil and about 15 percent of the natural gas. However, OPEC's exports of oil represent nearly 55 percent of the oil traded internationally. Although OPEC does not control the oil market, the cartel can significantly affect it—in 2001 its members collectively possessed more than 77 percent of the world's known crude oil reserves.

The supreme authority of OPEC is its conference, which consists of delegations from member countries and which meets at least twice a year—in March and September—and in extra sessions if necessary. At the conference, members analyze and discuss the current conditions in the world oil markets and make forecasts; they also make decisions about OPEC's future oil production policies. All decisions must be approved unanimously, and each country gets one vote in all matters.

OPEC's main tool for affecting the oil market is the setting of production ceilings for each member nation. These ceilings limit the amount of oil that the country can produce in a given time. Although formally every member retains absolute power of final decision about its production policies, once the ceilings are allocated at a conference and all delegations unanimously agree to the allocation, the countries must comply with the organization's decision.

OPEC has had mixed success in achieving its goals of oil price stabilization and support for steady demand. In the 1960s production expanded as demand grew at a very fast rate, so the cartel had little control over the supply of oil. However, by the 1970s the demand began to outgrow the supply of oil in non-OPEC countries. In 1973 OPEC raised its oil prices, triggering what eventually became known as the first oil crisis. The effect of higher oil prices was exacerbated by the Arab–Israeli war of

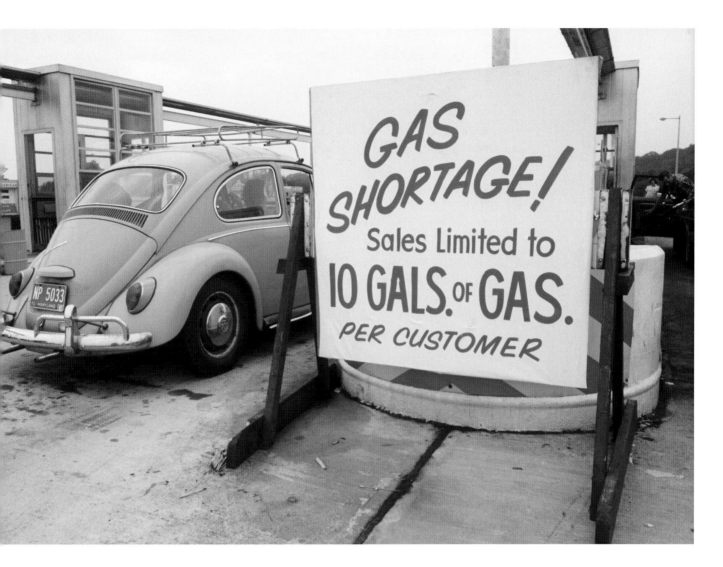

1973, during which the Arab members of OPEC stopped their exports of oil to countries supporting Israel. As a result, oil prices in the United States and Western Europe rose sharply and supplies became scarce.

During the 1980s OPEC set production ceilings for its members several times. However, several cartel nations ignored their limits. Consequently, supply of oil exceeded demand, and in 1983 OPEC was forced to cut its prices for the first time.

In the early 1990s oil prices remained relatively stable, with the exception of a brief price increase following Iraq's invasion of Kuwait in 1990. In 2008, volatility in crude oil prices roiled world economies. Prices rose from the low $80s per barrel in January 2008 to above $145 in July, before falling to around $30 at the end of the year. As a result, demand fell for the first time since the early 1980s. In 2009,

OPEC focused on returning a level of stability to both oil and gas markets.

In the late twentieth century OPEC's influence on the oil market was limited by the actions of other oil-producing countries, notably Russia. Russian oil companies pursue their own goals, which often involve expanding output; this undermines output contraction by the cartel. Since the 1990s Russian oil exports have been significant enough to affect OPEC's control of oil markets. As the cartel does not have perfect control of the world's supply of oil, its future success will depend on its ability to coordinate its actions with those of other oil-rich nations.

Further Research
Organization of Petroleum Exporting Countries
www.opec.org

—*Mikhail Kouliavtsev*

A gas station in Connecticut during the mid-1970s oil crisis.

Price Controls

Price controls are restrictions on prices used by governments to alter market outcomes. These controls typically take the form of a maximum price (a price ceiling) or minimum price (a price floor) in an individual market, although general price controls have sometimes been imposed in many markets simultaneously to try to contain inflation. Prices in markets are typically driven by supply and demand and have an important role in the efficient allocation of resources. However, markets do not necessarily lead to an equitable outcome for everyone, prompting policy makers to attempt to improve the market outcome.

The specific justification for intervention in a market may come from any of a number of sources, for example, concern for the welfare of the poor, the incomes of certain producers, or national security. Proponents of a higher minimum wage, for example, commonly cite the need for the working poor to earn enough to support themselves and their families. Milk price supports are typically justified by the need to generate adequate incomes for dairy farmers. Proponents of price protection for U.S. steel producers frequently stress the importance of a healthy domestic steel industry for national security. Economists are often skeptical about the social desirability of price controls and sometimes suggest that political expediency overrides genuine concerns about economic welfare when such controls are implemented.

A price ceiling is a legal maximum price that can be charged for a good or service. Governments impose price ceilings in markets where the prevailing price is perceived to be too high. Because the ceiling forces prices to be lower than they would be in an unregulated market, demand often outstrips supply: the quantity of the good or service supplied is often reduced while the quantity of the good or service demanded rises, usually resulting in a shortage. The intended beneficiary of the price ceiling is the consumer or purchaser of the good or service. Although some consumers may enjoy the benefit of the lower price, others may be left unable to secure the good or service at all. Black markets and other methods of evading the ceiling tend to develop as buyers look for ways to overcome the shortage and sellers accommodate them.

Rent control is a common example of a price ceiling. In some urban areas, rent control has been implemented to keep apartments affordable for people with limited incomes. Landlords may not be permitted to raise rent at all, or may be permitted to adjust rents only in small increments to stay even with the general inflation rate. Renters who are able to get rent-controlled apartments may benefit; however, price controls often have unintended negative consequences. In addition to a shortage of apartments and long waiting lists, some apartments may be taken off the market altogether as landlords convert buildings into condominiums or other uses not governed by the controls. Meanwhile, those buildings that remain apartments may be poorly maintained. With less rent coming

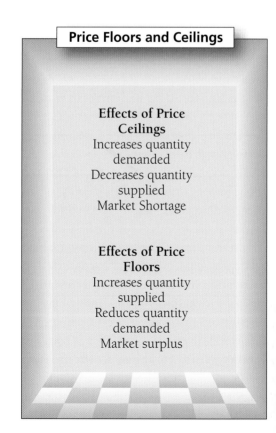

Price Floors and Ceilings

Effects of Price Ceilings
Increases quantity demanded
Decreases quantity supplied
Market Shortage

Effects of Price Floors
Increases quantity supplied
Reduces quantity demanded
Market surplus

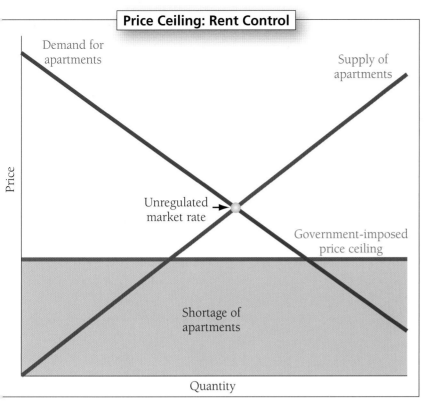

Price Ceiling: Rent Control

Demand for apartments

Supply of apartments

Price

Unregulated market rate

Government-imposed price ceiling

Shortage of apartments

Quantity

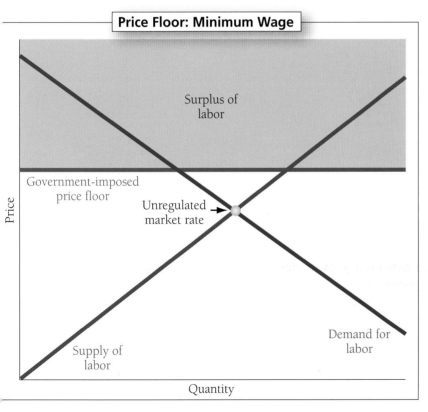

Price Floor: Minimum Wage

Surplus of labor

Government-imposed price floor

Price

Unregulated market rate

Supply of labor

Demand for labor

Quantity

These charts show the theoretical basis for price ceilings and floors. Normally, market rates are established by the intersection of supply and demand. However, when the unregulated market rate is deemed to be too high (in the case of rent) or too low (in the case of wages), a government-imposed price can be established to lower rents or raise wages. The imposition of a price ceiling sometimes creates a shortage (as in the case of apartments); the imposition of a price floor sometimes creates a surplus (as in the case of labor).

in and a long line of prospective renters looking for apartments, building owners have less incentive to service and renovate buildings than they would in an unregulated competitive market.

A price floor is a legal minimum price that can be charged in a market. Governments impose price floors when the market price is perceived to be too low. The intention is to benefit producers or sellers of goods and services, although once again unintended negative consequences are possible. A price floor set above the market equilibrium typically creates a surplus of goods or services on the market as suppliers wish to sell more at the higher price while users cut back in response to the higher price. The resulting market glut either finds its way illegally to buyers at discount rates, moves to other unregulated markets, or leaves sellers with undesired inventories. In some cases—agricultural markets, for example—the government has supported the price floor by buying the surplus on the market.

A common price floor is a minimum wage law. In the United States, the federal government has imposed some form of a minimum wage since the Great Depression. Intended to help low-income workers, the minimum wage has undoubtedly boosted the pay of millions of workers since its implementation. Although the real purchasing power of the minimum wage has generally fallen since the 1960s, many workers still enjoy a higher wage than they might in the absence of the law.

However, the minimum wage can have undesirable consequences. Although some disagreement has been voiced, many economists believe that when the minimum wage is increased significantly above the wage level that would otherwise prevail in the labor market, the unemployment rate will rise because of the surplus of labor. Among the groups likely to be hurt by a rise in unemployment are teenagers and others just entering the labor force and those already most economically disadvantaged. Here economists point to the trade-offs inherent in policy making: raising the income of those

Apartment buildings on New York City's Upper West Side. New York State's rent regulation laws cover about 1.2 million apartments, housing more than 2.5 million tenants, mostly in the New York City area.

minimum-wage workers who keep their jobs may come not only at the expense of the businesses that pay them, but also at the expense of those who lose jobs or cannot find jobs at all.

When a government imposes a price control in a single market, such as the labor market via the minimum wage, it is trying to create an outcome that is more equitable or otherwise desirable than the market would generate independently. Sometimes governments intervene to regulate prices in markets that are not competitive in the first place. For example, many public utilities are "natural monopolies"—industries in which having a single producer is more efficient than having many competing producers—and are typically regulated by the government.

In other areas, governments do not control prices directly but do exert influence on prices through taxes and subsidies. A subsidy, for example, will encourage increased production and lower prices to consumers, thus having an effect similar to a price ceiling without creating a shortage. However, the subsidy is costly to the government and therefore to taxpayers. In international trade, taxes on imports are called tariffs, and these tariffs can be used to protect domestic producers from foreign competition by increasing the price above what the market would otherwise dictate. For example, the steel industry in the United States has faced vigorous competition from foreign producers and has sought protection, citing its importance to national security and the need to keep workers employed.

Price controls are sometimes used by governments not to alter individual market outcomes but to control prices across the board. Such price controls are particularly enticing to policy makers during periods of high inflation. Nations worldwide have used price controls to limit inflation. In the United States, wage and price controls were attempted during the early 1970s by the Nixon administration. The root cause of inflation, however, is almost always the government's failure to control the growth of the money supply; thus price controls have typically had limited success. Although sometimes useful in the short run to slow the inflation rate, price controls can cause severe misallocations of resources and can stifle economic activity.

Prices play a critical role in a market economy because they indicate to consumers and producers where to allocate resources. High prices tell producers that a good or service is highly valued and that they should produce more, while also suggesting to consumers that a good or service is scarce and precious. However, high prices for necessities can hurt consumers,

Price Controls and the California Electricity Crisis

During the summer of 2000, price controls became a hot topic as California experienced a crisis in its electricity markets. On several occasions, demand for electrical power exceeded supply, resulting in sporadic blackouts in parts of the state. Along with power shortages, the wholesale price of electricity became extraordinarily volatile, peaking at hundreds of times its typical precrisis level.

With consumers at the retail level largely protected by a legal price ceiling, some utilities were caught in the middle, paying exorbitant prices to power generators but unable to recoup these costs from their customers. The state's largest utility, Pacific Gas and Electric (PG&E), declared bankruptcy. The state then spent billions of dollars purchasing electricity in the aftermath of the PG&E bankruptcy and the near-collapse of other utilities.

Supporters and critics of price controls interpret the crisis differently. Proponents of price controls for electricity blame the crisis on the deregulation of the wholesale power market several years earlier. They contend that if price caps had been in place in the wholesale market—in which utilities buy their power from generators—most of the financial crisis could have been averted. Opponents of price ceilings in electricity argue the opposite: had price caps been in place, they say, the shortages would have been even more severe and generators would have had less incentive to produce power. Furthermore, opponents of price controls argue, the cause of the financial crisis was not the soaring wholesale price but the price ceiling in the retail market, which failed to give consumers adequate incentive to reduce consumption.

sometimes even as the producers make huge profits. A similar situation occurs with low prices: the market is signaling buyers to consume more and producers to make less—consumers benefit, but producers may suffer. In situations where price controls are contemplated, policy makers must typically weigh the trade-off between the desirability of a more equitable or socially acceptable outcome and the distortion of incentives that price controls create.

Further Research

National Bureau of Economic Research

www.nber.org/digest/may05/w11114.html

An authoritative summary of a paper on the effect of price controls on pharmaceutical research.

New York State Rent Regulation Laws

www.nytimes.com/2009/02/03/nyregion/03rent.html

A news report on the New York State assembly's changing rent regulation laws in response to the economic recession.

U.S. Department of Labor

www.dol.gov/esa/whd/flsa

The Department of Labor establishes the federal minimum wage.

—*Randall E. Waldron*

Privatization

Privatization is the shift of government functions and assets into the private sector. Examples of privatization include replacing municipal garbage collection services with a private contractor, selling of ownership of a state industry or other asset to a private business or individual, and contracting with a private business to operate a state asset, as when a resort firm is hired to manage a state park. Privatization is important to businesses because it creates opportunities to expand and eliminates subsidized competition. Since the 1970s tens of thousands of enterprises throughout the world have been privatized.

Advantages of Privatization

The major advantage of privatization is the profit incentive. Because private businesses suffer losses and earn profits, they have incentives to manage assets efficiently. A manager whose division earns a profit, for example, often receives additional compensation or a promotion. Employees and managers of state-owned enterprises, on the other hand, are generally not subject to market discipline, and so lack those incentives. In particular, because civil service public sector employees and managers generally are compensated and promoted based on longevity of service rather than success, they lack the incentives to aggressively seek to lower costs that are present in private businesses.

State-owned and -operated enterprises are also subject to political interference. For example, a government may agree to raise wages for state workers to avoid labor unrest before an election, or it may divert investments or contracts to satisfy important constituents. Moving assets and services to the private sector can avoid many of these problems.

Another potential benefit of privatization is that it can force asset owners to face opportunity costs. For example, the Audubon Society owns a wildlife refuge in Louisiana where it has contracted for oil and gas production; Audubon uses the resulting profits to fund its wildlife preservation activities. However, the group opposes oil and gas production in the Arctic National Wildlife Refuge (ANWR).

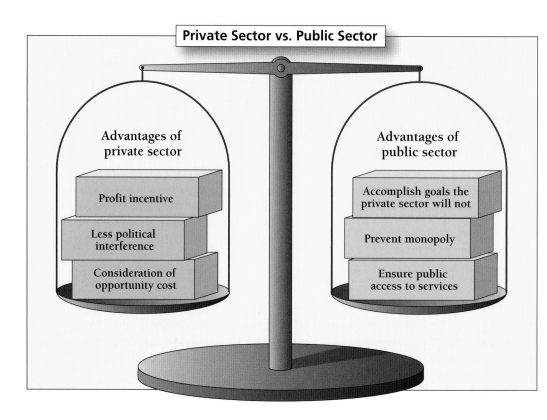

Private Sector vs. Public Sector

Advantages of private sector

- Profit incentive
- Less political interference
- Consideration of opportunity cost

Advantages of public sector

- Accomplish goals the private sector will not
- Prevent monopoly
- Ensure public access to services

British prime minister Margaret Thatcher, a leader of the privatization movement, in 1979.

On its own land, the environmental organization faced the opportunity cost of not exploiting the resources. On public land, however, those costs are borne by society as a whole, and the resource decision on public land must be made through political processes. When assets are held privately, decision makers must take opportunity costs into account.

Disadvantages of Privatization

State ownership of assets and provision of services is usually done to achieve specific goals. Privatization of some services and assets can frustrate accomplishment of the original goals. For example, many cities and towns in the United States created municipally owned public utilities to provide electricity because they feared investor-owned utilities would charge monopoly prices. Likewise, many local governments are investigating public ownership of broadband Internet networks within their borders and leasing the capacity to private businesses to prevent private cable companies from gaining

a monopoly. State ownership is one means of preventing monopoly profits.

State provision of services is often justified as necessary in cases where little profit is to be made—for example, to ensure access to particular services for the poor. Public primary and secondary education ensures public access to education without regard to income. (State ownership of schools is not required to achieve this goal, however, as the provision of vouchers and tax credits can enable underserved groups to gain access to privately provided services.) State ownership does provide greater public control of the content of education, however.

Strategies for Privatization

Studies by organizations like the World Bank have largely concluded that privatization can be beneficial when conducted properly. Private ownership of former state enterprises in both rich and poor countries has led to significant increases in profitability, service quality, service levels, and growth. Privatization of municipal services in the United States has produced increased productivity and quality of service. Not all privatizations are successful, however. Properly conducting privatization is key to its success. Among the most important factors are the following.

Rule of law. Privatization is successful only when the privatized business can operate in a market economy, which requires the rule of law. Privatized businesses must be able to rely on contracts and remain free of political interference.

Recognition of implicit property rights. Many interest groups feel they "own" state assets. A successful privatization must recognize these implicit claims on the assets when they are privatized. For example, one of the most successful privatizations was Prime Minister Margaret Thatcher's transfer of British public housing units to private ownership. Recognizing that the current tenants of the public housing felt they "owned" the right to remain in their homes, the Thatcher government privatized the units by offering to sell them at a discount to the tenants. By giving the tenants a good deal, the government converted these holders of implicit rights from potential opponents into supporters of privatization.

Avoiding overfragmentation of property rights. If privatization results in too many individuals holding claims to an asset, they may be unable to agree on how to manage their new property. For example, in Russia shares in many state enterprises were distributed to employees, managers, suppliers, customers, and other groups. The result was that each group was able to block the others from making use of the asset but was unable to implement its own preferred use, leaving many commercial buildings empty while new businesses operated from street kiosks.

Ensuring competitive market results. Simply transferring a monopoly firm or service from a public monopoly to a private monopoly may worsen the incentive problems, particularly if no regulatory structure is created to restrain the monopoly. Privatization of assets requires preprivatization division of the assets into small enough units to ensure no private monopoly results. In Britain's privatization of electricity generation plants, for example, the result was an oligopoly in generation rather than a competitive market because the government sold the plants in large groups rather than individually.

Ensuring fairness in the transfer. In theory, many of the benefits of privatization could be achieved by transferring state assets and services to any private owner. In practice,

Bolivian coca growers and union activists march on the road near Quemalia. Demonstrators demanded that the government reverse the privatization of state companies.

however, privatization is often politically impossible unless assets are fairly distributed. Many privatizations in formerly socialist countries have foundered because state ownership was replaced by "crony capitalism" in which politically well-connected individuals and groups secured former state assets at bargain basement prices.

Current Issues in Privatization

With the collapse of the Soviet Union and the revelation that Soviet claims of economic growth were false, support for direct state ownership of industrial resources also collapsed. As a result, much of current debate concerns how to privatize state-owned resources and whether to shift provision of services traditionally provided by state agencies into the private sector rather than whether private ownership is desirable.

One key debate centers on whose claims should be recognized in the privatization process. Should an enterprise be given to its employees, sold to the highest bidder, or allocated to all citizens through stock distributions? What should be done with the revenue generated by privatization? Should the new owner have responsibility for the enterprises' past conduct (for example, pollution) or have a clean slate? How should the transition be managed to minimize disruption of communities? All these questions require careful analysis and planning if privatization is to succeed.

In the United States, with relatively few state-owned enterprises, privatization has largely been discussed in terms of shifting service provision to the private sector to improve services. Proponents of education vouchers, for example, tout the benefits of a competitive education sector. Private investment of retirement accounts is offered as an alternative to social security. Municipalities consider shifting street repair, garbage collection, and other services to private firms. Almost any state service can be privatized by contracting with companies in the private sector. The question is: Do particular services have a sufficiently public character to justify their provision by the government?

Public services like garbage pickup are often cited as good candidates for privatization.

In 2008, the U.S. government initiated a financial stimulus and rescue program to aid the financial services sector. Government investment in troubled financial institutions, as well as other measures of the stimulus program that involved public-private partnerships, were criticized in some quarters as "backdoor privatizations."

Each privatization proposal must be justified individually. Many municipal privatizations in the United States fail because conditions are imposed that are designed to protect current employees' jobs; these conditions prevent the privatized entity from reducing labor costs. Although privatization has successfully transformed many state services and enterprises, it remains controversial. Successful privatization requires careful consideration of economic, regulatory, and political factors.

Further Research
Privatization Database
rru.worldbank.org/Privatization
This site provides information on privatization transactions of at least $1 million in developing countries from 2000 to 2007.

—*Andrew Morriss*

Productivity

Productivity equals the quantity of goods and services produced by each hour of work. The level of productivity in an economy significantly affects how much its workers earn and how well its people live. Workers in countries like the United States and Germany produce more for each hour they work than do workers in Mexico or Pakistan; U.S. and German workers are paid more in great part because they are more productive. Productivity growth is the result of making more goods and services without putting in more hours of work. Productivity growth is the wellspring of prosperity and is the reason people today have more and better goods than their grandparents had without working more hours.

Why Productivity Matters

Over time, an economy's growth rate equals the growth of its labor force (the increase in the number of people available for work) plus the growth in its productivity (the amount each worker produces). "Productivity isn't everything, but in the long run, it's almost everything," Paul Krugman, the Princeton University economist and *New York Times* columnist, has written. Average wages grow in line with productivity growth. Most people get most of their income from wages. Thus, as productivity increases, economic progress from one generation to the next increases also.

Productivity in the United States grew very rapidly (about 2.9 percent annually) in the 25 years following the end of World War II. Around 1973 productivity growth slowed mysteriously to about 1.3 percent annually. Economists still argue about the reasons for the falloff. Whatever the cause, slow productivity growth hurt wages and economic progress thereafter for more than two decades, producing an era that Krugman once called "the age of diminished expectations."

This slow growth in productivity was particularly disappointing and puzzling

because it coincided with the computer revolution; this phenomenon came to be known as the productivity paradox. "You can see the computer age everywhere but in the productivity statistics," Robert Solow, a Nobel Prize–winning economist at the Massachusetts Institute of Technology, observed in 1987. A surprisingly long time is often needed for a nation and its economy to determine how to harness a new technology. In the early part of the twentieth century, about two decades passed while businesses figured out how to get the most out of electricity, the new technology of that era. Only then did electricity yield an increase in productivity.

U.S. productivity quickened again around 1995, growing at an annual rate of 2.5 percent between 1995 and 2000. This surge in productivity was the essence of what was known as the New Economy, showing, according to most economic observers, that computers, communications technology, and the Internet were finally being used efficiently.

At the beginning of the twenty-first century, as the United States began recovering from the 2001 recession, the question of the strength of the productivity boom of the late 1990s remained unanswered. Few economists expected productivity to match the remarkable pace of the late 1990s, but few expected it to return to the dismal pace of the 1970s and 1980s. Seemingly small changes in the rate of productivity growth can have a great effect. A sustained half-percentage point rise in productivity results in the federal government collecting $1.2 trillion more from taxpayers over 10 years; a faster-growing economy also engenders more income and more profits.

Productivity in the United States grew rapidly for the quarter-century after World War II, slowed mysteriously around 1973, and then rose again around 1995.

U.S. Productivity Eras	
Annual growth in U.S. productivity, or output per hour of work.	
1947 to 1973	2.9%
1973 to 1995	1.3%
1995 to 2000	2.5%

Note: The annual growth in U.S. productivity, measured as output per hour of work.
Source: Bureau of Labor Statistics, http://www.bls.gov/lpc/iprdata1.htm (March 13, 2003).

Even workers who are not more productive themselves benefit when productivity grows. The typical barber, for instance, does not cut any more heads of hair in an hour today than barbers did 50 years ago. Yet barbers make more money today than they did 50 years ago. Why? Because rising productivity elsewhere in the economy has pushed up other workers' wages. If barbers today earned what barbers earned 50 years ago, no one would cut hair for a living. Barbers' wages have risen with everyone else's.

Why Productivity Growth Changes

What causes changes in the amount of output produced for each hour of work? Productivity growth often slows during recessions, or periods of reduced economic activity, and increases afterward, when businesses expand production rapidly without adding many new workers. The changes in productivity that matter, however, are best measured over long periods. Workers' productivity can be improved by equipping them with more and better machines that allow them to produce more in a normal workday. Another method is to invent a whole new way of doing something. Sending messages by e-mail instead of postal mail, for instance, can accomplish the same task with fewer hours of work; the Internet has no mail clerks or mail carriers. New techniques for organizing the workplace—for example, the assembly line in the early part of the twentieth century and self-managed work teams in the late twentieth century—can yield the same output with fewer workers and thus increase productivity. Training workers can also make them more efficient and thus more productive.

An automated Toyota assembly line in Miyazaki, Japan. Productivity has been improved through the incorporation of robotic equipment.

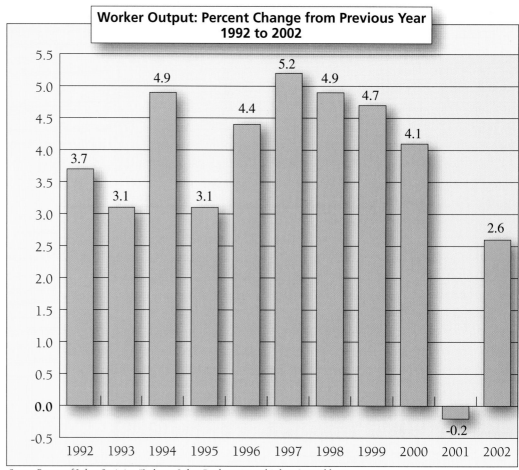

Worker Output: Percent Change from Previous Year 1992 to 2002

Source: Bureau of Labor Statistics, "Industry Labor Productivity and Labor Cost Tables," http://www.bls.gov/lpc/iprdata1.htm (April 3, 2003).

Most economists believe that spending more on research and development, investing more in new technologies, and improving the education of the population are the best ways for a society to try to increase the pace of productivity growth. Reorganizing an economy so that it uses resources more efficiently can also increase productivity. In the United States, the deregulation of important industries like trucking and airlines probably boosted productivity because it forced companies to compete with one another and find better ways of operating. Competition from imported goods accomplishes much the same goal by keeping U.S. producers under constant pressure to improve productivity. Information technology and reduced regulation helps lessen the friction in the economy—the time wasted on nonproductive tasks like filling out forms or counting parts—and, thus, helps increase productivity.

Why Productivity Sometimes Has a Bad Reputation

Productivity is sometimes blamed for layoffs. If Ford Motor Company can produce more cars with fewer workers, it will employ fewer people. For the individual worker, losing a job may be catastrophic, but for the economy as a whole, an increase in productivity is a benefit. A particular company or an entire industry may shrink, but, in a growing economy, other companies and industries spring up to employ people.

Agriculture is an example. In 1800 an American farmer needed 344 hours to produce 100 bushels of corn. A century later, a farmer needed 147 hours. By 1980 those 100 bushels took three hours of work. Richer land was farmed; better machinery and pesticides were used; labor-saving techniques were perfected. Many fewer workers were required to feed the American population. In 1800, 75 percent of all American

workers were farmers. By 1900 only 40 percent were. Only 3 percent of Americans now work on farms. The change was tough on nineteenth-century farm families, many of whom were forced off their farms or unable to employ their children. It destroyed some farm towns and a way of life. However, Americans overall are better off. They eat as much as or more than their grandparents did, but they spend much less time growing food, so they are freed to engage in other occupations—direct movies, teach math, read X rays, and give massages, for example. Although many fewer Americans work on farms, the country has food to spare, which can be traded with other nations for oil and other goods. The same process is happening to factories. They employ a shrinking fraction of American workers, but they produce more goods. Yet the U.S. economy continues to create more jobs almost every year.

Productivity grew rapidly in the last half of the 1990s, but the unemployment rate was lower than it had been in decades.

Some argue that information technology is different—that it will destroy jobs faster than new ones can be created. "Factory workers, secretaries, receptionists, clerical workers, salesclerks, bank tellers, telephone operators, librarians, wholesalers and middle managers are just a few of the many occupations destined for virtual elimination," warns author Jeremy Rifkin. "In the United States alone, as many as 90 million jobs in a labor force of 124 million are vulnerable to displacement by automation." Nearly all economists reject this view. Nonetheless, productivity growth does not guarantee that the benefits will be shared evenly. It pushes up the average wage, but wages for some workers may rise and wages for other workers may fall.

Although computers became ubiquitous in U.S. offices in the 1980s, about 15 years were to pass before their effect was felt in productivity growth.

Why Measuring Productivity Is Difficult

Productivity, like nearly everything in a modern economy, is usually gauged by the monetary value of a worker's output because comparing, say, tons of steel with numbers of heart transplants is very difficult. The market generally values what a heart surgeon can do in one hour more than it values the service that a waitress provides in an hour, so the heart surgeon is considered more productive.

Calculating productivity is easy in principle, hard in practice. The numbers published by the government are, at best, a good approximation of reality. Calculating the productivity of steelworkers is relatively simple. Steel companies can provide the government with the number of tons of steel each mill produces in a year and the number of hours the workers put in. The government divides the two to get a measure of tons of steel per hour of work. By comparing one year's figures with those of the next, the government calculates growth in productivity in the steel industry.

Measuring the output of high school teachers is much harder. Should it be measured by the number of students they teach? Or how much the students learn? Measuring the productivity of public health nurses, business consultants, television anchors, software writers, and many of the other people who work in service, rather than manufacturing, is similarly difficult.

Industries in which the product—personal computers, for example—keeps getting better also present difficulties in measuring productivity. The same number of hours may be required to design and build a computer as last year, but as this year's computer is much faster and smarter, the workers' output has increased—and thus their productivity has risen. The government tries to adjust for changes in the quality of the goods and services produced, but the precise adjustment is hard to make. The U.S. Labor Department's Bureau of Labor Statistics posts the latest productivity statistics and historical data on its Web site (http://www.bls.gov/lpc/home.htm).

Comparing productivity among countries is difficult, and different measures yield different results. By most measures, workers in the United States are the most productive in the world. Figures for Germany include both the very productive workers in what was once West Germany and the less productive workers in what was East Germany.

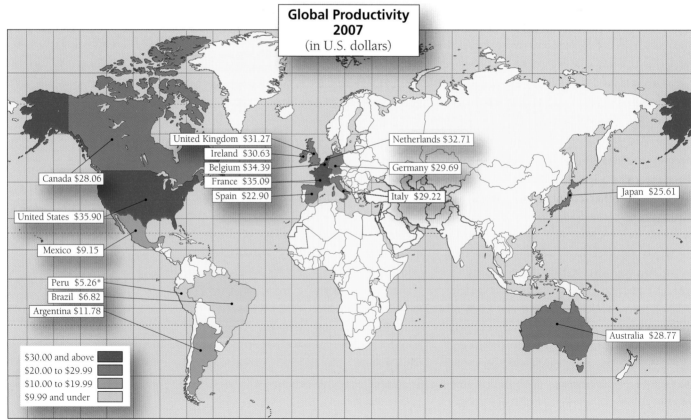

Global Productivity 2007
(in U.S. dollars)

United Kingdom $31.27
Ireland $30.63
Belgium $34.39
France $35.09
Spain $22.90
Netherlands $32.71
Germany $29.69
Italy $29.22
Japan $25.61
Canada $28.06
United States $35.90
Mexico $9.15
Peru $5.26*
Brazil $6.82
Argentina $11.78
Australia $28.77

$30.00 and above
$20.00 to $29.99
$10.00 to $19.99
$9.99 and under

Note: Measures dollar value of worker output per hour. *Peru figure dates from 1998
Source: University of Groningen

How should the productivity of this computer science teacher be measured? By the number of students he teaches, by the amount his students learn, or by some other measure?

Comparing productivity levels among countries is complicated by differences in the ways economies are measured, by changes in currency exchange rates, and by disagreements among economists about the most meaningful way to compare economies that differ markedly in the percentage of adults in the workforce. Most widely used measures rank U.S. workers as the most productive in the world. Economists generally expect the gap between U.S. workers and those in other countries to narrow as other economies learn from the United States and begin to use similar technologies. One of the big economic puzzles is the question: Why did the forces of the New Economy that yielded such an impressive surge in productivity in the United States in the late 1990s fail to produce a similar increase in other large, successful economies, like Germany, France, and Britain? Understanding productivity—why it grows more quickly in some countries than in others, and what governments, employers, unions, and colleges and high schools can do to spur its growth—

remains an area of research in economics that bears directly on the well-being of future generations.

Further Research
American Economics Association–Resources for Economists on the Internet
www.aeaweb.org/RFE
Site sponsored by the American Economics Association has links to Web-based resources.
Bureau of Labor Statistics
www.bls.gov/lpc/home.htm
The latest productivity statistics and historical data are posted on the BLS Web site.
OECD Productivity Database
www.oecd.org
The OECD Productivity Database, compiled by the Statistics Directorate, collates key productivity measures to allow international comparisons.
Recession 2008: A Matter of Terminology and Timing
www.sjsu.edu/faculty/watkins/rec2008.htm
A discussion of the U.S. 2008–2009 recession with reference to productivity and other issues from the economics department at San José State University, California.

—*David Wessel*

Protectionism

Economists generally agree that free trade is in the best interests of all countries. Free trade involves the ready movement of goods between countries, with every country having open access to other countries' markets. However, within many countries, some argue that free trade is harmful to either the country as a whole or certain groups within it. These groups will lobby their political representatives for a restriction on imports. In response, politicians can "protect" certain industries by limiting free trade by use of various protectionist measures. This protection does not come without costs.

Kinds of Protectionism

The most common ways to reduce imports into a country are by imposing tariffs and quotas. Tariffs are taxes placed on imported goods. Tariffs are of three kinds: ad valorem, specific, and compound. An ad valorem tariff is similar to a sales tax in that it is a percentage of the price of the product. A 10 percent ad valorem tariff imposes a 10 percent tax on the imported good. The tariff does generate revenue for a government. However, unlike a sales tax, governments rarely impose tariffs to raise revenues; tariff revenue in the United States accounts for only 1 percent of all government revenues.

A specific tariff involves a fixed amount of money per unit. For example, if Japanese carmakers were charged $100 for every car imported, that would be a specific tariff. Compound tariffs are a combination of ad valorem and specific tariffs. For example, in the United States imported wool blankets are faced with a 6 percent ad valorem tariff and a 1.8 cents-per-kilogram specific tariff.

Quotas involve a physical limit on the number of units of a particular product allowed to enter a country. The United States restricts the amount of cheese that can be imported with varying quotas that depend on the country exporting the cheese and the kind of cheese. For example, the United States allows only 1.85 million kilograms of Swiss cheese from Switzerland into the country. Other ways to restrict the amount of imports coming into a country exist; however, tariffs and quotas are the most used. Tariffs and quotas are sometimes imposed concurrently.

Effects of Protectionism

When trade restrictions are placed on imported products, the cost of those goods increases. In the case of the tariff, this tax will increase the price that consumers must pay. In the case of a quota, by reducing the amount of a good available in a country, the price of that product will rise. Local consumers will probably not buy as much. Protectionist measures harm local consumers as they must pay more for goods.

Tariffs and quotas do protect local jobs. Consumers will often turn to locally produced

Barriers to Trade		
Tariffs	**Quotas**	**Other**
• Ad valorem: percentage of price of product • Specific: fixed amount of money per unit • Compound: combination of ad valorem and specific tariffs	• Physical limit on number of units allowed into a country	• Prohibitions • Licensing schemes • Export restraint arrangements • Health and quarantine measures

Source: World Bank, "General Tariff Data," http://www.worldbank.org/data/wdi2001/pdfs/tab6_6.pdf (June 2, 2003).

products instead of the now relatively more expensive imported goods. As consumers buy less of the imported products and more of the local goods, local producers will increase their sales and hire more workers. Those who benefit from protection are the domestic producers of the goods and workers who are competing with imported products. When imports of cheese are restricted, U.S. cheese producers and workers in the cheese industry gain, but consumers pay a higher price for cheese than they would without the restrictions.

Debating Protectionism

A major rationale for protectionism is protection of local jobs. What typically occurs is that lower-priced imports are hurting local businesses, which then lay off their workers. With restrictions against the imported good in place, these local producers will be able to maintain their sales and employment levels. An argument heard often is that the low cost of labor in the exporting country is the basis for the low cost of imports.

However, many economists would say that low labor costs abroad are not a serious

In Switzerland two men move wheels of cheese with a forklift. The United States limits the amount of Swiss cheese that can be imported to protect domestic producers.

problem. The lower labor costs allow consumers to spend less for goods, saving them considerable money. Inexpensive foreign labor is often much less productive than are U.S. workers; as a result, the actual costs are not that much lower in the foreign countries. Even if they are, why not allow our consumers to buy from the country that can produce the best product at the lowest price?

Some argue that protectionist measures are necessary when other countries are engaged in unfair trade practices. These can include dumping (selling exported products below the cost of production) and foreign subsidies on production. Subsidies will lower a firm's production costs and therefore lower the price of the product on the international market. In such cases, the importing country may decide to place a tariff on the good to compensate for the production subsidy.

Tariffs were applied in the steel industry in the United States in 2002 in response to the fact that the European Union, South Korea, and Brazil were all heavily subsidizing local steel industries. Some criticized

the move as counter to the United States's professed support for free trade. However, when countries are not trading fairly, protectionist measures to level the playing field may be considered appropriate.

An additional argument for protection is national security, for example, in the case of oil. The United States would not want to be totally reliant on imported oil in case of war or other circumstances that do not allow the United States access to oil. Promoting some degree of self-sufficiency in certain kinds of products is desirable.

After a global recession began in 2008, many governments around the world implemented protectionist measures, including trade restrictions and subsidies. The G-20 countries agreed in November 2008 to avoid such measures, but by March 2009, 17 of the 20 countries had implemented trade restrictions.

Hidden Costs of Protectionism
The decision to protect local jobs at the expense of local consumers has costs. Consumers are harmed. When protec-

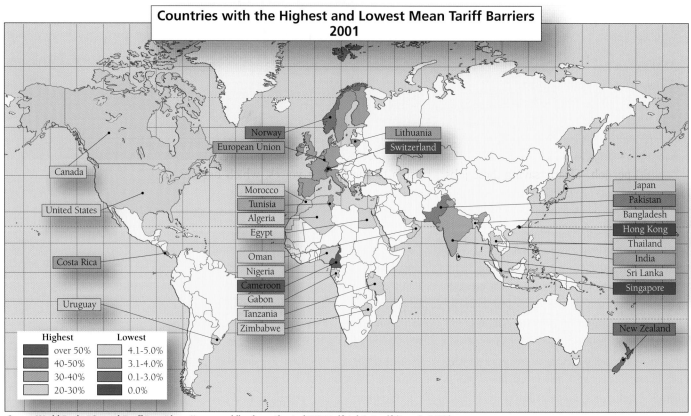

Countries with the Highest and Lowest Mean Tariff Barriers 2001

Highest		Lowest	
	over 50%		4.1-5.0%
	40-50%		3.1-4.0%
	30-40%		0.1-3.0%
	20-30%		0.0%

Source: World Bank, "General Tariff Data," http://www.worldbank.org/data/wdi2001/pdfs/tab6_6.pdf (June 2, 2003).

tions are established against lower-priced imports, the entire country may experience other economic costs. Economists have calculated the cost of each job saved from a number of different protectionist measures. For example, they found that restrictions on imported motorcycles cost Americans $150,000 per year per job saved. The annual cost for saving a job in the auto industry was $105,000 per job. Clearly saving these jobs was very expensive. In these two cases, the actual salaries of the jobs saved are significantly less than the cost of retaining that worker. So why do we protect these workers at such a high cost?

The answer lies in the politics of protectionism. Politicians, not economists, determine trade policies. Helping these workers and these industries to fight foreign competition through tariffs or quotas permits tremendous gains while each individual consumer pays a very small cost. Although the total costs to all U.S. consumers can be quite large,

the individual share is very low. Consumers usually do not complain when faced with higher prices; however, the industry and workers affected by the lower-cost imports lobby very hard for protection.

Economists argue that the benefits of protectionism are less than the losses and that countries should not engage in protectionist policies. Politicians, however, often listen to the loudest voices, which usually come from those harmed from the imports. Workers also vote. Therefore, politicians protect these workers and businesses, often at the expense of the consumers and the country as a whole.

Further Research
Interactive Tariff and Trade Dataweb
dataweb.usitc.gov
The United States International Trade Commission provides import statistics, export statistics, tariffs, future tariffs, and tariff preference information.

—*Tracy Hofer*

U.S. steelworkers march near the White House in February 2002 in support of the steel industry's demands for a high tariff on imported steel.

Recession

A recession is a downturn in a nation's economy. More precisely, it is a decline in a nation's gross domestic product (GDP)—a nation's total expenditure on all goods and services produced in its economy—for six months or more. Ten recessions have occurred in the United States since 1950, including one that began in 2008.

An expanding economy, one in which the GDP is growing, creates jobs, rising wages, and steady prices. These conditions give a sense of stability, confidence in the future, and optimism, encouraging people to invest their resources and engage in productive activity. Society benefits as goods and services become cheaper while wages increase. Recessions reverse these positive conditions. In recessions, unemployment increases, wages fall, and overall confidence suffers.

The causes of upturns and downturns in the economy are not well understood. One theory postulates that they result from events that affect specific companies or industries initially but then, through a "ripple effect," have broader impact. For example, in the early twentieth century Henry Ford perfected techniques for the mass production of cars, which created jobs as new workers were needed to both produce and subsequently maintain those cars. Other industries, including steel, road construction, and oil production, expanded because of the new technology, creating yet more jobs. The new jobs increased the earning power of workers and their ability to buy new goods and services; they produced economic growth.

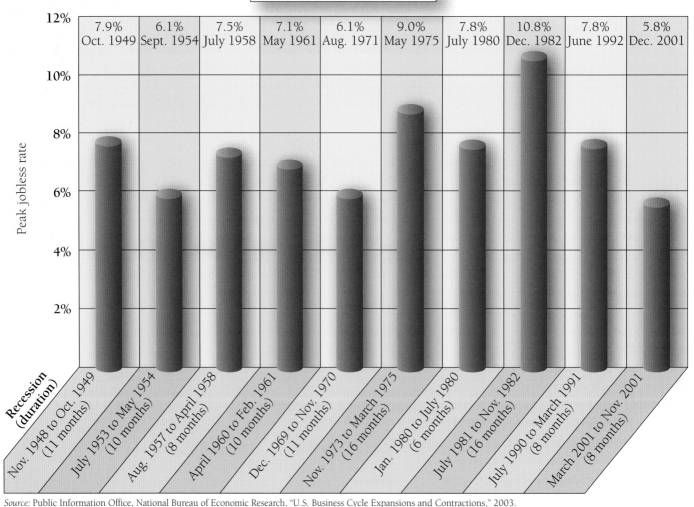

Source: Public Information Office, National Bureau of Economic Research, "U.S. Business Cycle Expansions and Contractions," 2003.

This process may also operate in reverse. If workers and company owners in a particular industry suffer a setback causing widespread losses of earnings and jobs, they will cut back on spending, and the ripple effect might push the economy toward or into a recession. One such recession occurred in 1973. Overseas oil producers colluded to increase prices dramatically. Demand for goods that used petroleum products dropped in response as the price for these goods rose. American car manufacturers were forced to reduce production of low-mileage vehicles that consumers no longer wanted. Hundreds of thousands of workers became unemployed in the automobile industry and in related industries; the entire economy went into a recession.

Another theory, developed by John Maynard Keynes, holds that recessions occur when people begin to spend less of their income. Events like the terrorist attacks in the United States on September 11, 2001, reduce optimism. Consumers lose confidence, saving more and spending less. Businesses react by reducing investment and employment. Unemployment then rises, wages fall, and the economy enters a recession. In these cases a recession might be said to occur because people acted as if one would occur.

The Great Depression of the 1930s is an excellent example. (A depression is a deep, prolonged economic downturn.) The decade of the 1920s was generally a period of optimism in the United States. People invested heavily and spent willingly on new consumer products. Businesses expanded, building new factories and hiring more workers, because consumers were willing to spend. The mood changed when the stock market crashed on October 29, 1929. Many investors suffered heavy losses and were unable to repay loans. Consequently, many banks were forced to close; many depositors lost their savings because their accounts were not insured. In the panic that followed, unemployment soared, spending dropped sharply, and the economy shrank dramatically. Government efforts to fix the

The gas crisis of the 1970s pushed the U.S. economy deep into recession.

economy did not work, and employment rates and consumer confidence remained low until the United States entered World War II in 1941.

The U.S. government uses several methods to try to prevent recessions. First, it serves as a guarantor of economic stability. It protects the value of currency, acts as a lender of last resort to banks, and guarantees (through a program of federal insurance) the security of bank deposits. All of

Gray's Papaya hot dog stand on New York's Upper West Side.

these measures foster economic confidence and optimism. Second, through the Federal Reserve system, the government monitors the economy and takes action to limit recessions when they do occur. It does this primarily through monetary policy. Monetary policy decisions made by the Federal Reserve Board of Governors have the effect of controlling the money supply. If a recession appears likely, the Fed has the power to purchase securities and to reduce the interest rates charged when banks borrow money at Federal Reserve district banks. These actions are intended to get more money into circulation, thus encouraging lending and giving businesses and consumers a greater incentive to spend and invest. The stimulus provided by increased spending and investment may then reignite economic growth.

Adjusting monetary policy does not always work. Six months or more may be needed for policy actions to take effect. To take timely, effective action, therefore, policy makers must try to predict future economic events. Often they are unable to provide accurate forecasts and, accordingly, fail to act in time to prevent a recession. Increases in the money supply can also overheat the economy—causing inflation

and thus introducing a new set of economic problems.

The government may also use fiscal policy—decreasing taxes, increasing spending, or both—in its efforts to stimulate a faltering economy. When the government increases spending (as it did in the buildup for World War II, for example), the demand for goods and services rises. This rise in demand increases employment and stimulates economic growth. Tax cuts are intended to work in a similar way: consumers who can keep an increased share of their income can presumably spend more. Fiscal policy changes may also fail, however. The necessary legislation may come too late to make a difference. New spending programs may be insufficient; tax cuts may be too small, or they may be targeted to benefit constituency groups for reasons unrelated to overall economic growth.

Government efforts to ensure economic stability and growth are also complicated by the degree to which national economies throughout the world have become interdependent. As world trade has increased, economic problems in one country can easily spread to others. For example, a nation in recession will be less able to purchase goods and services from other nations. The decrease in demand can cause job losses in other countries as producers of trade goods cut back. Similarly, economic shocks related to political instability or war can also have destructive ripple effects. In efforts to address international economic problems, many national governments now participate in cooperative efforts carried out through institutions like the International Monetary Fund and the World Bank.

Further Research
National Bureau of Economic Research
www.nber.org/cycles.html
A database of business cycles and contractions.
Recession
Recession.org
This site, founded in 1999, compiles news and research on topics relating to economic recession in the United States.

—*David Long*

Regulation of Business and Industry

In a market economy such as exists in the United States, price should ideally act as the information, incentive, and rationing mechanism that determines supply and demand. In practice, however, the operations of markets are not perfect. In addition, economies of scale and extraordinary capital requirements have resulted in the development of natural monopolies that dominate business in areas like public transportation, telecommunications, and power. Given the existence of market imperfections and of monopoly power, free markets alone cannot guarantee equitable distribution of resources in a complex industrial society. As a consequence, U.S. governments have established regulatory bodies to promote fair trade practices and to safeguard citizens.

The U.S. Congress, state legislatures, and local governments have all created commissions empowered to establish and enforce standards for specific activities in the private sector. Members of regulatory agencies are generally appointed by the executive branch of government and serve for fixed terms. The commissions are empowered to impose regulations that have the force of law. They may also conduct hearings and rule on whether their regulations are being followed.

Railroad Regulation

Railroads were the first big businesses in the United States. Rapid expansion between 1860 and 1880, however, resulted in excess railroad capacity. As a consequence, railroads attempted to maximize their returns by adopting a number of discriminatory price practices. Outraged by unfair treatment, in the early 1870s farmers and other businesses successfully pressured several midwestern states to pass regulatory laws that established commissions to set maximum rates, prohibited charging exorbitant rates

for short hauls, and generally made illegal price discrimination based on the identity of the shipper or place of shipment. The U.S. Supreme Court in *Munn v. Illinois* (1877) upheld a state's right to regulate railroads and other businesses "clothed with a public interest" within its boundaries. In *Wabash, St. Louis and Pacific Railway Company v. Illinois* (1886), the Court, however, ruled that the efforts of Illinois to regulate rates between states infringed on the federal government's exclusive control of interstate commerce.

In 1887 Congress passed the Act to Regulate Commerce, which brought all railroads engaged in interstate commerce under federal regulation. The act also established the Interstate Commerce Commission (ICC), the first permanent federal regulatory agency. The five-member ICC was empowered to oversee the management of the railroads, hear complaints stemming from violations of the act, and require railroads to file annual reports using uniform accounting practices.

The ICC was the prototype for later federal regulatory agencies. Like its precursors at the state level, it was composed of members with specialized knowledge of the railroads. Permanent and independent, the ICC gained recognition as an impartial and nonpartisan body capable of equitable regulation. The Hepburn Act of 1906 increased the membership of the ICC from five to seven and empowered the commission to fix just and reasonable maximum rail rates, to establish uniform accounting methods, and broaden the commission's jurisdiction to

Interstate Commerce Commission 1887 to 1995	
Mandate: Regulate surface transportation, including <ul><li>railroads</li><li>trucking companies</li><li>bus lines</li><li>freight forwarders</li><li>water carriers</li><li>oil pipelines</li><li>transportation brokers</li><li>express agencies</li></ul>	**Powers:** <ul><li>set rates</li><li>investigate rate issues</li><li>establish uniform accounting methods</li><li>consolidate railroad systems</li><li>manage labor disputes in interstate transport</li><li>enforce desegregation of passenger terminal facilities</li></ul>

U.S. Courts and Restraint of Trade

Era	Court Position
1880s to late 1930s	Courts follow "rule of reason." Restriction of competition is not unlawful if it does not involve predatory practices.
Late 1930s to 1970s	Control of a large market share considered to be per se illegal.
1970s to 2000s	Courts focus on the degree of competition rather than the number of firms in an industry.

include sleeping-car companies, ferries, oil pipelines, terminals, and bridges.

Antitrust Regulation

In the last decades of the nineteenth century, fear of monopoly power and the abuse that was associated with the consolidation of many industries, most notably the monopolistic behavior of Standard Oil, led to passage of the Sherman Antitrust Act in 1890. The act outlawed "every contract, combination in the form of trust or otherwise, or conspiracy in restraint of trade." In 1914 Congress approved the Federal Trade Commission Act to further advance the government's efforts to prevent unfair methods of competition in interstate commerce. The act established the five-member, bipartisan Federal Trade Commission (FTC). The FTC was charged with collecting annual and special reports from corporations; these reports were and are used to assess industry concentration and impact on competition. The FTC was also authorized to investigate charges of unfair business practices including misbranding and misleading advertising, to publish its findings, and to issue cease and desist orders in cases where illegal practices were found to exist.

Establishment of the FTC acknowledged that industrial growth demanded a complex system of government regulation, but until the late 1930s the courts followed the "rule of reason" with respect to restraint of trade. That is, courts held that restriction of competition was not unlawful if it did not involve predatory practices like collusion among independent firms. Given this narrow legal interpretation, large size alone was insufficient for a finding of violation of antitrust laws.

After 1938, however, the Justice Department and courts began to rule that control of a large market share was per se illegal, and prosecutions of antitrust cases dramatically increased. The government won most of these cases, but the courts imposed relatively minor penalties. In the 1970s the courts moved away from per se interpretation of the law, focusing on the degree of competition rather than the number of firms in an industry. This shift in interpretation was at least partly responsible for the government's dropping its case against IBM in 1982. The recognition of the importance of global competition led the Justice Department to approve the Boeing Aircraft Corporation's acquisition of its major domestic competitor, McDonnell Douglass, in 1997. The prosecution of Microsoft in the late 1990s involved issues of both predatory behavior and stifling of competition, but even in that case, the initial ruling that called for the company's breakup was reversed.

During the 1920s the FTC's role in safeguarding consumers against deceptive sales practices became well established, and, by the early 1930s, more than 90 percent of the complaints issued by the agency involved issues of consumer deception. The FTC is authorized to impose a variety of remedies, including affirmative disclosure that provides additional information about an advertised product; corrective advertising that requires a firm to sponsor additional advertising to correct the effects of its previous misleading ads; and restitution or refunds to consumers who have been misled by deceptive advertising.

The New Deal

The Great Depression of the 1930s called into question the efficacy of the free market system. With the U.S. economy on the brink of collapse, President Franklin D. Roosevelt between 1933 and 1938 sponsored legislation that began or expanded federal regulation of many aspects of business. Roosevelt's New Deal included the Emergency Banking Relief Act (1933), which provided for government supervision of U.S. banks, while the

Glass–Steagall Act (1933) separated commercial and investment banking functions and insured bank deposits through the Federal Deposit Insurance Corporation. The Securities Exchange Act (1934) established the Securities and Exchange Commission (SEC) and required the registration and disclosure of information concerning securities traded on exchanges. The Federal Communications Commission (1934) was created to regulate communications by telegraph, cable, and radio, while the Federal Housing Administration (1934) came into existence to insure loans for new home construction and for repairs to existing housing.

To aid farmers, the New Deal effectively removed agriculture from the free market by creating a system of acreage allotments and price supports. To assist industrial workers, the New Deal created the National Labor Relations Board (1935) to oversee negotiations between management and labor. The Motor Carrier Act (1935) put buses and trucks engaged in interstate commerce under the control of the ICC. The Public Utility Holding Company Act (1935) gave the Federal Power Commission authority to regulate interstate transmission of electric power, gave the FTC authority over interstate transmission of gas, and gave the SEC jurisdiction over the financial practices of utility holding companies. The Merchant Marine Act (1936) created the U.S. Maritime Commission to develop the American merchant marine, and the Wagner–Steagall Act (1936) created the U.S. Housing Authority to assist in the development of low-rent housing. The Food, Drug, and Cosmetic Act (1938) extended the FTC's control over the advertising of food, drugs, and cosmetics, and the Civil Aeronautics Act (1938) created the Civil Aeronautics Authority to regulate air transport rates and assure the stability of the air transport industry.

The proliferation of federal agencies during the New Deal reflected confidence in the ability of expert commissions to provide the most equitable oversight of the economy. In his book *The Administrative Process* (1938), James Landis, a former member of the SEC, best articulated the rationale for administrative regulation. He argued that the executive,

On March 9, 1933, President Franklin Roosevelt signs the Emergency Banking Relief Act.

Regulation of Business and Industry

1870s
Several midwestern states pass regulatory laws to outlaw price discrimination by railroads.

⬇

1877
In *Munn v. Illinois* the U.S. Supreme Court upholds a state's right to regulate railroads.

⬇

1887
Act to Regulate Commerce passed.

⬇

1890
Sherman Antitrust Act passed.

⬇

1906
Hepburn Act passed.

⬇

1907
Wisconsin and New York become the first states to establish public service commissions to oversee public utilities.

⬇

1914
Federal Trade Commission Act passed.

⬇

1933 to 1938
Many regulatory laws and agencies established as part of the New Deal: Emergency Banking Relief Act (1933), Glass–Steagall Act (1933), Securities Exchange Act (1934), Federal Communications Commission (1934), Federal Housing Administration (1934), National Labor Relations Board (1935), Motor Carrier Act (1935), Public Utility Holding Company Act (1935), Merchant Marine Act (1936), Wagner–Steagall Act (1936), Food, Drug, and Cosmetic Act (1938), and Civil Aeronautics Act (1938).

⬇

1964 to 1975
Regulatory agencies established: Equal Employment Opportunity Commission (1964), National Transportation Safety Board (1966), Council on Environmental Quality (1969), Environmental Protection Agency (1970), National Highway Traffic Safety Administration (1970), Occupational Safety and Health Administration (1970), Consumer Product Safety Commission (1972), Mining Enforcement and Safety Administration (1973), and Materials Transportation Bureau (1975).

⬇

1974
Economist Alfred Kahn establishes basis for deregulation of some industries.

⬇

1978
The U.S. Airline Deregulation Act passed.

⬇

1982
The U.S. government drops its antitrust case against IBM.

⬇

1997
Justice Department approves Boeing Aircraft's acquisition of its major domestic competitor, McDonnell Douglass.

⬇

2001
Decision to break up Microsoft reversed.

legislative, and judicial branches of government were ill prepared to address complex, modern issues; in contrast, regulators possessed expertise that was developed "only from that continuity of interest, that ability and desire to devote 52 weeks a year, year after year, to a particular problem."

Social Regulation

The first wave of regulatory activity in the United States focused on maintaining competition in an era of business consolidation; the second arose from the market failures associated with the Great Depression. The third wave of regulation was directed at protecting consumers, employees, and the general public interest from corporate harm. These latest efforts gave the government oversight of many of the most important areas of corporate decision making, including hiring, employee work conditions, product safety standards, and pollution control. They have also had a major impact on virtually all industries.

Between 1964 and 1977 Congress created 10 federal regulatory agencies: the Equal Employment Opportunity Commission (1964), the National Transportation Safety Board (1966), the Council on Environmental Quality (1969), the Environmental Protection Agency (1970), the National Highway Traffic Safety Administration (1970), the Occupational Safety and Heath Administration (1970), the Consumer Product Safety Commission

(1972), the Mining Enforcement and Safety Administration (1973), the Materials Transportation Bureau (1975), and the Office of Strip Mining Regulation and Enforcement (1977). These agencies greatly enlarged the size of the federal government and substantially raised government expenditures as well as business costs related to compliance with regulatory mandates.

Regulatory efforts during the 1960s and 1970s brought business and nonbusiness interests into sharp opposition. Earlier regulatory eras often found business working with government in shaping regulatory legislation. In the 1960s and 1970s, by contrast, civil rights activists, consumer groups, and environmental protection advocates joined with other public interest organizations to lobby for regulatory legislation, and, in many cases, business was left out of the process of administrative policy formulation.

State Regulation

The term *public utility* is used to identify a range of industries that provide services like transportation, communication, electrical power, gas, and water that are used by the general citizenry. Although utilities are typically private, investor-owned firms, competition does not characterize these markets. Instead, the importance of economies of scale and a desire to take advantage of those efficiencies led to the emergence of natural monopolies—only one provider of a specific

Eras of Regulatory Activity		
Era	Regulatory Focus	Business Role
1880s to 1930s	• Maintaining competition	Business works with government in shaping regulation.
1930s to 1960s	• Correcting market failures • Using expert commissions to provide equitable oversight of the economy	
1960s to 1970s	• Protecting consumers, employees, and general public from corporate harm	Business is often left out of the process of policy formulation.
1980s to 2000s	• Deregulating key industries, including transportation, banking, and telecommunications • Enforcing social and environmental regulation	

Quantifying the amount spent on and the amount saved by federal regulation can be difficult. Such estimates are important, however, in assessing whether the regulation is useful. (Agencies use different methods for assessing expenditures and savings—thus the great variance in the estimates provided.)

Estimated Annual Costs and Benefits of Federal Regulation
April 1995 to September 2001
(in millions of 2001 dollars)

Federal Agency	Estimated Annual Costs	Estimated Annual Benefits
Agriculture	2,249 to 2,271	2,938 to 5,989
Education	362 to 610	655 to 814
Department of Energy	1,836	3,991 to 4,059
Health and Human Services	2,988 to 3,067	8165 to 9,182
Housing and Urban Development	150	190
Department of Labor	361	1,173 to 3,557
Department of Transportation	1,756 to 3,808	2,400 to 4,312
Environmental Protection Agency	41,523 to 42,326	29,140 to 66,092
Total	51,225 to 54,429	48,652 to 67,602

Source: Federal Register 67, no. 60, March 28, 2002.

service in a given area—as the earliest electrical power, gas, water, and telephone utilities developed in the United States.

Local and state governments acknowledged efficiencies associated with a single, large utility provider, but they also recognized the need to protect consumers from abuses associated with monopoly power. In 1907 Wisconsin and New York became the first states to establish public service commissions to oversee public utilities; by 1913 nearly all the other states had followed their example. The state commissions were charged with assuring that the operation of utilities conformed to the public interest with regard to pricing and provision of service.

Given the charge to oversee rates and to determine conditions of service, regulators have often been involved with decisions that in other kinds of firms are under the control of management. This circumstance produced conflict as early as the 1920s in relation to issues like the fair value of the property owned by utilities, equitable returns for utility stockholders, and reasonable utility rates. From the 1920s until the late 1960s, however, technological innovation and increasing economies of scale produced a situation where consumers benefited from declining rates in many regulated industries, while investors in those utilities enjoyed increasing returns.

After 1970 utilities, particularly those providing electric power, faced new challenges as technological improvements slowed, fuel charges rose, and demands for costly environmental safeguards increased. Utilities applied for rate increases, but state commissions, many of which were staffed by lawyers, tended to ignore economic considerations. In 1974, however, economist Alfred Kahn became chairman of the New York Public Service Commission. Arguing that "applied microeconomics is the exciting new frontier of public policy," Kahn encouraged the New York commission to employ economic analysis

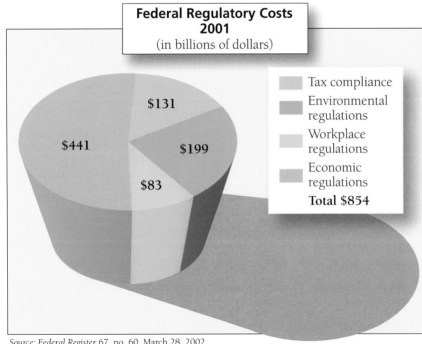

Federal Regulatory Costs 2001
(in billions of dollars)

$131

$441

$199

$83

Tax compliance

Environmental regulations

Workplace regulations

Economic regulations

Total $854

Source: Federal Register 67, no. 60, March 28, 2002.

in its regulatory efforts. This analysis led New York state to introduce a new rate structure for electric power that took into account the actual costs of serving business and residential customers. It also led New York to unbundle telephone charges so that consumers would not subsidize business customers or pay for services like directory assistance if they did not use them.

Kahn's work in New York gained national attention. Many other state agencies copied his pricing structures. Even more important, the use of economic analysis, which Kahn helped promote, had the long-term effect of suggesting, during the decades that followed, the need to deregulate some industries.

Deregulation

The administration of President Jimmy Carter took up the banner of deregulation. Carter believed that excessive regulation inhibited efficiency in many industries, and he accepted the argument that regulatory agencies had often been captured by the interests they had been designed to control. Among the industries he identified for deregulation were the airlines, trucking, and railroads; in addition, he supported decontrol of natural gas prices.

In 1978 Congress passed the United States Airline Deregulation Act. The act abolished the Civil Aeronautics Board, left airlines free to establish rates and routes, and opened the industry to new entrants. The act is noteworthy because it reversed a century-long trend of increasing government intervention in the economy. Two years later, the Motor Carrier Act began the deregulation of interstate trucking by giving firms greater control over rates and by making it easier for new businesses to enter the industry. Also in 1980 the Staggers Rail Act curtailed the ICC's powers to set rail rates. (The ICC was disbanded in 1995.) Carter's deregulation strategies were essentially pragmatic; the trend toward greater deregulation and increased limits on regulatory agencies would intensify and become more ideological during the administration of Ronald Reagan, who was elected in 1980.

During a press conference, U.S. Consumer Product Safety Commission chairwoman Ann Brown demonstrates how the seat of the Option 5 High Chairs separates from the frame, allowing the child to fall to the ground. Retailer Costco recalled about one million of the chairs after receiving 57 reports of injuries.

The last decades of the twentieth century witnessed two divergent trends in regulation of business and industry. The introduction of new kinds of competitors into industries long considered to be natural monopolies promoted deregulation of the transportation, banking, and telecommunications industries. Deregulation of the banking sector, however, was considered one of the causes of the meltdown in the financial services industry in 2008, a trigger for the global recession that followed; this led to a reconsideration of deregulation in general and some calls for greater regulation of key industries. The social and environmental regulation initiated in the 1960s and 1970s remains in force and appears likely to have a lasting impact on the relationship between business interests and those of the larger society.

Further Reading

The Future of Financial Services Regulation
financialservices.house.gov/hearing110/hr102108. shtml
The transcript and webcast of hearings in the U.S. House of Representatives in October 2008.

—Marilyn Lavin

Risk Management

Risk refers to the possibility of loss or injury, especially in situations marked by uncertainty. People put themselves at risk by driving on icy roads, by investing in the stock market, and by petting a strange dog; everything might turn out fine, but each action also might lead to trouble, minor or serious. The variation in possible outcomes creates the sense of risk.

In day-to-day operations, businesses always take some degree of risk: the new supplier might be unreliable, the new product line might not appeal to customers, or the chief financial officer might embezzle money. The potential loss lies in the future in each case, and the future is uncertain. Risk management refers to business practices designed to reduce the possibilities of loss that arise from uncertain knowledge about the future.

Aspects of Risk Management

Risk management involves three steps: identifying sources of potential losses, evaluating potential losses, and selecting means for responding to loss exposures. After these steps are completed, businesses and individuals can implement and administer a risk management program.

Identifying Sources of Potential Losses. People who study risk describe potential losses by reference to different kinds of sources: perils, hazards, and exposures. A peril is an immediate cause of a loss. Common perils include fire, hail, tornadoes, earthquakes, and hurricanes.

A hazard is a more general condition that lies behind the occurrence of a loss, increasing its probability of occurrence, its severity, or both. Some hazards are physical conditions in the environment that increase the risk of loss. Examples might include a poorly lit stairwell in an apartment building or old, frayed wiring in a warehouse. Other hazards are moral: conditions in which somebody or some organization might benefit from a loss and might therefore have reason to feel ambivalent about the risk in question. If an insurance policy guarantees reimbursement for the cost of a new computer when an old one is stolen, for example, the insured owner of an old computer may be less than diligent about preventing its theft. The moral hazard in such a case need not involve outright dishonesty. It might be a matter of inattention or carelessness augmented by the prospect of benefiting from loss.

Exposure in a risk situation is the kind of loss faced by the person or company at risk. A property loss exposure is associated with real property (a beachfront hotel might be leveled by a hurricane, for example) and personal property (an automobile might get dented). A liability exposure involves the

Sources of Risks		
Type	**Definition**	**Examples**
Peril	• An immediate cause of loss	• Fire • Tornadoes • Earthquakes • Terrorism
Hazard	• Physical conditions in the environment that increase risk of loss • Moral conditions in which someone might benefit from a loss	• Physical: poorly lit stairway • Moral: insurance policy guaranteeing replacement of stolen property
Exposure	• Type of loss faced by person or company at risk	• Property loss: personal or real property • Liability: lawsuits

possibility that a person or business might face lawsuits (a restaurant might be sued by a customer alleging food poisoning, for example) and therefore incur an obligation to pay money damages.

Managing risk uses various methods to identify potential losses. One approach is the physical inspection of a business or home to identify potential perils, hazards, and exposures. Inspectors from an insurance company might advise owners of a nursing home, for example, that they face a risk of liability arising from inadequate supervision of aides. Some potential losses can be anticipated by reviews that identify losses that have occurred in the past. An analysis of a firm's financial statements might provide clues to the present loss exposures of the firm. Businesses may also use risk questionnaires and interviews with employees to learn about areas of potential exposure. By identifying problems, businesses decrease their chance of ignoring exposures that could lead to catastrophic losses.

Evaluating Potential Losses. The second step in the risk management process is to evaluate potential losses, estimating their probable frequency and severity. Loss frequency is the probable number of losses that may occur during a given period—for example, the number of accidents a business's fleet of delivery trucks is likely to be involved with in the next year. Loss severity is the potential size of the losses. From frequency and severity estimates, potential loss exposures can be ranked. Ranking enables an individual or business to decide which loss exposures deserve the most attention.

Responding to Loss Exposures. The third step in risk management is to consider various responses to loss exposures. Businesses rely on two main approaches: risk control and risk financing.

Risk control involves techniques that reduce the frequency and severity of losses, including avoidance of certain hazards and implementation of safety programs. Just as an individual can avoid the risk of being

killed in a bungee cord accident by finding another recreational activity, a business can avoid some liability exposures by declining to offer certain products or services. Insurance companies prohibited by state law from linking their prices (insurance premiums) to varying degrees of risk, for example, may respond by withdrawing from that sector of the insurance market.

Living with Risk
Avoiding all risks is impossible; it is also undesirable. One could avoid the peril of

Underwriters at Lloyd's of London in England.

Steps in Dealing with Risk

Identify sources of potential losses

⬇

Evaluate potential for exposure

⬇

Respond to loss exposures
(such as risk control and risk financing)

automobile crashes by refusing ever to ride in an automobile, but the alternatives—riding a horse, walking, staying home—would strike many people as unsatisfactory and would, in any case, introduce new forms of risk. Risk is associated, moreover, with positive outcomes as well as losses. Some economists contend that profitable economic activity is linked with risks taken in a climate of uncertainty. For

individuals and businesses, therefore, acting to control the frequency, severity, or unpredictability of losses that cannot be avoided is the preferred course. The frequency of fires might be reduced by prohibiting smoking in areas with flammables present, for example; losses from fires might also be reduced by the installation of sprinkler systems.

To handle risks that cannot be avoided or adequately controlled, individuals and businesses often turn to some form of risk financing. One kind of risk financing is risk retention. An individual practices risk retention when he or she knows of a certain risk and decides nonetheless to keep at least part of it. For example, a driver may decide to retain the risk of a fender bender (in part) by purchasing a car insurance policy with a $500 deductible (driver agrees to pay for all damage to the car

A crystal and glass gift shop in Olympia, Washington, after an earthquake in 2001.

under $500). He retains $500 worth of risk, and in return his insurance premiums are reduced. Alternatively, the driver could choose to adopt a funded risk-retention program by setting money aside to pay for damage to his car in case of an accident.

Another kind of risk financing is transfer—a shifting over of risk to somebody else by means of a legal agreement. Transfer may be achieved through contracts, hedging, incorporation of a business, or the purchase of insurance. Transfer of risk by contract occurs, for example, when a purchaser of an automobile also purchases an extended warranty. The risk of loss from defects in the automobile is then shifted to the issuer of the warranty. Hedging is a means for transferring the risk of unfavorable price increases by buying and selling contracts on an organized exchange like the Chicago Board of Trade or New York Stock Exchange. For example, an airline may try to reduce the risk of spikes in aviation fuel prices by buying contracts for the delivery of set amounts of aviation fuel at a fixed price at a known date in the future. Some business owners shift risk by incorporation. Laws governing incorporation generally prevent business creditors from taking personal assets belonging to owners, even when the owner's business owes a debt.

For many individuals and businesses, insurance is the most feasible method for transferring risk. It often provides a relatively inexpensive means to address potential losses. In return for premium payments, the insurer agrees to pay for certain losses in the event of specified contingencies, for example, illness or a failed shipment of goods. The insuring company can offer such protection because it pools risks from a large group of individuals or businesses—betting, in effect, that only a small percentage of them will make valid claims in a given year.

The purchaser of insurance must avoid buying either too little or too much protection. Insufficient coverage may leave the purchaser vulnerable to huge financial losses. Buying too much insurance, however, shifts

risk that might better be retained. Risk is present even in efforts to reduce risk.

Risk is uncertainty about the occurrence of a loss. Minimizing the negative aspects of not knowing the future is the essence of risk management. Risk management entails identifying potential losses, evaluating them, selecting appropriate means for responding to loss exposures, and implementing a risk management program. Insurance is the most common technique used for managing risk.

A company that relies on a fleet of trucks might need to evaluate its loss frequency—the probable number of lost or damaged trucks during a given time.

Further Reading
Risk Management Magazine
www.rmmagazine.com
The magazine published by the Risk and Insurance Management Society offers many articles online; the Society (www.rims.org) publishes a daily online newswire service and provides a useful Resources area on its home page.
Software Engineering Institute
www.sei.cmu.edu/risk/
A discussion of risk management from Carnegie Mellon University.

—*Carl Pacini*

Service
Economy

The United States is often described as having a service economy, or an economy in which the majority of employment and business revenues are generated by services, as opposed to manufacturing or agriculture. The United States is not alone; the wealthy countries of Europe and Asia are also service economies. Indeed, many economists see a natural transition to services as

One definition of services is that they are based on a relationship, such as attorney to client, rather than on the sale of objects such as chairs.

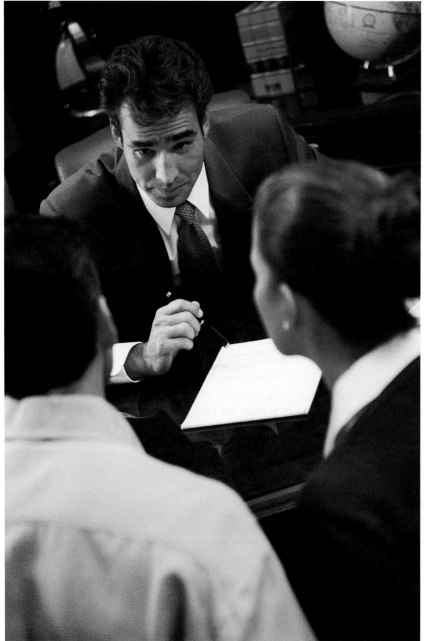

countries become wealthier: poor countries rely on agriculture, better-off countries rely on manufacturing, and wealthy countries rely on services.

If a service economy is defined as one where the majority of employment is in the service sector, then the United States developed a service economy during the 1950s. The importance of the service sector has only grown: in 1960 more than 55 percent of the workforce was employed in the service sector; by 2000 that number was more than 70 percent and by 2005 more than 80 percent. During the 1970s, a period of economic stagnation, some observers wondered if a service economy was a "no-growth" economy. The 1980s was a decade of low productivity gains, and some argued that improving productivity in a service economy was next to impossible. During the 1990s, as the gap between rich and poor increased, some fingered the service economy as the culprit.

The increasing importance of the service sector has created significant issues for policy makers and economists who fall back on strategies and theories developed during the industrial era. For example, a common approach for federal governments seeking to boost their economies is to reduce the amount of taxes companies pay when they make major capital investments in their businesses. However, a service economy is less capital intensive—it relies less on expensive factories and machinery—than is a manufacturing economy, so the effect of such a tax reduction may be muted. The erosion of the U.S. industrial base that has accompanied the rise of the service economy has also caused considerable distress for some workers, as manufacturers have relocated factories abroad and well-paying, often unionized, manufacturing jobs held by older workers have been lost.

What Is a Service Economy?
Considerable confusion exists about what the service economy is and how it works. No official or traditional definition of services exists. In fact, services were once reg-

ularly defined by what they are not: any activity that does not qualify as manufacturing or agriculture is in the service sector. By this definition, services became the category for "everything else" that is happening in an economy.

When "everything else" has been the fastest-growing segment of the economy for decades, however, more precise definitions are needed. One definition of the service sector is that it produces immaterial objects. As one magazine put it, a service can be bought or sold, but it cannot be dropped on the floor. Services can have results that are quite material, however. For example, a haircut cannot be dropped on the floor, but a person who gets a haircut will notice tangible difference in his hair.

Thus, a second definition of the service sector is that service produces a change in the condition of a good or a person. A man who hires a barber to cut his hair has changed the condition of his hair. A man who hires a lawyer to get him a divorce has changed his marital condition.

Both definitions point to a peculiar issue for policy makers and economists: services are very hard to measure. A factory worker produces a certain number of goods, which can be counted. A farm likewise produces a specific amount of grain or milk that can easily be measured. How should the output of a hairdresser be measured? Weighing the hair or counting the haircuts misses an essential aspect of what makes the service—the haircut—worth buying. A doctor may see many patients, but if they all die from preventable causes, the doctor is not adequately performing medical services. As a result, some observers have called for new methods of measuring the worth of a business and its output, but little consensus exists on what those new methods should be.

Yet another definition of services is that a service produces a relation—doctor–patient, lawyer–client—rather than a thing. Defining services in this way suggests that communication is more important in a service economy than in an industrial economy because two

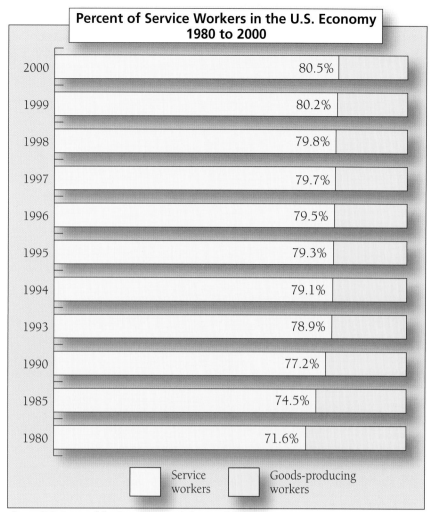

Percent of Service Workers in the U.S. Economy 1980 to 2000

Year	Service workers
2000	80.5%
1999	80.2%
1998	79.8%
1997	79.7%
1996	79.5%
1995	79.3%
1994	79.1%
1993	78.9%
1990	77.2%
1985	74.5%
1980	71.6%

☐ Service workers   ☐ Goods-producing workers

Source: U.S. Bureau of the Census, *Statistical Abstracts of the United States,* 2001, Washington, D.C., Government Printing Office, http://www.census.gov/prod/2002pubs/01statab/labor.pdf (March 26, 2003).

people generally need to interact to produce a relation. It also suggests that the consumer in a service economy has a different role from the consumer in a manufacturing economy. A person buying a refrigerator has only to pay for it for the transaction to be a success, but a person visiting a doctor has to tell the doctor all sorts of things, for example, what hurts, personal and family medical histories, and must constantly respond for the medical visit to be a success.

Labor in the Service Economy
Services are difficult to define partly because the service sector is far from homogenous. Service jobs encompass low-paying jobs, for example, waiting on tables and answering phones, as well as high-paying professions, for example, doctors, lawyers, consultants, or investment bankers.

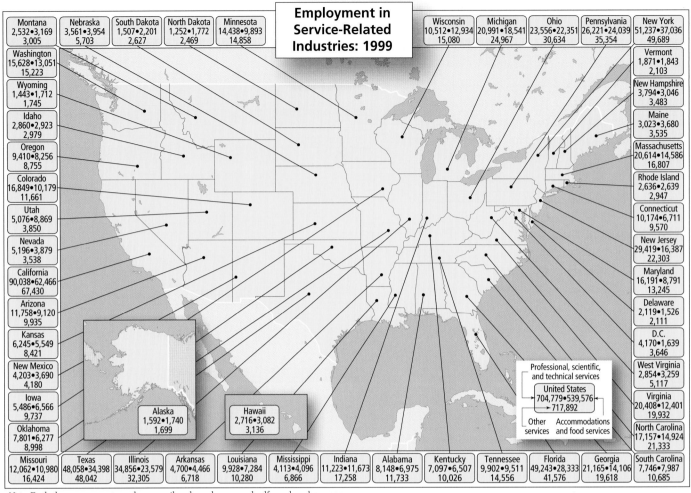

Employment in Service-Related Industries: 1999

State	Professional, scientific, and technical services • Other services	Accommodations and food services
Montana	2,532•3,169	3,005
Nebraska	3,561•3,954	5,703
South Dakota	1,507•2,201	2,627
North Dakota	1,252•1,772	2,469
Minnesota	14,438•9,893	14,858
Wisconsin	10,512•12,934	15,080
Michigan	20,991•18,541	24,967
Ohio	23,556•22,351	30,634
Pennsylvania	26,221•24,039	35,354
New York	51,237•37,036	49,689
Washington	15,628•13,051	15,223
Wyoming	1,443•1,712	1,745
Idaho	2,860•2,923	2,979
Oregon	9,410•8,256	8,755
Colorado	16,849•10,179	11,661
Utah	5,076•8,869	3,850
Nevada	5,196•3,879	3,538
California	90,038•62,466	67,430
Arizona	11,758•9,120	9,935
Kansas	6,245•5,549	8,421
New Mexico	4,203•3,690	4,180
Iowa	5,486•6,566	9,737
Oklahoma	7,801•6,277	8,998
Vermont	1,871•1,843	2,103
New Hampshire	3,794•3,046	3,483
Maine	3,023•3,680	3,535
Massachusetts	20,614•14,586	16,807
Rhode Island	2,636•2,639	2,947
Connecticut	10,174•6,711	9,570
New Jersey	29,419•16,387	22,303
Maryland	16,191•8,791	13,245
Delaware	2,119•1,526	2,111
D.C.	4,170•1,639	3,646
West Virginia	2,854•3,259	5,117
Virginia	20,408•12,401	19,932
North Carolina	17,157•14,924	21,333
Alaska	1,592•1,740	1,699
Hawaii	2,716•3,082	3,136
Missouri	12,062•10,980	16,424
Texas	48,058•34,398	48,042
Illinois	34,856•23,579	32,305
Arkansas	4,700•4,466	6,718
Louisiana	9,928•7,284	10,280
Mississippi	4,113•4,096	6,866
Indiana	11,223•11,673	17,258
Alabama	8,148•6,975	11,733
Kentucky	7,097•6,507	10,026
Tennessee	9,902•9,511	14,556
Florida	49,243•28,333	41,576
Georgia	21,165•14,106	19,618
South Carolina	7,746•7,987	10,685

Professional, scientific, and technical services
United States → 704,779•539,576 → 717,892
Other services   Accommodations and food services

Note: Excludes government employees, railroad employees, and self-employed persons.
Source: U.S. Bureau of the Census, *County Business Patterns,* Washington, D.C., Government Printing Office, 2000.

The service sector is usually broken down into smaller sectors. One sector that became considerably larger in the 1960s and 1970s was government jobs. Because government is essentially a service for its citizens and does not produce material goods, it is considered part of the service sector. Education and health care are also considered part of the service sector.

Consumer services include jobs in retail, restaurants, and hair salons. Consumer service jobs tend to pay low wages; they also tend to require little education. Although these jobs might be the stereotypical form of service sector employment, in reality the percentage of people employed in consumer services has declined over the past several decades, mainly because of decreasing employment of maids and other household servants.

In economic terms, services are labor intensive, not capital intensive like manufacturing. A manufacturer relies largely on equipment and machinery—capital—to perform; a service business relies on its people. Indeed, some service businesses acknowledge this by referring to their employees as "human capital."

The relational aspect of services also makes the individual service provider a very important figure. For example, a doctor must spend years in school and get special accreditation before she may practice medicine. Even so, she might not be a good doctor, and society considers her performance to be so important that she can be sued or even imprisoned for not doing her job correctly.

The labor-intensive aspect of services led to speculation that services could not take advantage of economies of scale (the lower costs of making things that often result from making more of them). For instance, a doctor is only one person and can see only a certain number of patients a day.

However, during the 1990s service industries did appear to be able to organize around economies of scale. The consulting industry, for example, became increasingly dominated by large firms, which had the effect of spreading administrative costs over a larger group of employees. The rise of that industry in itself also suggested economies of scale at work: a group of people with extremely specialized knowledge who set up a consulting firm then apply that knowledge to several different companies concurrently—thus the specialized knowledge is applied to more places for less cost.

Producer Services

An increasingly important part of the service sector is producer services, or services sold to businesses. This sector includes finance, insurance, real estate, legal services, consulting, and so on. Producer services have grown as businesses have become larger, more international, and more complex. A business interested in starting operations abroad, for example, will probably employ a number of producer-service professionals to determine where to locate the operation, to help it navigate unfamiliar laws and regulations, and to finance the venture. The business may hire those workers from outside, or it may have in-house departments dedicated to various kinds of producer services.

Producer services have also grown because of changes in manufacturer opera-

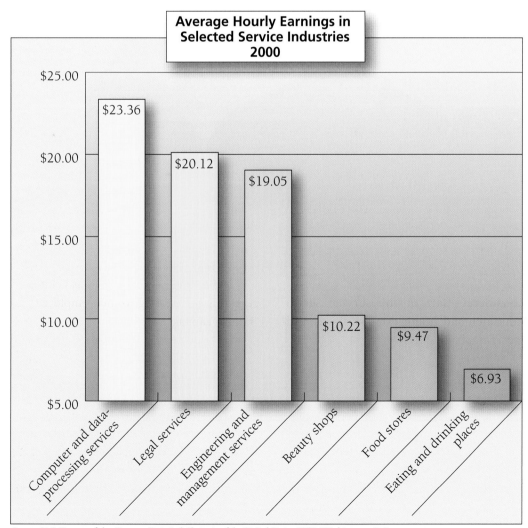

Source: U.S. Bureau of the Census, *Statistical Abstracts of the United States,* 2001, Washington, D.C., Government Printing Office, 2002.

tions. Ironically, one of the reasons that the manufacturing economy has declined is greater hiring from the service sector by manufacturers. Manufacturers have become increasingly reliant on technology and automation, which changes the kind of worker they tend to hire. A manufacturer can install an automated assembly line, with robots networked to a computer monitor that displays their status. Instead of hun-dreds of manufacturing-sector workers, the manufacturer needs only a handful—plus many service-sector workers to service the robots, design the networking software, and address computer problems.

If producer services blur the line between the manufacturing and service sectors, they can also blur the line between goods and services. Purchase a computer assembled by those in the manufacturing

Salaries for service workers vary widely depending on the service. Computer consultants are some of the best-paid service workers.

sector and it comes with software created by those in the service sector. It also may come with a service contract, which requires service-sector employees to fulfill.

Blurring the line between selling services and selling goods has always been the norm in restaurants but is increasingly becoming the norm in other fields as well because services add value to goods, giving them a competitive edge in the marketplace. Most consumers would rather buy a computer that comes with software and a service contract rather than a computer that needs basic software installed.

As a result, economists are increasingly viewing the service sector as a complement to manufacturing and a benefit to the national economy. In a service economy, goods and manufacturing do not disappear because many of the services revolve around them. Instead, goods and manufacturing are bolstered by services—goods are more competitive, manufacturing companies are more profitable, and workers are more productive.

Of course, adjustments by workers are required. If, as seems likely, manufacturing industries employ more and more service-sector workers, the old-fashioned manufacturing job, which paid fairly well and demanded more physical strength and endurance than education, is going to become even more endangered.

Service-sector jobs, in contrast, tend to either pay quite well or pay poorly; the determining factor is usually education and training rather than size and strength. Indeed, the gap in wages and employment is growing between workers with a college education and those without. Workers, especially women, have responded by seeking more education. From 1982 to 2007 the percentage of American workers with some college education rose from 33 percent to 61 percent.

The late 1990s were a time of high growth and increasing productivity that seemed to put to rest some of the earlier concerns about the service economy. Clearly, manufacturing will not disappear

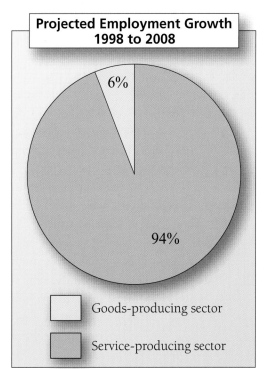

Projected Employment Growth 1998 to 2008

6%

94%

☐ Goods-producing sector

☐ Service-producing sector

Source: Bureau of Labor Statistics, "Service Sector Dominant Source of New Jobs," *MLR: The Editor's Desk,* 1999, http://www.bls.gov/opub/ted/1999/Nov/wk5/art05.txt (March 26, 2003).

and goods will continue to matter, even as the service sector remains dominant. As economists continue in their attempts to understand the service economy, more optimistic assessments are coming to the fore: services may be less vulnerable to recession and allow American products to compete globally. Current understanding of the service economy may not be any more accurate than past assessments, but as services seem here to stay, ample opportunity will be available to find out.

Further Research
Coalition of Service Industries
www.uscsi.org
CSI is a trade organization dedicated to the development of U.S. domestic and international policies that enhance the global competitiveness of the U.S. service sector through bilateral, regional, multilateral, and other trade and investment initiatives.
USA Economy in Brief
www.america.gov/publications/books/economy-in-brief.html
A U.S. Department of State publication that discusses the role of the service economy.

—*Mary Sisson*

Socialism

Socialism is a political ideology that maintains that economic equality is necessary for genuine human freedom. Socialists, accordingly, work to replace the capitalist system of competition and private property with a system based on cooperation and common ownership.

Despite these unifying themes of egalitarianism and anticapitalism, historically socialists have been divided over two main issues. First, reform versus revolution: Could the capitalist system be reformed through the democratic process or must it be overthrown by revolution? Second, collectivist versus libertarian socialism: Should a socialist economy be run by the government or by the workers themselves?

The Origins of Socialism

Socialists sometimes trace their origins to slave uprisings in the classical world, to peasant rebellions against the feudal system, or to the radicalism of the English Civil War in the 1640s. Socialists may draw inspiration from these episodes, yet no identifiable lineage connects these incidents to modern socialist thought, which is a product of the Industrial Revolution.

The term *socialism* was first used in the 1830s to describe the ideas of the utopian socialists Robert Owen, Charles Fourier, and Henri de Saint-Simon. Owen was a Welsh industrialist and social reformer who made three major contributions to the development of socialism: his experiments in collective living and working at New Lanark in Scotland and later New Harmony in Indiana; his theoretical views on the importance of the social environment in the formation of the human character; and his leadership of the first national trade union confederation in Britain. Fourier, a French social theorist, also advocated experimental communities. The creation of small-scale

Plans for New Harmony, Indiana, a utopian socialist community founded by Robert Owen in 1825.

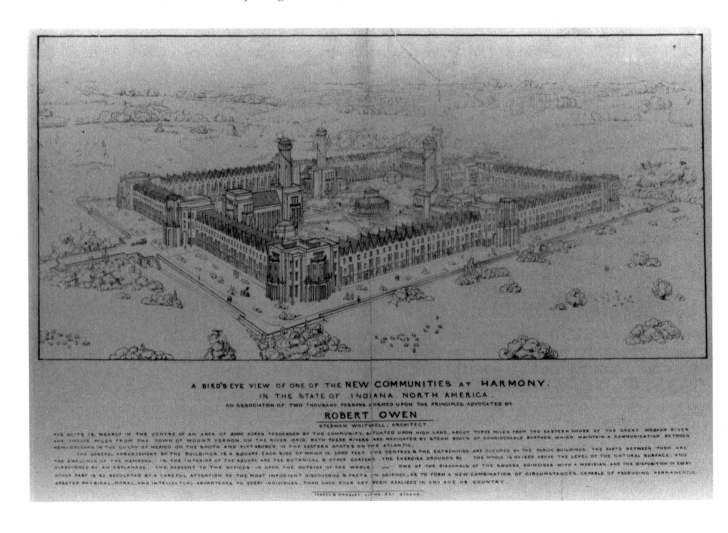

A BIRD'S EYE VIEW OF ONE OF THE NEW COMMUNITIES AT HARMONY.
IN THE STATE OF INDIANA NORTH AMERICA
AN ASSOCIATION OF TWO THOUSAND PERSONS FORMED UPON THE PRINCIPLES ADVOCATED BY
ROBERT OWEN
STEDMAN WHITWELL, ARCHITECT.

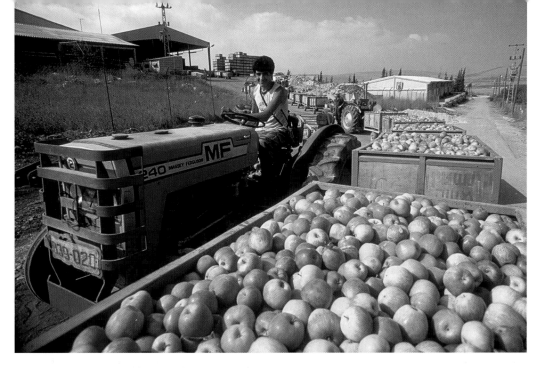

Apples being transported from a kibbutz in Israel.

cooperatives has continued to be a part of the libertarian socialist tradition and can still be seen, for example, in the Israeli kibbutz movement. Saint-Simon, another French thinker, took part in both the American and French Revolutions. His ideas on the achievement of social justice through industrialization directed by experts marks the start of collectivist socialism's interest in economic planning.

Marxism

The nineteenth-century German intellectual Karl Marx, along with his collaborator Friedrich Engels, rejected utopian socialism and worked to develop a theory of scientific socialism that would identify the laws of historical development, analyze the nature of capitalist society, and provide a strategy for the achievement of a communist society. They first set out their ideas in *The Communist Manifesto* (1848). Marx advanced three main arguments. First, all societies are divided along class lines. Second, every society has a class of exploiters and exploited. Third, history is driven forward toward communism by class conflict.

Marx contended that in a capitalist society the ruling class uses its economic power to shape society's ideas and culture to disguise the exploitation of the working class. Marx predicted that the capitalist system would impoverish the workers, who would then become receptive to the ideas of communist agitators. In most cases, the capitalists would have to be overthrown in violent revolution. Society would then enter its socialist phase, in which industry would be taken over by the state. In the later communist phase, the state would "wither away" and society would be organized on the principle of "from each according to his capacity, to each according to his needs."

Russia experienced the world's first communist revolution in 1917. Vladimir Lenin, the revolution's leader, was succeeded in 1928 by Joseph Stalin. Stalin initiated a drastic program of forced economic development directed by a totalitarian state. Stalin's exiled rival, Leon Trotsky, developed a Marxist critique of Soviet bureaucracy and organized revolutionary parties to work against state rule and for communist societies based on workers' control. Trotsky was murdered by Stalin's agents in 1940.

The Stalinist model was imposed on Eastern Europe by the Red Army at the close of World War II. Only Yugoslavia successfully pursued a communist path independent of the Soviet Union. In Hungary in 1956 and Czechoslovakia in 1968, attempts by communist governments to assert greater independence from Moscow were militarily thwarted by Soviet invasions.

In 1949 Mao Zedong led the communists to power in China. Mao developed a version of Marxism adapted to the conditions of developing countries, making the peasantry the agents of revolution. Both China and the Soviet Union backed communist parties and guerrilla movements in Asia, Latin America, and Africa. The expanding communist world was substantially weakened, however, by the Sino–Soviet split of the late 1960s, brought about by ideological differences and traditional rivalries between the two great powers.

Communism eventually collapsed in the early 1990s, brought down by its inability to sustain military expenditures, by the immense inefficiencies of its planned economies, and by tensions within the Soviet bloc, especially in Eastern Europe. Most former communist states have since converted to democracy and the market economy, with varying degrees of success. Others have been plagued by ethnic conflict, especially the new republics of the former Yugoslavia. The People's Republic of China has maintained its communist system of government while making the transition to a market economy. Residual communist countries, for example, Cuba and Vietnam, are also liberalizing their economies. Only North Korea remains relatively unchanged.

The Social Democratic Tradition

West European social democracy, or democratic socialism, is a strand of socialist thought that has developed independently of Marxism. Social democrats want to use the democratic process to reform capitalism in the direction of greater equality. They trace their origins to the German socialist Eduard Bernstein and his book *Evolutionary Socialism* (1899). Reformists argue that capitalism has changed since Marx began writing about it in the 1840s. Working men (and later women) have acquired the right to vote. Labor and socialist political parties have emerged. Trade unions have improved workers' pay and conditions. A growing number of worker-capitalists have even bought shares in businesses. Thus, proletarian revolution has become unnecessary, even counterproductive. From the early twentieth century onward, European leftists criticized capitalism increasingly in ethical, rather than economic, terms.

In the years following World War II, most West European countries created comprehensive welfare states (governments that devote a large measure of their expenditures to providing benefits to individuals) and mixed economies (economies that are partly market-driven and partly government-controlled, in which the state takes over key industries). In *The Future of Socialism* (1956), British Labour politician Anthony Crosland argued that socialists had achieved their principal goals; consequently, no further state ownership was

A socialist rally in Madrid, Spain, in 1995.

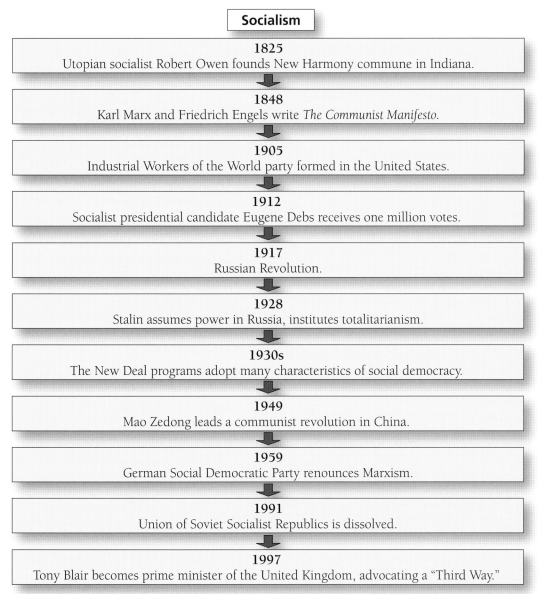

Socialism

1825
Utopian socialist Robert Owen founds New Harmony commune in Indiana.

1848
Karl Marx and Friedrich Engels write *The Communist Manifesto.*

1905
Industrial Workers of the World party formed in the United States.

1912
Socialist presidential candidate Eugene Debs receives one million votes.

1917
Russian Revolution.

1928
Stalin assumes power in Russia, institutes totalitarianism.

1930s
The New Deal programs adopt many characteristics of social democracy.

1949
Mao Zedong leads a communist revolution in China.

1959
German Social Democratic Party renounces Marxism.

1991
Union of Soviet Socialist Republics is dissolved.

1997
Tony Blair becomes prime minister of the United Kingdom, advocating a "Third Way."

necessary, and the Left should instead concentrate on creating a more equal society through the redistribution of wealth by means of taxation and social spending. In 1959 the German Social Democratic Party renounced Marxism and proclaimed that it was now a "people's party," not a "workers' party."

In the mid-1970s the model favored by social democrats was put under severe pressure by concurrent rises in unemployment and inflation. Governments throughout the developed world responded with antiinflationary monetary policies, the privatization of state industries, greater free market competition, and welfare reform. In some countries, Britain, the United States, and Canada among them, these policies were championed by conservative politicians and opposed by social democrats. In Australia, New Zealand, and Spain, the reforms arose from social democratic governments.

At the turn of the twenty-first century, social democrats continue efforts to modernize their ideology. The former British Labour Party prime minister Tony Blair has joined with centrist politicians from outside the social democratic tradition, including former U.S. president Bill Clinton, to advocate the "Third Way," which seeks to reconcile the market economy with social justice, a policy orientation also advocated by the administration of U.S. president Barack Obama.

We are entering tonight upon a momentous campaign. The struggle for political supremacy is not between political parties merely, as appears upon the surface, but at bottom it is a life and death struggle between two hostile economic classes, the one the capitalist, and the other the working class.

The capitalist class is represented by the Republican, Democratic, Populist and Prohibition parties, all of which stand for private ownership of the means of production, and the triumph of any one of which will mean continued wage-slavery to the working class. . . .

The Republican and Democratic parties, or, to be more exact, the Republican-Democratic party, represent the capitalist class in the class struggle. They are the political wings of the capitalist system and such differences as arise between them relate to spoils and not to principles.

With either of those parties in power one thing is always certain and that is that the capitalist class is in the saddle and the working class under the saddle.

Under the administration of both these parties the means of production are private property, production is carried forward for capitalist profit purely, markets are glutted and industry paralyzed, workingmen become tramps and criminals while injunctions, soldiers and riot guns are brought into action to preserve "law and order" in the chaotic carnival of capitalistic anarchy.

Deny it as may the cunning capitalists who are clear-sighted enough to perceive it, or ignore it as may the torpid workers who are too blind and unthinking to see it, the struggle in which we are engaged today is a class struggle, and as the toiling millions come to see and understand it and rally to the political standard of their class, they will drive all capitalist parties of whatever name into the same party, and the class struggle will then be so clearly revealed that the hosts of labor will find their true place in the conflict and strike the united and decisive blow that will destroy slavery and achieve their full and final emancipation.

In this struggle the workingmen and women and children are represented by the Socialist party and it is my privilege to address you in the name of that revolutionary and uncompromising party of the working class. . . .

I shall not stand alone, for the party that has my allegiance and may have my life, the Socialist party, the party of the working class, the party of emancipation, is made up of men and women who know their rights and scorn to compromise with their oppressors; who want no votes that can be bought and no support under any false pretense whatsoever.

The Socialist party stands squarely upon its proletarian principles and relies wholly upon the forces of industrial progress and the education of the working class.

The Socialist party buys no votes and promises no offices. Not a farthing is spent for whiskey or cigars. Every penny in the campaign fund is the voluntary offerings of workers and their sympathizers and every penny is used for education.

What other parties can say the same?

—Eugene Debs, speech to the Socialist Party Convention, 1904

American Socialism

In contrast to most other Western democracies, the United States has never accepted socialism as a mainstream political idea. Historians have suggested several possible explanations. First, as a wealthy society, the United States has avoided some of the material hardships that gave rise to socialist movements elsewhere. Second, America affords greater social mobility than Europe. Consequently, socialism's language of class has less appeal to Americans. Third, during the cold war, communist and socialist ideas were tainted by association with the Soviet Union.

Socialism has not been altogether absent from the American political experience. The late nineteenth century witnessed the growth of radical farmers' movements, principally in the Midwest. A militant trade union movement, the International Workers of the World, known as the Wobblies, was formed in 1905 to achieve socialism through strike action. In the presidential election of 1912, American Socialist Party leader Eugene Debs garnered a million votes; an American Communist Party was founded in 1919.

During the 1930s the Roosevelt administration's New Deal shared many characteristics of social democracy and, in the 1960s, the antipoverty programs of the Kennedy and Johnson administrations owed much to the ideas of the American socialist Michael Harrington. At the beginning of the twenty-first century, Democratic Socialists of America is the principal American affiliate to the social-democratic Socialist International.

Marxist communism has been discredited by its record of political repression and economic failure, and communist parties around the world have gone into decline. By contrast, the social-democratic tradition shows signs of recovery after two decades of serious electoral and ideological challenges. However, whether the advocates of the "Third Way" will revive social democracy or merge it with mainstream liberalism is still to be seen.

Further Reading

Heaven on Earth: The Rise and Fall of Socialism
www.pbs.org/heavenonearth/
Web site accompanying a PBS documentary.

History of Economic Thought Web Site
homepage.newschool.edu/het//index.htm
Home page of the New School University's repository of links and information on economic history and theory.

Marxists Internet Archive
www.marxists.org
This archive of writings that are Marxist or relevant to the understanding of Marxism includes a students' section with background information on the history of Marxist thought.

—Peter C. Grosvenor

Subsidy

Subsidy is financial assistance granted by a government to a private person, association, or corporation to support an undertaking considered beneficial to the public. Subsidy may come in the form of direct financial contributions or it may be indirect aid, for example, tax breaks, low-interest loans, inexpensive insurance, and low purchase prices for land and natural resources. Subsidy also describes financial assistance granted by one country to another.

Every year, billions of U.S. tax dollars are spent on subsidizing a vast array of American businesses, industries, and services. In addition, the federal government regularly subsidizes other countries through, for example, liberal trade policies and direct assistance packages. The general consensus is that the United States must engage in these forms of subsidy to promote the health of the national economy and general public welfare. Rarely, however, do policy makers fully agree on who should get what. Indeed, although most agree that government subsidy of big business and industry should be reduced, enacting legislation that reflects this ideal has proven to be difficult for members of Congress, who must balance their constituents' concerns with those of the country as a whole.

Why Subsidize?

The word *subsidy* often carries a negative connotation: the media regularly warn about government spending that benefits big business and industry at the cost of American taxpayers. At the same time, U.S. subsidy policies are partly responsible for making the United States the world's leading economic power. For instance, in the nineteenth century the federal government developed a system of subsidies to encourage individuals and companies to make the high-risk move to the western states. Legislation during this time made land free for homesteaders, developed railroads, waterways, and irrigation systems, and offered rock-bottom prices for the purchase of land containing natural resources. Without these various forms of subsidy, the West would never have developed and flourished as it did. State and federal governments still apply similar subsidy principles to support the growth of new technologies in industries like defense and energy.

Subsidy has also proven to be instrumental in strengthening weakened economies. For example, in the 1930s, when the U.S. economy was ravaged by the Great Depression, Congress passed New Deal legislation, including the Agricultural Adjustment Administration, which helped to control crop overproduction by paying farmers to leave their land fallow. Other forms of subsidy, for example, the Civilian Conservation Corps and the Tennessee

Two U.S. Civilian Conservation Corps enrollees work on the construction of a building in Arkansas in 1937.

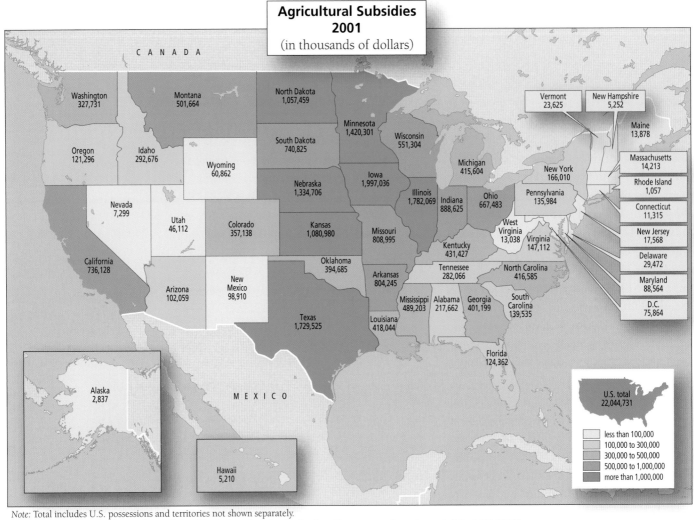

Agricultural Subsidies 2001

(in thousands of dollars)

CANADA

Washington 327,731

Montana 501,664

North Dakota 1,057,459

Minnesota 1,420,301

Vermont 23,625

New Hampshire 5,252

Maine 13,878

Oregon 121,296

Idaho 292,676

Wyoming 60,862

South Dakota 740,825

Wisconsin 551,304

Michigan 415,604

New York 166,010

Massachusetts 14,213

Rhode Island 1,057

Nebraska 1,334,706

Iowa 1,997,036

Pennsylvania 135,984

Connecticut 11,315

Nevada 7,299

Utah 46,112

Colorado 357,138

Kansas 1,080,980

Illinois 1,782,069

Indiana 888,625

Ohio 667,483

West Virginia 13,038

Virginia 147,112

New Jersey 17,568

Delaware 29,472

California 736,128

Missouri 808,995

Kentucky 431,427

Maryland 88,564

D.C. 75,864

Arizona 102,059

New Mexico 98,910

Oklahoma 394,685

Arkansas 804,245

Tennessee 282,066

North Carolina 416,585

South Carolina 139,535

Mississippi 489,203

Alabama 217,662

Georgia 401,199

Texas 1,729,525

Louisiana 418,044

Florida 124,362

MEXICO

Alaska 2,837

Hawaii 5,210

U.S. total 22,044,731

less than 100,000
100,000 to 300,000
300,000 to 500,000
500,000 to 1,000,000
more than 1,000,000

Note: Total includes U.S. possessions and territories not shown separately.

Source: U.S. Department of Agriculture, National Agriculture Statistics Service, http://www.nass.usda.gov/research (March 23, 2003).

Valley Authority, reduced unemployment and provided environmental and development assistance to depressed regions. Although much New Deal–era legislation is no longer in effect, its principles still influence U.S. subsidy policy.

Another important form of subsidy occurs when state and federal governments help industries provide a necessary public service that would otherwise not be profitable. For example, in the 1920s the federal government began subsidizing private airlines for delivery of mail. In part because of this policy, the airline industry grew and carriers began to transport passengers. The industry is now so essential to the health of the U.S. economy that, after the 2001 terrorist attacks, Congress quickly passed a $15 billion aid package to ensure the survival of the industry.

Other industries that receive this kind of federal and state support include health care, education, railroads, and home and road construction.

With all of these tax dollars being funneled into domestic business and industry, why should the United States subsidize other countries? The United States may do so to generate goodwill, assist a war effort that is deemed important to national security, or to help stabilize a country's economy—increasingly important in an era of globalization, when one region's economic distress may effectively destabilize the world economy. The United States does not work alone in providing such subsidies. The International Monetary Fund (IMF), an organization of 185 countries, was established to encourage economic growth in member countries and promote financial cooperation. To fulfill that mission, the IMF often provides temporary financial assistance to countries that are threatened by excessive debt or currency devaluation.

Subsidy Controversies

Despite these clear benefits of subsidy, U.S. policy makers have been sharply criticized for continuing subsidy policies that primarily benefit huge corporations rather than small businesses and individuals who are more clearly in need of assistance. U.S. farm policy has come under particular scrutiny in recent years. In the first decade of the twenty-first century, $73 billion in federal subsidies will go to farms, but 47 percent of the payments go to 8 percent of the nation's farms—the wealthiest of them; 60 percent of the nation's farms receive no crop subsidies at all. Critics have demanded that the federal government reduce this level of spending and redirect it to less wealthy farms. In addition, concern has been expressed that such subsidy policies do more harm to the

economy than good: because agricultural subsidies often come in the form of the government paying farmers a fixed price for crops, farmers are motivated to overproduce without regard for real market prices.

Congress has been criticized for "pork barrel" spending, or legislation that subsidizes special projects for particular districts and states. Through pork barrel spending, federal money is channeled into unnecessary military bases, prisons, and VA hospitals to keep them in operation, and waterway, bridge, and highway construction that would typically be paid for with state money. "Pork" does not benefit the country at large; it serves the narrow interests of legislators' districts and states. Thus, pork barrel spending is largely considered to be a method of securing reelection—at a cost to U.S. taxpayers of billions of dollars a year "Pork barrel" spending was a central issue in the heated 2008 presidential campaign, as Republican candidate John McCain made cutting "pork" and other government spending a key part of

Senator John McCain led a bipartisan initiative to curb the use of "pork" in spending bills in 2009.

A farmer fertilizes wheat in Tennessee, where farmers received $195 million in USDA subsidies in 2006.

his electoral platform. Although McCain did not win the election, it brought the issue to a wide audience.

Such wasteful subsidy policies may go hand in hand with environmental degradation. Government-supported mining, farming, ranching, irrigation, logging, and oil and gas drilling enterprises are allowed to deplete natural resources, pollute air and groundwater, and destroy whole ecosystems. Often the government foots the bill for environmental cleanup costs, rather than holding the companies themselves responsible. Taxpayer and environmental organizations like Friends of the Earth, Taxpayers for Common Sense, and U.S. PIRGs (Public Interest Research Groups) lobby Congress for reform of subsidy policies that are doubly costly in their wastefulness and the harm they do to the environment.

With special interest groups spending millions of dollars a year in lobbying on Capitol Hill, government cannot seem to wean big businesses from the federal dollar. Despite talk about cuttings subsidies, in practice, Congress has often done the reverse—not only maintaining but also expanding federal aid to favored industries and pork barrel projects. However, cuts in subsidy spending must be approached with caution: U.S. businesses must remain competitive with other countries that provide similar subsidies. Hence, at the beginning of the twenty-first century, U.S. policy makers have a mandate to enact subsidy reforms that promote taxpayer rights at the same time that they preserve national health, economic and otherwise.

Further Research
How to Spend an Extra $15 Billion
www.washingtonpost.com/wp-srv/nation/
    interactives/farmaid
An in-depth investigation into agricultural subsidies
    by reporters from the *Washington Post*.

—*Andrea Troyer and John Troyer*

Sustainable Development

Historically, environmental protection has been considered the enemy of economic growth. Sustainable development strives to reconcile these two goals, meeting the needs of the present without compromising the ability of future generations to meet their own needs. The concept has revolutionized the way in which many businesses view environmental issues. Nevertheless, the concept is problematic and controversial, and its usefulness for solving Earth's ongoing environmental crisis remains uncertain.

What Is Sustainable Development?

Until recently, economists and environmentalists seldom saw eye-to-eye. The publication of *The Limits to Growth* (1972), an influential but highly pessimistic report by the Club of Rome, a think tank concerned with global problems, prompted a debate on whether unchecked economic growth threatened to severely deplete natural resources. In *Small Is Beautiful* (1973), British environmentalist E. F. Schumacher advocated lower economic growth and small-scale local development to protect the environment. Oxford economist Wilfred Beckerman replied with an argument that "small is stupid" because "economic growth is still a necessary condition for remedying most of the serious environmental problems facing the world, particularly in developing countries."

The concept of sustainable development suggested a way of moving beyond this polarized economy-versus-environment debate. The basic concept of sustainable development is the belief that economic development can proceed without exhausting the natural resources on which all life ultimately depends.

If environmentalists view sustainable development as a way to control what they

A crowded train station in Bhopal, India, in 1984; more than 200,000 people were forced to flee the city because of the Union Carbide industrial accident that killed 2,500 people and injured another 50,000.

consider to be the worst excesses of industry and commerce, businesses see the concept as a new path to competitive advantage. According to H. N. J. Smits, CEO and chairman of Dutch banking group Rabobank, "Sustainable development, far from being a new and restrictive condition to industrial and financial progress, provides the keys that will unlock all the major markets of the future." For example, oil companies might redefine themselves as energy supply companies and base their businesses on sustainable energy forms like solar power. This would bring not just environmental benefits but also ensure the longer-term viability and profitability of oil companies as petroleum reserves dwindle.

Political entities like the European Union also note the economic advantages of sustainable development; Europe's member states adopted their first joint sustainability strategy in June 2001, arguing that the strategy would deal "with economic, social and environmental policies in a mutually reinforcing way." The World Business Council on Sustainable Development confirms this view: "Sustainable development is about ensuring a better quality of life for everyone, now and for generations to come. Thus it combines ecological, social, and economic concerns, and offers business opportunities for companies that can improve the lives of the world's people."

Several attempts have been made to define sustainable development more clearly.

A 1987 report, *Our Common Future* (also known as the Brundtland report after its chair, Norwegian politician Gro Harlem Brundtland), proposed that key elements of sustainable development include: using growth to eliminate poverty and meet basic human needs in developing countries; conserving and enhancing natural resources; developing environmentally appropriate technologies; and combining economic and environmental factors in decision-making processes. Others have since offered strategies for realizing the promise of sustainable development. In 1991 the International Chamber of Commerce published a 16-point Business Charter for Sustainable Development, which seeks to integrate environmental concerns into key aspects of business management, including customer relations, employee training, and relationships with vendors and suppliers.

For all these attempts at clarification, no single definition of sustainable development has emerged. Indeed, as *Economist* environment editor Frances Cairncross has written: "The appeal of the phrase is that it means so many different things to different people. Every environmentally aware politician is in favor of it, a sure sign that they do not know what it means."

The Pros and Cons of Sustainable Development

The value of the sustainable development concept may depend less on how clearly it can be defined than on how much of a difference it makes in practice. Supporters of the idea point to considerable progress in some industries, but critics remain doubtful. Forestry, for example, has witnessed high-profile initiatives like the Forestry Stewardship Council (FSC), an international labeling initiative that encourages consumers to choose wood products harvested from sustainable forests and to avoid timber from tropical rain forests. However, according to the FSC, only about 0.02 percent of the world's forests are managed sustainably. Moreover, economic studies suggest that, although global incentives to conserve

Humanity has the ability to make development sustainable—to ensure that it meets the needs of the present without compromising the ability of future generations to meet their own needs. The concept of sustainable development does imply limits—not absolute limits but limitations imposed by the present state of technology and social organization on environmental resources and by the ability of the biosphere to absorb the effects of human activities. But technology and social organization can be both managed and improved to make way for a new era of economic growth. The commission believes that widespread poverty is no longer inevitable. Poverty is not only an evil in itself, but sustainable development requires meeting the basic needs of all and extending to all the opportunity to fulfill their aspirations for a better life. A world in which poverty is endemic will always be prone to ecological and other catastrophes.

—*Our Common Future* (The Brundtland Report),
World Commission on Environment and Development, 1987

U.N. Commission on Sustainable Development Indicators

Social	Environmental	Economic	Institutional
Equity • Poverty • Gender equality **Health** • Nutritional status • Mortality • Sanitation • Drinking water • Health care delivery **Education** • Education level • Literacy **Living conditions** • Housing • Security (crime) • Population (population change)	**Atmosphere** • Climate change • Ozone layer depletion • Air quality **Land** • Agriculture • Forests • Desertification • Urbanization **Oceans, seas, and coasts** • Coastal zone • Fisheries **Fresh water** • Water quantity • Water quality **Biodiversity** • Ecosystem • Species	**Economic structure** • Economic performance • Trade • Financial status **Consumption and production patterns** • Material consumption • Energy use • Waste generation and management • Transportation	**Institutional framework** • Strategic implementation of sustainable development strategy • International cooperation **Institutional capacity** • Information access • Science and technology • Disaster preparedness and response

Source: U.N. Commission on Sustainable Development, "Indicators of Sustainable Development," http://www.un.org/esa/sustdev (March 10, 2003).

The U.N. Commission on Sustainable Development has outlined a large number of indicators, which include social, economic, institutional, and environmental factors.

forests or manage them sustainably may be in place, old-style industrial logging continues to provide much better financial returns, especially from a national perspective—a major disincentive to the adoption of sustainable development practices.

Other industries have also moved toward sustainability. The chemical industry in North America, Europe, and Australia has established a program called Responsible Care that, among other achievements, has encouraged companies to reduce toxic emissions, communicate with local communities, and persuade suppliers to join them on a journey of progressive environmental improvement. Critics argue that voluntary regulatory programs are simply a ruse to avoid tougher, government-imposed regulations in the aftermath of chemical disasters like the explosion at the Union Carbide chemical factory in Bhopal, India, in 1984.

Sustainable development is problematic for other reasons. One difficulty is that some industries can more easily integrate the concept into their operations. Information technology companies find sustainable development much easier to embrace than, for example, oil companies, whose core business, according to most definitions, can never be remotely sustainable.

Another problem is the difficulty of assessing whether local efforts toward sustainable development are having a similar effect on a global scale. For example, cities

---

Achieving Sustainable Development

In its report *Sustainability through the Market*, the World Business Council on Sustainable Development suggested seven keys to sustainability:

- increasing innovation (developing "new ways to improve lives while boosting business");
- practicing eco-efficiency (for example, implementing energy-saving technologies that save more money than they cost);
- increasing dialogue between companies, governments, and local communities;
- influencing customer choices by making the benefits of sustainability clearer and more compelling;
- encouraging markets to take more account of environmental and social concerns;
- using markets to reach and improve the lives of the poorest people;
- and "establishing the worth of Earth"—making sure the true environmental and social costs of our use of resources are appreciated.

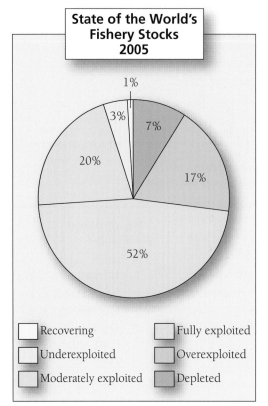

State of the World's Fishery Stocks 2005

1%
3%
7%
20%
17%
52%

☐ Recovering ☐ Fully exploited
☐ Underexploited ☐ Overexploited
☐ Moderately exploited ☐ Depleted

One indicator of the degree to which sustainable development has or has not been achieved is world fish stocks, many of which are overexploited.

Source: United Nations Food and Agriculture Organization. *The State of World Fisheries and Agriculture.*

in industrialized nations have achieved major improvements in air and water quality over recent decades through tougher legislation and greater public awareness of environmental issues. Some of these gains are the result of the gradual transition from manufacturing to service economies in the developed world. Yet developed countries still need manufactured goods, many of which are now produced in developing countries that have less stringent environmental regulations. Sustainability gains in developed nations may, therefore, have been counterbalanced by environmental and social losses in developing nations.

Some environmentalists view the concept of sustainable development with suspicion, believing it may be used as a public relations exercise to disguise business-as-usual industrial attitudes with environmental platitudes—a technique these environmentalists call "greenwash." They cite, for example, the way oil companies have set up token solar energy ventures, while simultaneously supporting organizations like the Global Climate Coalition, a Washington,

D.C.–based lobby that campaigns against the science of climate change and the political efforts to address it. Economists like Wilfred Beckerman are also skeptical: "If 'sustainable development' is interpreted . . . as implying that all other components of welfare are to be sacrificed in the interests of preserving the environment in the form it happens to be in today, then it is morally indefensible."

Overall, so-called sustainability indicators, for example, plummeting fish stocks, animal species in decline, rising human population in developing nations, and deteriorating freshwater resources, suggest the world has never been further from sustainable development. According to Dr. James Baker, head of the U.S. National Oceanic and Atmospheric Administration, "there is a global consensus that we must make our development sustainable." That much is evident in statements from organizations, the World Bank, for instance, which argue for sustainable economic growth that can eradicate poverty, and the World Business Council on Sustainable Development, which highlights the profitable business opportunities offered by improving people's lives.

Further Reading
Center for Sustainable Global Enterprise
www.johnson.cornell.edu/sge
This center, at Cornell University, looks at the interaction of business and sustainability.
Learning for Sustainability
www.learningforsustainability.net
A Web site offering Internet resources on sustainability and governance.
U.N. Division for Sustainable Development
www.un.org/esa/dsd
The United Nations operation provides research and resources on international sustainable development issues.
World Bank
www.worldbank.org
Home page of the World Bank.
World Business Council for Sustainable Development
www.wbcsd.org
The WBCSD is a CEO-led, global association of some 200 companies.

—Chris Woodford

Tariff

A tariff is a tax associated with the import or export of goods and services. These taxes are also referred to as customs duties. Tariffs can be structured as a percentage of the price of the item or as a flat, per unit tax. For instance, the government could place a tariff of 10 percent on all imported automobiles; this charge is referred to as an ad valorem tariff (*ad valorem* is Latin for "according to the value"). Alternatively, the government could simply charge a flat rate of $1,500 per automobile; such charge is called a specific tariff.

Tariffs have a long history and have been used quite extensively throughout U.S. history as a way for the federal government to raise tax revenues. Prior to the creation of the federal income tax in 1913, a major portion of U.S. government revenues came from tariffs on trade. In 1900 tariff revenues contributed about 50 percent to federal government revenues. Later in the century, however, tariff revenues had shrunk dramatically to only about 1.5 percent of federal government revenues.

Between 1945 and 2001 the worldwide level of tariffs was reduced by almost 95 percent as a result of two factors. First, the General Agreement on Tariffs and Trade (GATT) specifically targeted tariffs for reduction within a multilateral, mutually negotiated framework. Second, as tariffs have fallen out of favor, a pernicious cousin to the tariff—quotas—has risen to take their place as the preferred method of protecting domestic industries and their workers. GATT created the World Trade Organization, which is the forum for international trade negotiations. Negotiations subsequent to GATT, known as the Doha Development Agenda, began in 2001 but ended in stalemate in 2008.

Tariffs violate economic efficiency because they reduce the gains from trades that accrue through specialization and exchange. The logic of gains from trade extends from trade among individuals to trade among complex societies. The initial reason for people to trade is either to obtain something they do not have access to or to take advantage of the productivity gains inherent to specialization and exchange. When one party specializes in the production of, say, automobiles, many productivity gains result. However, for specialization to be worthwhile, people must be free to trade. To the extent that tariffs reduce trade, they reduce productivity gains.

Because tariffs create both winners and losers in the economic system, they are linked to the concept of protectionism. The following example uses the United States and a $50 tariff on imported bicycles to illustrate the effects of a tariff. At least six important groups are affected when tariffs are placed on bicycles: foreign bicycle producers, foreign bicycle workers, domestic bicycle producers, domestic bicycle workers, domestic bicycle consumers, and the government.

Under the tariff, foreign bicycle producers are required to pay $50 for each bicycle exported to the United States; they would

A cartoon from 1921 mocks the Republican Party's reliance on tariffs.

CURES ALL THE ILLS OF MAN OR BEAST

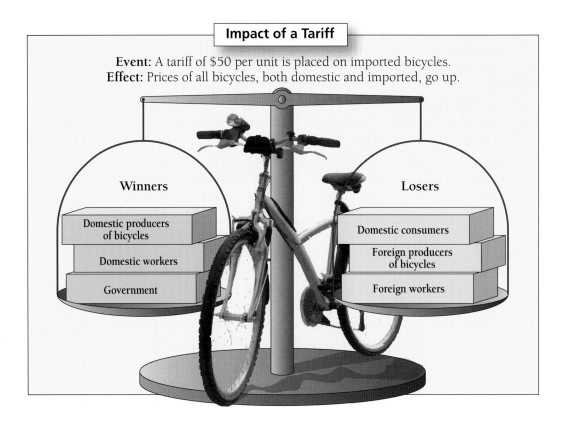

Impact of a Tariff

Event: A tariff of $50 per unit is placed on imported bicycles.
Effect: Prices of all bicycles, both domestic and imported, go up.

Winners
- Domestic producers of bicycles
- Domestic workers
- Government

Losers
- Domestic consumers
- Foreign producers of bicycles
- Foreign workers

treat the charge as a cost of production. As a direct result, the price of imported foreign bicycles rises. Domestic consumers respond by buying fewer foreign bicycles. Therefore, foreign producers and their workers lose under the tariff. On the other hand, a tariff will benefit domestic bicycle producers and workers. As the prices of the imported bicycles rise, consumers will buy more domestic bicycles because their price, relative to foreign bicycles, has fallen.

The fifth group affected is domestic consumers of bicycles. Consumer choice becomes increasingly limited, and the tariff is a tax that ultimately increases the price of all bicycles. The final major group affected by a tariff is the government, which receives the tariff revenues of $50 per bicycle. States are banned from imposing tariffs so, in the United States, the federal government receives all tariff revenues. Thus, the winners are domestic producers and workers in the import-competing industry and the government. The losers are domestic consumers, foreign producers, and foreign workers.

The pattern of winners and losers creates a tendency for government to enact tariffs: domestic industries and organized labor are typically well represented in lobbying the government for favorable treatment. This effort is aided by two realities faced by consumers. First, most consumers know little about how tariffs affect prices. Second, consumers, unlike industries, are not a well-organized group with lobbying power capable of delivering votes and making campaign contributions.

Further Reading
World Trade Organization
www.wto.org
Home page of the World Trade Organization.
—*Bradley K. Hobbs*

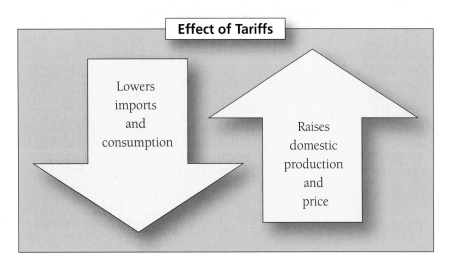

Effect of Tariffs

Lowers imports and consumption

Raises domestic production and price

Wealth Distribution

The issue of wealth distribution has dominated world history for hundreds of years. It has been the cause of wars, revolutions, and dramatic political changes across the globe. These conflicts resulted in new forms of government and affected the lives of billions of people. The distribution of wealth is how the income, property, and productive resources of a society are apportioned among its members. A society with an equal distribution of wealth would see all citizens with the same amount.

Historical Perspective

Most of history has featured a dramatically unequal distribution of wealth worldwide, with a small number controlling the vast majority of the wealth. In kingdoms with larger populations, for example, China, Japan, and most of Europe, such control was maintained through a system called feudalism. In brief, feudalism involved the rulers granting land to nobles in exchange for loyalty; the nobles then allowed peasants residency in return for working the land, paying taxes, and serving as soldiers.

The poor benefited because they received protection provided by the nobles. The cost of this system to the poor was twofold. First was a rigid social structure in which the peasants had no political rights. Second, as few employment opportunities were available outside of farming and peasants were not free to leave the estates, feudalism kept the great majority of the peasants poor. The feudal system worked to the great advantage of the land-owning nobles.

Feudalism gradually evolved into less onerous forms of government, with peasants slowly gaining some rights in Europe as the Crusades, the growth of cities, and other events unfolded. This trend accelerated with the beginning of the Agricultural Revolution, starting about 1500. Farm production increased because of better

technology, new crops, and better farming methods. By the 1700s increased agricultural efficiencies led to a surplus labor force because fewer farmers were needed. About the same time, the Industrial Revolution began and the poor migrated to the cities to work in the new factories.

Conditions in the cities were abysmal: low pay, unsafe working conditions, and long hours. Rapid urbanization, first in England and then in other parts of Europe, was accompanied by the creation of slums and unsanitary living conditions. However,

An 1873 wood engraving entitled "Two Christmas Dinners," from Frank Leslie's Illustrated Newspaper, *shows the contrast between rich and poor in the nineteenth century.*

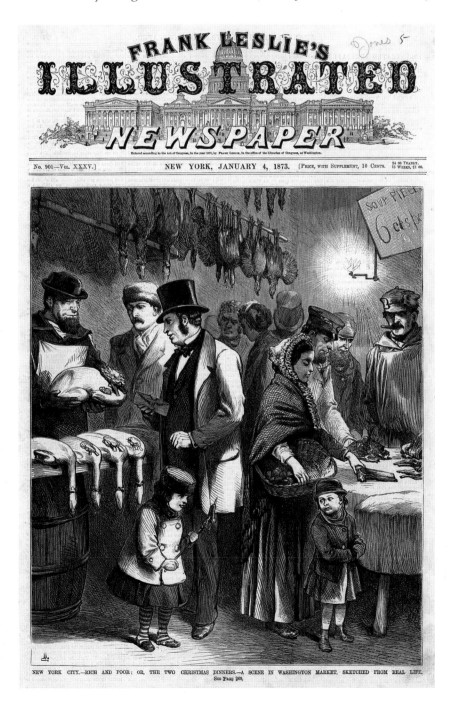

another consequence of the Industrial Revolution was the rise of a new social class, the newly rich. These were men who became wealthy by starting their own businesses. Such means of generating wealth had dramatic political and economic effects on Europe and the United States.

Many of the newly rich embraced a political philosophy called liberalism. Most prominently asserted by Adam Smith (1723–1790), liberalism called for less government interference in the economy and increased economic freedoms. The liberals also demanded political rights from the ruling conservatives, which resulted in the gradual spread of male suffrage, the right to vote. The gradual redistribution of wealth during the Industrial Revolution led to greater political rights for the newly rich and greater economic opportunities for all. However, liberals shared many of the attitudes the "old money" held about the poor: both felt that poverty was a natural condition and that the solution to being poor was hard work. Thus, neither liberals nor conservatives offered a direct solution to the mass poverty of the urban slums.

A second and related consequence was the development of Marxism. Karl Marx (1818–1883) was repulsed by liberalism and considered it to be a way to continue the suffering of the proletariat—his term for the large majority who were the working poor. He forecast that this system would eventually fall to a worldwide revolt of the poor in response to their horrid conditions of life and labor. Marxism called for a drastic change in the distribution of political power and wealth in society. In brief, Marx argued for total economic and political equality, with universal suffrage and public ownership of all means of production. Such changes were to be accomplished through a violent overthrow of the rich by the poor.

Marx's predictions of worldwide revolution were not realized for several reasons. First, Adam Smith's assertion that liberalism would ultimately improve living standards for the poor and middle class proved to be correct. Gradually the working hours, pay, and working conditions of European and U.S. workers improved. Second, the capitalist nations gradually enacted social and economic reforms to address the worst excesses of capitalism. Voting rights were expanded in Europe and the United States, child labor laws enacted, and other laws passed to improve working conditions and living standards for the poor.

Wealth Distribution in the Modern Era

Economists generally agree that, at least in developed countries, wealth gradually became more equally distributed until roughly 1970. Government policies like unemployment insurance, old age insurance (pensions), and progressive income tax codes all worked to redistribute wealth, benefiting the poor more than the rich. This period also saw the "golden age" of the middle class, especially in the United States. The country experienced an extended economic expansion after World War II, maintaining high levels of employment.

U.S. Aggregate Income: Percentage Received by Each Fifth of Households 1970 to 2000						
Year	Lowest fifth	Second fifth	Third fifth	Fourth fifth	Highest fifth	Top 5 percent
1970	4.1	10.8	17.4	24.5	43.3	16.6
1975	4.4	10.5	17.1	24.8	43.2	15.9
1980	4.3	10.3	16.9	24.9	43.7	15.8
1985	4.0	9.7	16.3	24.6	45.3	17.0
1990	3.9	9.6	15.9	24.0	46.6	18.6
1995	3.7	9.1	15.2	23.3	48.7	21.0
2000	3.6	8.9	14.9	23.0	49.6	21.9

Source: U.S. Bureau of the Census, *Current Population Survey,* http://www.census.gov/hhes/www/income.html (April 29, 2003).

Combined with relatively strong unions, workers maintained high wages that ensured good living standards.

The early 1970s brought economic instability and other changes in the economy. Inflation eroded the purchasing power of consumers, hurting the poor the most. Concurrently, foreign competition eroded the profits of U.S. and European corporations, reducing their ability to pay high wages. Previously well-paid manufacturing jobs were moved to developing nations as corporations attempted to cut costs.

About the same time the nature of work began to change. Service sector jobs, for example, in health care and tourism, grew as manufacturing declined. Employers began to demand more sophisticated skills, especially computer usage, in return for high wages. The result of these changes was reduced opportunity for low-skilled workers to earn middle-class wages. Unions, which previously had been able to force employers to pay higher wages, were weaker in these fields. Unions also experienced a general decline in their overall power because of political changes and the decline of manufacturing jobs.

Determining Wealth

Education has become the most important predictor of a worker's income and potential to become wealthy. The average earnings chart above shows that in every case, more education results in a higher average income for all workers. For example, the income difference between the average college graduate and high school graduate is roughly $32,500 for men and $20,000 for women.

The chart above also highlights two other points. First, those who earn the most on average have advanced degrees in law, medicine, and other fields. Second, it also shows a dramatic difference between the earnings of men and women. Many factors account for this, including women having a more prominent role in child rearing, as well as a pay bias toward men in some fields.

The chart may also lead to the conclusion that income and wealth are concentrated

Average Earnings by Educational Attainment 2006

	No high school diploma	High school diploma only	Bachelor's degree	Master's degree	Doctorate
Male	$24,072	$37,356	$69,818	$87,981	$116,473
Female	$15,352	$23,236	$43,302	$53,209	$77,968

Note: Year-round, full-time workers.
Source: U.S. Bureau of the Census, *Current Population Survey,* http://www.census.gov/hhes/www/income.html (April 29, 2003).

in the hands of the most educated. However, this is not entirely the case. Studies indicate that although some of the richest individuals in the United States are highly educated doctors, lawyers, and so on, most are not members of the intellectual elite, nor are they children who inherited large estates. The majority of the wealthiest Americans are first-generation rich—those who have started and run their own businesses.

The explosion of wealth in Silicon Valley, California, the center of computer industry innovation, illustrates this trend. The second half of the 1990s witnessed a tremendous business boom in Internet applications and a concurrent expansion in start-up companies creating new software. Most of these companies were founded

Economic Mobility in the United States

A fundamental premise of the U.S. economy is that all citizens have the opportunity to improve their economic well-being. This important idea suggests a relationship between work and income that gives people an incentive to work hard to get ahead.

Economic mobility measures how often Americans increase or decrease their incomes compared with national averages. Economic mobility is measured in quintiles, or fifths, of the U.S. working population. Thus, the top quintile is the richest 20 percent of Americans.

Personal income changes over the average person's lifetime. In general, income rises with age, education, and work experience, and peaks in a person's forties and fifties. After this point people generally move down in income quintiles because of retirement or reduction in working hours.

Studies of the American economy indicate substantial economic mobility. Between 25 and 33 percent of adults move into a new income quintile each year; over the course of a decade, 60 percent move into a new tax bracket. Thus, the poor can increase their incomes and the rich can fall back. The total rate of mobility has remained constant for the past several decades: the fortunes of specific individuals change often, the proportion of people in each quintile has remained stable. Overall opportunity has not increased despite numerous government initiatives.

Factors Leading to Increased Inequitable Wealth Distribution in the United States after 1970

- Inflation eroded purchasing power, affecting poor most.
- Foreign competition eroded U.S. businesses' ability to pay high wages.
- Well-paid manufacturing jobs moved to developing nations.
- General decline in power of unions prevented them from forcing higher pay.
- Shift to Information Age economy reduced opportunity of low-skilled workers to earn middle-class wages.

by people with middle-class backgrounds who had four years of college or less. This group was unique more for its talent and energy than formal education—many of them had dropped out of college, or did not attend at all.

Technology companies competed for the best employees by using stock options (the right for employees to buy ownership). The combination of luck, talent, and hard work, as well as a concurrent stock market boom, resulted in many of these entrepreneurs becoming extremely wealthy before they turned 30.

The rapid pace of change in the computer industry illustrates an important point about wealth in the United States. Wealth can be obtained through hard work and talent, but once a family becomes wealthy it will not necessarily remain so. In most cases, family fortunes do not last beyond the second or third generation. Many of the dot-com millionaires lost their fortunes with the dot-com crash of 2000. A

similar pattern was followed by those people who earned high bonuses from the financial services industry between 2001 and the crisis in the sector in 2008, during which many major banks failed.

The stock market collapses in 2000 and 2008–2009 raise concerns about stock ownership as a means of wealth generation. Roughly 50 percent of Americans have invested in the stock market as a means to build wealth. The rich tend to have far more invested, and thus see greater changes in their fortune with the movements of the markets. Such volatility is partly responsible for the widening gap between rich and poor from the 1990s and a shrinking of this gap with the stock market declines that followed. Despite the vicissitudes of the market, over the long term the trend of greater stock ownership should allow for more Americans to build wealth.

Global Distribution of Wealth

The distribution of wealth can also be considered both internally—distribution within one nation—and between countries. The global distribution of wealth is starkly unequal. For the purposes of study, nations are usually divided into three kinds. The first are called developed nations, which include the countries of western Europe, the United States, Canada, Japan, South Korea, and Taiwan. In general, these nations are comparatively wealthy because they industrialized successfully. As a result, their living standards and incomes tend to be the highest in the world.

The second tier of nations includes some that are in the process of industrializing or

Aggregate Income of Selected Nations: Percentage Share by Each Fifth of Households 1998

	Lowest fifth	Second fifth	Third fifth	Fourth fifth	Highest fifth
Austria	10.4	14.8	18.5	22.9	33.3
Brazil	2.5	5.7	9.9	17.7	64.2
China	5.5	9.8	14.9	22.3	47.5
India	9.2	13.0	16.8	21.7	39.3
Italy	7.6	12.9	17.3	23.2	38.9
Mexico	4.1	7.8	12.5	20.2	55.3
Nigeria	4.0	8.9	14.4	23.4	49.4
United States	4.8	10.5	16.0	23.5	45.2

Source: The World Bank, *World Development Report*, 1998–1999.

Percent of Population Living on Less than $1.25 per Day 1990 to 2005				
Region	1990	1996	2002	2005
East Asia and the Pacific	54.7	36.0	27.6	16.8
Eastern Europe and Central Asia	2.0	4.6	4.6	3.7
Latin America and the Caribbean	9.8	10.8	11.0	8.4
Middle East and North Africa	4.3	4.1	3.6	3.6
South Asia	51.7	47.1	43.8	40.3
Sub-Saharan Africa	57.9	58.7	55.1	51.2
World	41.6	34.4	30.6	25.2

Source: World Bank, 2008

that have wealth from exporting oil. This group includes Mexico, Saudi Arabia, and much of eastern Europe. The remaining countries are referred to as lesser- (or under-) developed nations. In general, the average income is well below $1,000 per year and quality of life measures are far behind those of the more advanced countries.

The table gives aggregate income data from eight countries, showing the share of income received by each quintile of society; the first fifth represents the poorest and the highest the richest. This table reveals several facts. No nation in the world has an equal distribution of income. Austria comes the closest, and even in that country the richest 20 percent earn more than three times the income of the poorest 20 percent. The higher the income bracket a person occupies, the greater amount of income received.

The second trend shown by this table is that the poorer the country, the more concentrated the income is in the top fifth. For example, the richest 20 percent of Brazil's population earns roughly twice as much as the other 80 percent of Brazilians. The wealthy have several economic advantages in poorer countries. One is access to education—many poor countries are unable to offer free public education to all citizens. Another is that poor countries tend to have corrupt governments dominated by the rich. Thus the wealthy get richer and the poor are kept from gaining ground.

Wealthier nations generally operate on principles that reduce wealth inequalities in society. All have democratic governments and varying depth of commitment to the idea of addressing wealth inequities through government spending and taxation policies. These traditions are strongest in Europe and Japan and are somewhat weaker in the United States.

Experts disagree about the future of the world's wealth distribution. Some are pessimistic, asserting that the decline of well-paying manufacturing jobs and other changes in the nature of work suggest that only the highly educated will prosper in the future. Others are optimistic, arguing that governments now have a much better understanding of poverty and are undertaking programs to mitigate it. Moreover, they maintain that advances in medicine and other areas do improve the quality of life for the poor, as will the spread of democracy and capitalism. In either case, neither group predicts a solution to poverty or a dramatic change in how the wealth of the world's countries is apportioned. The highly educated and entrepreneurial will continue to do well, while the less educated and unfortunate will lag behind.

Further Research
Poverty around the World
www.globalissues.org/article/4/poverty-around-the-world
A comprehensive article looks at the issue of poverty in developing countries, including the initiatives of the World Bank and methods of measuring poverty.

—*David Long*

World Bank

The World Bank is a group of organizations based in Washington, D.C., that is funded by the international community and lends money to countries for economic development. Originally known as the International Bank for Reconstruction and Development (IBRD), it was established in 1944 to provide loans for postwar economic regeneration. More recently, the World Bank has concentrated on providing both economic and technical assistance to developing countries, with an increasing focus on relieving global poverty.

The Creation of the World Bank

Along with its sister organization the International Monetary Fund (IMF), the IBRD was created at the United Nations Monetary and Financial Conference held at Bretton Woods, New Hampshire, in July 1944. On the premise that "it is in the interest of all nations that postwar reconstruction should be rapid . . . [to] . . . aid political stability and foster peace," the conference proposed the establishment of a new international organization that could both increase the amount and share the risks of foreign investment. The IBRD would "assist in providing capital through normal channels at reasonable rates of interest and for long periods for projects which will raise the productivity of the borrowing country."

After commencing operations in June 1946, the IBRD made its first loans to help with postwar reconstruction. Within three years, the focus of its activities had shifted subtly and the bank began to concentrate on providing funds to help poorer countries with more general economic development. This also brought a shift in the territory of its operations from the nations of Western Europe, which had sought economic help with rebuilding their war-torn industries and economies, to the developing nations of Africa, Asia, and Latin America.

Since that time, the World Bank (still formally known as IBRD) has created a number

World Bank

1944
The International Bank for Reconstruction and Development created.

1946
Bank makes first loans to help with postwar reconstruction.

1955
Bank forms Economic Development Institute to provide technical assistance to member countries.

1956
Bank establishes International Finance Corporation to promote private investment in developing countries.

1962
Bank creates International Development Association to provide long-term loans to debtor nations.

1966
International Center for Settlement of Investment Disputes formed to resolve disagreements between governments and private foreign companies.

1988
Multilateral Investment Guarantee Agency formed to encourage internal investment by developing nations.

1993
World Bank withdraws from financing dam on India's Narmada River due to environmental protests.

2008
World Bank has 185 members and provides developing nations with a total of $24.7 billion in loans.

of related institutions to help advance different aspects of its work. In 1955 the bank's Economic Development Institute (EDI) was formed to provide technical assistance to member countries. In 1956 the bank established its International Finance Corporation (IFC) to promote private investment in developing countries. In 1962 the bank created the International Development Association (IDA) to provide long-term loans to nations that are heavily in debt. In October 1966 another World Bank institution, the International Center for Settlement of Investment Disputes (ICSID), was formed to resolve disagreements (for example, when governments try to nationalize a company's assets) between member governments and private foreign companies that invest in their countries. The bank's most recent offshoot, the Multilateral Investment Guarantee Agency (MIGA), was formed in 1988 to encourage internal investment by developing nations by offering guarantees against the risks involved. Collectively, the IBRD, IFC, IDA, ICSID, and MIGA are known as the World Bank Group.

The bank is controlled by its members through a board of governors and executive directors. Members appoint the governors, who meet once a year. The governors, in turn, control the board of 21 executive directors who are responsible for determining the bank's policies and approving loans.

Five directors are appointed by the bank's largest shareholders; the remainder are elected by the governors. Overall control of the bank rests with its president, who is by tradition appointed for a five-year term by the United States—the bank's largest shareholder. Although the IBRD, the IFC, and the IDA are separate institutions, considerable overlap exists among them: only World Bank members can join the IFC and the IDA, and the three organizations share the same president, board of governors, and executive directors.

The bank is probably the world's biggest provider of financial assistance to developing economies. In fiscal year 2008 it provided over 100 developing nations with a total of $24.7 billion in loans, $13 billion through the IBRD and around $11.2 billion through the IDA. In 2008 the biggest share—23 percent—of new IBRD lending (some $5.7 billion) went to Africa, 19 percent went to Latin America and the Caribbean, and East Asia and the Pacific accounted for a further 18 percent. Membership in the bank is constantly growing. In 1982, for example, the bank had 142 members; by 2008 membership had reached 185.

World Bank Operations

In some ways, the bank works like an ordinary commercial bank. Its stated purpose is

The World Bank Group				
The International Bank for Reconstruction and Development	The International Development Association	The International Finance Corporation	The Multilateral Investment Guarantee Agency	The International Center for Settlement of Investment Disputes
Established: 1945 Members: 185 Cumulative lending: $446 billion	Established: 1960 Members: 168 Cumulative lending: $193 billion	Established: 1956 Members: 181 Committed portfolio: $32.2 billion	Established: 1988 Members: 173 Cumulative guarantees issued: $19.5 billion	Established: 1966 Members: 155 Total cases registered: 288
Aims to reduce poverty in middle-income and creditworthy poor countries by promoting sustainable development through loans, guarantees, and nonlending services.	Provides interest-free credits to world's poorest countries.	Invests in sustainable private enterprises in developing countries; provides long-term loans and guarantees.	Encourages foreign investment in developing countries by providing loan guarantees.	Provides international facilities for conciliation and arbitration of investment disputes.

Source: World Bank, 2009

- The Poorest Countries: We are helping overcome poverty and spur sustainable growth in the poorest countries, especially in Africa.

- Post-conflict and Fragile States: We are addressing the special challenges of countries that are emerging from conflict or seeking to avoid the breakdown of the state.

- Middle-income Countries: We are building a competitive menu of development solutions for middle-income countries, with customized services as well as finance.

- Global Public Goods: We are playing a more active role in regional and global issues that cross national borders, including climate change, infectious diseases, and trade.

- The Arab World: We are working with partners to strengthen development and opportunity in the Arab world.

- Knowledge and Learning: We are a learning organization: we increasingly leverage the best global knowledge to support development.

to make loans to developing economies; to make loans, it must have both capital and working funds. Capital is provided (subscribed) by member countries that contribute different amounts according to the relative strength of their economies. Members pay around 8.5 percent of their subscribed capital but must be ready to pay the remainder on request. The bank also generates working funds by offering bonds on the world's capital markets and by collecting interest and repayments on the loans it makes. The bank is virtually self-financing, earning almost as much money in interest and repayments as it grants in the form of loans; it has been profitable every year since its creation in 1946 and has never needed to call in the fully subscribed capital.

Unlike commercial banks making ordinary loans to private citizens, the World Bank takes a close interest in how members use its money. Usually (and sometimes in partnership with the IMF) it attaches stringent conditions to its loans ("conditionality"), requiring nations to adopt agreed

economic development strategies known as Structural Adjustment Programs (SAPs), which have often proved intensely controversial. Money is generally provided only for specific projects for which borrowers have been unable to get loans in the commercial market at reasonable terms. World Bank loans have often been associated with massive infrastructure projects like hydroelectric power plants, highways, ports, pipelines, and airports, but most of the bank's loans are now made for agricultural and rural development projects. Money is lent both to member governments and to private companies operating in member states (governments must guarantee the loans). Often the bank's staff provides technical as well as financial assistance with particular projects.

Since the 1980s the bank has focused much of its attention on projects that benefit the poorest people in the poorest nations; part of its mission statement is "to fight poverty with passion and professionalism for lasting results." In the past the World Bank has frequently been criticized for imposing a one-size-fits-all development strategy on its borrowers, for example, by stipulating SAPs that prioritize debt repayment over public spending, require the privatization of public services, or force nations to grow cash crops for export rather than food for a sometimes undernourished home population. Largely as a response, the bank has developed a Comprehensive Development Framework in which each borrower country owns its own Poverty Reduction Strategy (a development plan to reduce poverty through macroeconomic, structural, and social policies), while the bank owns a parallel Country Assistance Strategy that determines how much financial and technical support it will provide. The bank continues to target its efforts at the poorest nations with task forces focusing on low- and middle-income nations. The high-profile Heavily Indebted Poor Countries (HIPC) Initiative, launched in 1996, aims to provide relief for developing nations suffering most from the problems of long-term debt.

Issues and Controversies

Measuring the effectiveness of the World Bank's policies and programs—averaged over many different projects, across the entire developing world, over its half-century of existence—is difficult. The bank points to general gains in developing nations in areas like life expectancy (risen from 55 to 65 years), infant mortality (reduced by 50 percent), and adult literacy (doubled). Nevertheless, the bank readily acknowledges that considerable challenges remain.

The bank's policies have repeatedly been attacked by campaigners on environmental and Third World development issues. Critics charge that the bank, along with the IMF and a consortium of commercial banks, has knowingly perpetuated and exploited the Third World debt crisis for the overall financial benefit of the developed world in a throwback to colonial days. Environmental groups claim that the bank continues to finance what they maintain are environmentally suspect practices in developing nations, including growing crops with large amounts of agri-chemicals and pesticides, logging endangered forests, encouraging the use of fossil fuels, constructing massive highways and dams, and incinerating toxic waste. Critics have had some successes in challenging the World Bank. For example, in the 1990s the World Bank withdrew from a highly controversial plan to finance the Sardar Sarovar hydroelectric dam on India's Narmada River after finding itself the target of a worldwide environmental campaign. Further, the adjustment of the World Bank's one-size-fits-all policies is the result, in no small part, of pressure from opponents around the world.

The World Bank and its associated organizations will continue to play a definitive role in development for the foreseeable future. As the bank becomes increasingly sensitive to criticism, it is likely to adopt more strategies along the lines of the HIPC Initiative and to try to convince critics that its efforts are truly making a difference in world poverty. Whether its policies are an essential aid to economic development in poorer nations or sometimes contribute to the very problems they claim to relieve is likely to remain a matter of intense debate.

A protester in the guise of former World Bank president James Wolfensohn marches in the streets of Washington, D.C., during anti-globalization protests.

Further Research
Bretton Woods Project
www.brettonwoodsproject.org
Created as an independent initiative by a group of British nongovernmental organizations (NGOs), the Bretton Woods Project presses for increased transparency and civil society participation in World Bank and IMF policies and interventions.
World Bank
www.worldbank.org
Home page of the World Bank.

—*Chris Woodford*

Glossary

arbitration   Method of resolving disputes by use of a neutral third party to hear arguments and make a ruling.

asset   Something of value.

asset management   Process of managing money and other items of value to make them grow in value.

balance of payments   Record of all transactions between the residents of one nation and the residents of all foreign nations.

bankruptcy   Legal process that allows a company or individual to restructure debts.

barriers to entry   Factors discouraging competition in a market.

bear market   Period of declining stock prices.

best practice   Standard of comparison used in businesses that takes companies or individuals who operate most efficiently as a benchmark.

bonds   Certificates stating that a firm or government will pay the holder regular interest payments and a set sum on a specific maturity date.

bull market   Period of rising stock prices.

capital   Money or wealth that is put at risk to fund a business enterprise.

capital, human   Skills and experience of workers.

capital, intellectual   Knowledge used in production of a good or service.

capitalism   Economic and social system based on private ownership of the means of production; goods and services are allocated through the coming together of supply and demand in the competitive free market.

collective bargaining   Negotiations between management and a union to establish a labor contract.

commodity pricing   Condition that exists when intense competition results in the price of a good being set only slightly above its cost of production.

communism   Economic and social system based on group ownership of the means of production; goods and services are allocated by the central government.

conglomerate   A company that grows by merging with or buying businesses in several different industries.

consumer price index (CPI)   Measure of the overall price level of goods.

corporation   Company owned by stockholders.

corporatism   Economic and social system wherein national economic policy is negotiated between representatives of government, employers' organizations, and trade unions.

cost-benefit analysis   Evaluating the monetary and nonmonetary gains and losses that ensue from making various choices.

deficit   Cash shortfall resulting from a government spending more than it takes in in taxes and other revenues.

demand   Amount of a good or service consumers will purchase at different prices at a given time.

depression   Recession of unusual length and severity.

deregulation   Process of removing government restrictions on business.

derivatives market   Trading of financial assets based on other instruments; futures and options are derivatives with their values determined by the movement of stock and commodities prices.

development economics   Study of how a society can achieve high productivity and better living standards.

disinvestment   Decline of the total amount of capital goods in an economy.

distribution of wealth   How the assets of a society are divided among its members.

diversification   Allocation of money among different kinds of assets to minimize risk and maximize long-term results.

dividend   The part of a corporation's profits paid to its stockholders.

due diligence   Researching a company to evaluate the benefits and risks of a merger or an investment

economies of scale   Declining average cost of production that results from increasing output.

elasticity   Sensitivity of supply and demand to changes in a good's price.

environmentalism   Set of political ideas based on people protecting and restoring the environment.

export subsidy   Payments made by governments to domestic producers of a good; intended to allow the producers to sell their products at low prices.

fair market value   Price at which property would change hands between a willing buyer and a willing seller when both are fully informed about the asset.

Federal Reserve   Central bank of the United States; it is responsible for the orderly operation of the banking system, monitoring the economy, and conducting monetary policy.

fiscal policy Process of managing economic expansions and contractions by adjusting government spending to stabilize incomes and economic performance.

foreign exchange Financial instruments, including currency and checks, used for making payments between countries.

futures Financial arrangement in which those involved agree on a set price, quantity, and date for an exchange in the future.

General Agreement on Tariffs and Trade (GATT) Influential series of agreements designed to encourage world trade.

globalization Process of world economic integration driven by a combination of free trade and information technology.

gross domestic product (GDP) Estimate of the value of goods and services produced within a country over a given period.

gross national product (GNP) Estimate of the value of goods and services produced by a country over a given period, including those goods and services produced by national entities outside the nation's physical boundaries.

hedging Method used by individuals or businesses to make financial transactions to protect against future price changes.

hyperinflation Period of dramatic price increases caused by an increase in the money supply.

import substitution Encouraging economic development by limiting imports to encourage domestic production.

income inequality Differences in income between various groups.

initial public offering The first time a company sells stock to the public.

incubator Private or publicly funded entity that provides facilities and support staff for small businesses.

index Mathematical measurement tool that uses a variety of data for input and comparison.

infrastructure Transportation, communications, education, and financial systems of a country.

insolvency A financial condition in which an individual is unable to pay his or her debts as they come due, or a condition in which liabilities exceed assets.

investment Present use of resources to enable greater production in the future.

Keynesian principles Theories of economist John Maynard Keynes; the idea that governments can positively influence the business cycle through spending on taxation policies.

knowledge workers People who use knowledge, rather than manual labor, to earn income.

laissez-faire Policy of minimal government interference in an economy.

liberalism In economics, the belief that a nation's wealth can achieve the greatest increase with minimum government interference with trade.

liquidity The ease with which assets can be converted into cash without a decline in value. **money supply** Amount of money in an economy.

macroeconomics Study of an economy as a whole.

management Work done by people responsible for guiding formal organizations toward their intended purposes.

market capitalization Total value of a corporation's outstanding shares.

market economy Economic system wherein decisions are made in markets and based on the forces of supply and demand.

mediation Method of dispute resolution in which a neutral party hears the positions of both sides and assists them in reaching a settlement by offering expert opinion and suggestions.

mercantilism Belief that wealth is the foundation of a powerful nation and that national economic policy should therefore be based on attempting to maximize exports and minimize imports.

microeconomics Study of the decisions made by individuals and firms.

monetarism Economic theory that holds that government regulation of the money supply is key to stable economic growth.

monetary policy Government's use of its power over the money supply to influence economic growth and inflation.

most-favored nation Designation that guarantees all nations accorded that status will receive equal treatment when trading with one another.

nationalization Government takeover of private industries.

nonprofit Self-governing organization dedicated to supporting some public purpose.

opportunity cost Alternatives that are lost when a choice is made.

outsourcing Contracting with other companies for the performance of specific production tasks.

pork barrel spending Legislation that subsidizes special projects for particular districts or states with the intention of serving the narrow interests of legislators or interest groups.

price fixing One or more businesses colluding to charge prices higher than the normal market would determine.

private property Property held by individuals either singly or in voluntary associations rather than being held by the state.

privatization Sale of government providers of goods and services to the private sector.

productivity   Amount of work that can be completed in a given time.

profit   The amount left over after the cost of doing business has been subtracted.

progressive tax   Tax that is imposed at a higher percentage on individuals with higher incomes.

protectionism   Government action that partly shields domestic industries from foreign competition; tariffs and quotas are forms of protectionism.

public goods   Goods that everyone can enjoy equally and no one can be excluded from; fresh air and national defense are public goods.

quota   A predetermined limit on the amount of foreign goods that can enter a country.

rate of return   Percentage by which revenues achieved exceed the cost of investment.

recession   Period in which overall economic output declines.

regressive tax   Tax that places a greater proportional burden on people with lower incomes.

regulation   Government action intended to promote fair trade practices and to safeguard citizens.

reserve requirements   Percentage of deposits banks and other depository institutions must keep in cash or on account with the Federal Reserve.

return on investment   Percentage change in the value of an asset.

risk management   Process of identifying sources of potential losses, evaluating potential losses, and selecting means for responding to loss exposures.

secondary market   A stock exchange; the New York Stock Exchange is a secondary market.

securities   Stocks, bonds, and other financial instruments.

service economy   Economy in which the majority of employment and business revenues are generated by services.

socialism   Economic system based on equality and group ownership of the means of production.

stagflation   Condition of simultaneously rising unemployment and inflation.

stakeholders   Active participants in corporate decisions.

stock   Part ownership in a corporation.

stock options   Rights of employees (granted by employer) to buy shares in a company at a certain price at some point in time.

subsidiary   A business controlled by another business.

subsidy   Financial payment from a government to support a business endeavor.

supply   Amount of a good or service producers will provide at different prices and at a given time.

sustainability   Rate of economic growth that is compatible with planetary welfare and the needs of future generations.

sustainable agriculture   A method of farming that attempts to minimize human impact on the environment.

sustainable development   Promotion of economic growth in a manner that minimizes effects on the natural and cultural environment.

tariff   Tax on imported goods.

tradable allowance   Environmental policy that allows producers of pollution to buy and sell emissions credits to achieve an overall reduction in pollution.

trade deficit   When a nation buys more from abroad than it sells.

trade surplus   When a nation sells more goods to other nations than it buys from other nations.

transnational corporation   Corporation that operates in many different countries.

valuation   Process of estimating an asset's relative worth.

venture capital   Private funds used to start or expand a business.

wealth distribution   How the wealth of a society is divided among its members.

yield   Return on an investment.

Index

Page numbers in **boldface** type indicate complete articles. Page numbers in *italic* type indicate illustrations or other graphics.

A

advertising, 19, 22, 178
agriculture, 27, 209
  productivity, 166–167
  subsidies, 179, 199, 201, *202*
AIG, 51
airlines, 66, 179, 200
  deregulation, 62, 63, 166, 183
Andersen, Terry L., 76–77
Annunziata, Robert, *50*
antitrust laws, 65, 83, 114, 136, 178
arbitration, **6–8**
AT&T deregulation, *63*, 64–65
auto industry, 46–47, 96, 97, 120, 173, 174, 175

B

balance of payments, **9–10**, 115, 116, 122
balance of trade, 9, **11–13**, 122
bankruptcy, 13, 14, 52, 60, 66, 70, 89, 91, 159
banks, 128, 138–140
  bailout funds, 52, 60, 163
  deregulation, 64, 183
  failure, 14, 66, 91, 175, 212
  regulation, 175–176, 178–179
  See also central banks
Beckerman, Wilfred, 203, 206
Bhopal disaster, 76, 205
black markets, 156
board of directors, 48–50, 58–59
bonuses, 52
Bové, José, 98
Bretton Woods agreement, 28, 30, 115, 214
Breyer, Stephen, 62, 63
Brezhnev, Leonid, 41
bribery, 19, 22, 23, 24
Bright, John, 26
Bruntlandt, Gro Harlem, 204
Bureau of Labor Statistics, 45, 46, 47, 111, 168
business cycles, **14–17**, 26, 28, 97, 99, 174, 212
  corporate governance, 51–52
  economic growth, 69, 70, 71
  macroeconomics, 127–129
  See also recession
business ethics, **18–24**, 26, 48, 51–52, 53–56, 60

C

Cairncross, Frances, 204
California electricity crisis, 66, 159
Capital Account, 9–10
capitalism, **25–31**, 54, 70, 123, 194, 195, 196, 198, 210
  business cycles, 14–16
  See also free market
Carson, Rachel, 54, 74
cartel, **32–33**, 113, 153–155, 175
Carter, Jimmy, 62, 183
Castro, Fidel, *38*, 39
central banks, 69, 70, 80, 86, 116.
  See also Federal Reserve System
CEO (chief executive officer), 49–52, 59
Chicago Board of Trade, 34, *35*, 187
Civil Aeronautics Board, 62, 63, 183
Civilian Conservation Corps, 28, 74, 199
class conflict, 36, 195, 210
classical school (economics), 14, *129*
climate change, 73, 206
Clinton, Bill, 63, 64, 66, 197
Club of Rome, 74, 203
Cobden, Richard, 26
cold war, *38–41*, 78, 95, 198
collaterized debt obligations, 52
collectivization, 36, 37, 195
commodities, **34–35**, 89–91
common markets, 121–122
communism, 27, 28–29, 31, **36–41**, 195–196
  failures, 41, 62, 95, 196, 198
comparative advantage, 118, 135
competition. *See* free market
compound tariff, 170
computer age, 164, 167, 168, 211–212
Conference Board, 42, 43, 44
consumer confidence, 175
Consumer Confidence Index, **42–44**
Consumer Leasing Act, 83
Consumer Price Index, **45–47**, 111, *114*, 127, *128*
Consumer Product Safety Commission, 55
consumer protection, 55, 82–85, 178, 181, 182
contractionary fiscal policy, 86, 87
Corn Laws (Britain), 26

corporate governance

corporate governance, **48–52**, 58–59, 60
  business ethics, 18–24
  human capital, 105–107
  See also management
corporate social responsibility, 19–22, **53–56**
  environmentalism, 77
corporation, **57–61**.
  See also multinational corporation; trusts
cost-benefit comparison, 135
cost-of-living, 45, 47, 69, 99, 114
cost push theory, 112, 113
credit. *See* interest rates
Crosland, Anthony, 196–197

D

Debs, Eugene, 198
debt, U.S., 86, 87, 128
deficit nation, 9–10, 11
deficit spending, 28, 86, 87, 128
demand pull theory, 112–113
deregulation, 30, 31, 55, **62–66**, 159, 166, 183
discount prices, 96–97, 157
discount rates (bank), 139–140
dividends, 57
division of labor. *See* specialization
dot.com boom, 51, 210–211
dumping, 172

E

earned income tax credit, 125
economic efficiency, 134, 135, 136–137, 182, 183, 207
economic growth, 26, **67–71**, 87, 111, 210–211
  determinants, *128*
  environmentalism, 72, 77
  gross domestic product, 100–103, 127
  income distribution, 108, 110
  macroeconomics, 127–129, 134
  productivity, 164–169, 174
  service economy, 193
  sustainable development, 203–205
economic indicators, 17, 42, 43, 44, 127
  Consumer Price Index, 45–47
  macroeconomics, *128*, 129
economic mobility, 211
economies of scale, 177, 191
education, 26, 163, 200
  wealth distribution, 211, 213
Ehrlich, Paul, 72
electricity, 164, 179, 182, 183
  deregulation, 65–66, 159

E (continued)

Emerson, Ralph Waldo, 74
employment. *See* labor market
endangered species, 74, 206
Engels, Friedrich, 36, 196
Enron, *51*, 52, 60
entrepreneurs, 25, 68, 133, 210, 211–212
environmentalism, 31, 54–55, 71, **72–77**, 217
  business ethics, 19, 22, 24
  multinationals, 144
  regulations, 181, 183
  subsidy reform, 202
  sustainable development, 203–206
Environmental Protection Agency, 55, 74, 181
Equal Employment Opportunity Commission, 55, 181
ethics. *See* business ethics
euro (currency), 80, 81, 121
European Central Bank, 80
European Coal and Steel Community, 78
European Union, 12, **78–81**, 121, 172, 204
exchange rates, 28, 30, 80, 115
executive compensation, 50–52, 60
external benefits, 136
Exxon oil spill, 55, 74

F

Fayol, Henri, 130
Federal Deposit Insurance Corporation, 57, 179
Federal Reserve System, 69, 128, 129, 138–140, 176
Federal Trade Commission, 22, **82–85**, 178, 179
financial services
  crisis (2008), 125, 163, 212
  deregulation, 64, 66, 183
  regulation, 178–179
fiscal policy, 15, 16, 69, **86–88**, *127*, 128, 129
  business cycles, 15, 16, 176
food safety, 76
Ford, Henry, 54, 174
Foreign Corrupt Practices Act, 21, 24
forest sustainability, 204–205
Fourier, Charles, 194
fraud, 22, 84–85
free market, 25–31, 95, 110
  business cycles, 14–15
  cartels vs., 32–33
  deregulation, 62–66, 183
  economic growth, 68
  environmentalism, 76–77
  productivity, 166
  unfair practices, 82, 83, 178

New Economy, 164, 169
Newton, Isaac, 25
New York Stock Exchange, 17, 187
Nike, 97–98, 142–143
Nixon, Richard, 30, 39, 159
nonprofit entities, **147–148**
North American Free Trade Agreement, 12, 31, 121–122
nuclear power, 55–56, 65, 74

O
Obama, Barack, 63, 197
Occupational Safety and Health Administration, 55, 125, 181
off-balance-sheet loans, 52
oil, 172, 204, 205, 206
 cartels, 32, 33, 153–155, 175
 price shocks, 30, 72–73, 108, 112, 175
oil spill, 55, 74
oligopoly, 135
O'Neal, Stanley, 52
opportunity cost, **149–150**, 160–161, 186
Organisation for Economic Co-operation and Development, **151–152**
Organization of Petroleum Exporting Countries, 32, **153–155**
Our Common Future (1987 report), 204
Owen, Robert, 36, 194
ozone layer, 72

P
pensions, 52, 54, 112
Phillips Curve, 113
phishing fraud, 84–85
physical capital, 68
pollution. See environmentalism
Pol Pot, 39
population growth, 72, 206
pork barrel spending, 201–202
poverty, 26, 71, 93, 109, 110, 210, 213
 sustainable development, 204, 206
 World Bank, 214, 216
preferred stock, 57
price ceiling, 156, 159
price controls, 30, 114, 137, **156–159**, 177
price fixing, 32–33, 113, 153, 154–155, 173
price floor, 157
prices
 business cycles, 14, 15, 16

commodity futures, 34
consumer index, 45–47, 127
deregulation, 62, 65, 66, 183
globalization, 96–97
microeconomics, 134, 135
protectionism, 170, 171, 208
 See also inflation
privatization, 30, 31, 66, **160–163**
producer services, 191–193
productivity, 113, **164–169**, 193
 business cycles, 14, 15, 16
 cartel curbs, 33, 154
 economic growth, 67, 70, 174
 human capital, 106
 as leading economic indicator, 43
 microeconomics, 126, 127, 134–35
 See also gross domestic product
profit sharing, 54
Progressive Era, 27, 63
property rights, 68, 77, 162
protectionism, 12–13, 16, 26, 27, 30, 81, 94–95, 159, **170–173**
 types, 120
public interest groups, 147, 148, 181
public utilities, 64–65, 158–159, 161, 179, 181–183
Public Works Administration, 28
Pullman, George, 53–54

Q
quota, trade, 12, 13, 120, 121, 122, 170

R
railroad rate regulation, 177–178, 181
Reagan, Ronald, 30–31, 55, 62, 183
recession, 17, 51–52, 69, 70, 108, 125, **174–176**
 financial services deregulation, 183
 labor market, 125
 productivity, 164, 165
 protectionism, 172
recycling, 54–55, 76, 77
regulation of business and industry, 27, 55, 63, 65, 74, 77, 136, **177–183**
 business ethics, 22–23
 Federal Trade Commission, 82–85
 price controls, 30, 114, 137, 156–159
 See also deregulation

rent control, 156–157
resource allocation, 159
restraint of trade, 178
revenue tariff, 120
Ricardo, David, 26
Rifkin, Jeremy, 167
ripple effect, 174, 175, 176
risk management, **184–187**
 futures, 35, 89, 90
 opportunity cost, 150
 subprime mortgages, 52
Rome, Treaty of (1957), 78, 79
Roosevelt, Franklin D., 27, 28, 64, 178, *179*, 198
Roosevelt, Theodore, 6, 74

S
Saint-Simon, Henri de, 194, 195
sanitation, 26, 209
Sarbanes-Oxley Act, 22
 major provisions, *24*
Saro-Wiwa, Ken, 145
savings, 68, 112
scarcity, 134–135, 149, 150, 159
Schultz, Theodore, 104
Schumacher, E. F., 76, 203
Schuman, Robert, 78
Securities and Exchange Commission, 179
self-interest, 25, 68, 76
service economy, 108–109, **188–193**, 206, 211
 human capital, 104–107
shareholders, 20, 21, 48–52, 57–58, 59, 60
Sherman Antitrust Act, 83, 178
shortages, 95, 156
short-selling, 90
Silicon Valley, 98–99, 211–212
Smith, Adam, 10, 21, 25–26, 62, 65, 67, 68, 119–120, 210
 microeconomics, 134
Smits, H. N. J., 204
social cost, 70
social democracy, 196–197, 198
socialism, 26, 31, 36, **194–198**
Social Security, 28, 114
social services, 26, 28, 53–56, 147, 148
solar power, 204, 206
Solow, Robert, 164
special drawing rights, 116
specialization, 25, 26, 67, 118, 134–135, 207
specific tariff, 120, 170
speculation, 17, 27, 35, 91
SRI funds, 56
stagflation, 30, 113
Stalin, Joseph, 27, 37–38, 195
Standard and Poor 500 Index, 17, 56

state regulation, 181–182
steel industry, 172
Stigler, George, 62, 63
stock market
 business cycles, 14, 16–17, 28, 175, 212
 corporate scandals, 52
 federal regulation, 179
 futures markets, 89–91
 risk, 187
 See also shareholders
stock options, 51, 52, 212
Structural Adjustment Programs, 216
subprime mortgage crisis, 52
subsidy, 159, 172, **199–202**
 export, 120
Summers, Lawrence, 63, 64
supply and demand, 14, 25, 95, 113, 135, 159, 177
 determinants, *135*
 oil, 154–155
sustainable development, 77, **203–206**

T
tariff, 12–13, 16, 26, 27, 120, 121, 170, 172, **207–208**
taxes, 86, 87, 125, 128, 129, 176, 210
 business cycles, 16, 28
 exemptions, 147, 148
 income distribution, 108, 109–110
 microeconomics, 136–137
 subsidies, 199, 200
telephone service, 182, 183
 deregulation, 63, 64–65, 183
terrorism, 66, 140, 152, 175, 200
Thain, John, 52
Thatcher, Margaret, 30, 62, 81, *161*, 162
"Third Way," 197, 198
Thoreau, Henry David, 74
Tito, Josip, 39
trade deficit, 9–10, 11, 112
trade surplus, 11, 12, 122
trade unions. *See* unions
tragedy of the commons, 76
transportation deregulation, 183
Trotsky, Leon, 37, 195
trusts, 26–27, 82, 83, 178
Truth in Lending Act, 83
Tylenol tampering, 55

U
unemployment, 40–41, 108, 112, 125, 138, 200
 business cycles, 14, 17, 26, 69, 70, 125, 175